S. Dryden (Sylvanus Dryden) Phelps

Holy Land with Glimpses of Europe and Egypt

A Year's Tour

S. Dryden (Sylvanus Dryden) Phelps

Holy Land with Glimpses of Europe and Egypt
A Year's Tour

ISBN/EAN: 9783337189402

Printed in Europe, USA, Canada, Australia, Japan

Cover: Foto ©Andreas Hilbeck / pixelio.de

More available books at **www.hansebooks.com**

HOLY LAND

WITH

GLIMPSES OF EUROPE AND EGYPT:

A YEAR'S TOUR.

BY S. DRYDEN PHELPS, D.D.

Twenty-two Engravings.

New-York:
SHELDON & COMPANY, 335 BROADWAY.
BOSTON: GOULD & LINCOLN.
1863.

LIST OF ILLUSTRATIONS.

MELROSE ABBEY	Frontispiece.
PALM TREES	Title-page.
BUNYAN'S COTTAGE AT ELSTOW	25
HOSPICE OF ST. BERNARD	62
FLORENCE FROM THE SOUTH-EAST	102
THE NILE AT OLD CAIRO	162
GHAWAZEE OR DANCING GIRLS	169
RUINS OF KARNAK AT THEBES	173
HOUSE WITH A CHAMBER ON THE ROOF OR WALL	193
HOUSE-TOP OR ROOF AND BATTLEMENTS	193
WOMEN WEEPING AT A GRAVE	198
POOL OF HEZEKIAH, OLIVET, ETC	203
WAILING PLACE OF THE JEWS	214
ABSALOM'S TOMB (RESTORED)	220
BETHANY	222
BETHLEHEM	242
THE DEAD SEA FROM THE NORTH-WEST	248
THE JORDAN, AT THE SUPPOSED PLACE OF CHRIST'S BAPTISM	252
JERUSALEM FROM THE NORTH-EAST	282
CAPERNAUM AND SEA OF GALILEE	356
SKIN BOTTLES AND WATER-JARS	360
VALE OF NAZARETH	366

PREFACE.

"WHAT travelers the Americans are! I find them everywhere," said a solid, intelligent, good-natured English lady as she reached, almost out of breath, the top of the last flight of stairs in the lofty tower of the great Cathedral of Notre Dame in Antwerp, and looked a few feet above where I had just climbed to the highest accessible point. She might have added, if she had looked over the lists of our publishers, "and how many books of travels they write!" Every author, I suppose, perceives—though others may not—reasons sufficient to justify his publication. He differs, perhaps, in some important respects, from others who have gone over the same ground, or he has so wrought up, arranged, and condensed his materials as to present in a life-like manner just what is most desirable and interesting to readers generally.

I have given a sketch of my whole tour in a single volume, and I do not know of another writer who has brought the results of a journey of like extent into so small a space. In this purposed and labored brevity, the first part of the book is necessarily a rapid narrative of sights and scenes by the way; but the chapters on Palestine—a land of the deepest interest to all who prize the sacred Scriptures—I have extended and amplified as the subject seemed to demand. I have endeavored to present accurate *pictures* of the places and scenery where I traveled, so that the reader, by using as it were my eyes, may have a kind of stereoscopic view of the same localities. To the general reader, to the student or the Bible, to the tourist through the same countries—and who does not desire or intend sometime to make the journey?—I trust this volume will be found both useful and entertaining. In preparing the materials of my daily journal for the press, I have consulted several works on the Holy Land, and have derived especial aid from Dr. Thomson's "Land and the Book," Stanley's "Sinai and Palestine," and the "Hand-book of Syria and Palestine," compiled by Rev. J. L. Porter.

While visiting, in Florence, the observatory of Galileo where by his improved telescope he made wondrous discoveries in the heavens, the saintly spirit of my precious mother, in her seventy-fifth year, passed to her glorious home beyond the stars. And while ascending the Nile, near the place where the infant Moses was found in the flags of the river, my youngest child, a bright and darling boy in his fourth year, was taken up to the bosom of the Good Shepherd. To their blessed memories, and to my beloved Christian Flock, by whose approval and kind liberality the journey was undertaken, I dedicate this volume.

New Haven, Conn., 1862.

CONTENTS.

I.—THE PASSAGE—IRELAND—SCOTLAND.

Embarking—Sea-life—Iceborgs—Whales—Saint Johns—Services—Land ho!—Queenstown—Cork—Blarney Castle—Sabbath in Killarney—The Lakes—Gap of Dunloe—Fourth of July Celebration—Limerick—Dublin—Presbyterian Assembly—Revival—Belfast—Dr. Cooke—Giant's Causeway—Round Towers—Trip to Scotland—The Highlands—Lochs Lomond and Katrine—Stirling Castle—Edinburgh—Abbotsford..9

II.—ENGLAND—WALES—NOTED PLACES.

Rural Scenery—Excursion to Caernarvon—Its Castle—Liverpool—Rev. Stowell Brown—Dr. Raffles—Bedford—Bunyan's Cottage—Cardington—Kettering—Northampton — Olney — Stratford-on-Avon — Leamington — Oxford—Southampton—Stonehenge—Isle of Wight......................................22

III.—LONDON—BUNHILL FIELDS—PREACHERS.

Greatness of London—Saint Paul's—Westminster Abbey—British Museum—Hampton Court—Windsor Castle—Houses of Parliament—Bunyan's Tomb—Smithfield—Spurgeon's Preaching—Dr. Cumming—Hall, Noel, Landels, and Brock—Prayer Meetings...31

IV.—FRANCE—BELGIUM—HOLLAND—THE RHINE.

Across the Channel — Rouen — Paris — Grand Military Pageant — American Chapel—Churches and Religion—The People—Parisian Attractions—Versailles — Belgian Scenery — Brussels — King Leopold — Waterloo — Antwerp—Churches—Rubens—Dutch-Land, Cities and Scenery—Aix-la-Chapelle—Tomb of Charlemagne—Relics—Cologne—On the Rhine—Drachenfels—Mayence—Frankfort—Heidelberg—Baden-Baden—Strasbourg—A Famous Clock......40

V.—SWITZERLAND—A TOUR IN THE ALPS.

Mountain Scenery — Rail-Carriages — Geneva—Dr. Malan—The Arve—Mont Blanc—Chamouny—Flegere—Mer de Glace—Glaciers—Tete Noir—Martigny—Grand Saint Bernard—Dogs—The Morgue—Moonlight Drive—Baths of Leuk—Gemmi Pass—Thun—Interlachen—Swiss Lakes........................55

VI.—THE SWISS—ALPINE JOURNEYS—GERMANY.

Characteristics—Cottages—Productions—Sabbath Observance — Dust-Stream—Wengern Alp—Jungfrau — Avalanches — Grindelwald — Great Scheideck—Storm — Reichenbach — Happy Valley—Handek—Grimsel—Rhone Glacier—Furca—Devil's Bridge—Home of Tell—Ascent of the Rigi—Storm—Predicament — Mount Pilatus — Lucerne — Zurich — Constance — John Huss—Rhine Falls—Lake Constance—Augsburg..................... 67

CONTENTS.

VII.—BAVARIA—AUSTRIA—ITALY—VENICE.

Munich—Art Galleries—Churches—Cemetery—Russian Bath—German People—The Tyrol—Salzburg—Mozart—Kufstein—Deep Well—A Criminal—Innsbruck—Wounded Soldiers—Brenner Pass—In Italy—Verona—Attractions of Venice—Gondolas—Murano and Lido—Padua—Solferino...................62

VIII.—MILAN—MANTUA—BOLOGNA—FLORENCE—PISA.

Milan Cathedral—Last Supper—Incident—Birth-place of Virgil—Bologna—Apennines—Rural Aspects—People Excited—Productions—Florence—Pitti Palace—Uffizi Gallery—Churches—Mr. Powers—Protestant Services—A Singular Prisoner—Fiesole—Galileo's Observatory—Baptism and Funeral—Benefits of Travel—Contrasts—Pisa—Baptistery—Campo Santo—Cathedral—Leaning Tower—Leghorn to Rome...94

IX.—ROME—ITS CHURCHES—THE VATICAN—TIVOLI.

The Eternal City—Churches—Raphael's House—Saint Peter's—Interior, Roof, and Ball—Saint Paul's—Saint John Lateran—Holy Staircase—Paul's Hired House—Mamertine Prison—Tasso's Tomb—Cemetery of the Capuchins—The Vatican—Galleries—Paintings—Quirinal Palace—Spada—Festival in Sistine Chapel—The Pope—American College—Excursion to Tivoli—Hadrian's Villa 109

X.—OLD ROME—COLISEUM—CATACOMBS—CHRISTMAS.

Ruins—Fountains—Capitol—Forum—Arch of Titus—Coliseum—Appian Way—Catacombs—Christmas Holidays—Pope and Cardinals at Saint Peter's—Bambino—Pope at the Church of the Jesuits—Priests and People—Romanism at Home—Villas and Studios—Pincian Hill—Italian Sunset................121

XI.—NAPLES—POMPEII—VESUVIUS—BAIÆ—MALTA.

New Year—Rome to Naples—Herculaneum—Pompeii—House of Diomede—Borbonico Museum—Ascent of Vesuvius—Lava—Tomb of Virgil—Puteoli—Lake Avernus—Ruins of Baiæ—Malta..135

XII.—EGYPT—ALEXANDRIA—CAIRO.

"Land of Egypt"—Oriental Sights—Donkey Riding—Cleopatra's Needle—Pompey's Pillar—Catacombs—Pasha's Palace—Bazaars—Alexandria to Cairo—Sight of the Pyramids—Phases of Eastern Life—Wedding—Mosques—Queer Test—Dancing Dervishes—Shoobra Gardens—Petrified Forest—Heliopolis—Aged Sycamore—Fine Obelisk..144

XIII.—LAND OF MOSES—LIFE ON THE NILE.

Sacred Associations—Missionaries—Salutation—Dragoman Engaged—On the Nile—Our Party—Climate—River—Soil—Productions—Irrigation—Scenery—Villages—Sand Storms—Girls—Fellaheen—Our Crew—Devotions—Fare—Festival—Ghawazee—Funeral—Quarrel.......................................158

XIV.—THEBES—ITS TEMPLES AND TOMBS—DOWN THE RIVER.

Grandeur of Thebes—Luxor—Mustapha Aga—Karnak—Temples—Colossal Statues—Tombs of the Kings—Mummy Pits—Down the Nile—Sights—Adventures—Turkish Dignitary—Female Wrath 171

XV.—MEMPHIS—THE PYRAMIDS—THE RED SEA.

Pyramids of Sakkara—Image of Remeses—Tomb of Apis—Pyramids of Ghizeh—A Dream—Insolent Arabs—Ascent of the Great Pyramid—Interior—The Sphinx—Leaving the Nile—Excursion—The Desert—Mirage—Red Sea—Passage of the Israelites—Wells of Moses.................................182

CONTENTS. vii

XVI.—PALESTINE—JOPPA TO JERUSALEM.

Entering the Holy Land—Joppa—House of Simon—Oranges—Gate of the City—Peter's Vision—Dorcas—Hedges of Cactus—Plain of Sharon—Philistia—Lydda—Ramleh—Women Weeping at a Grave—Latron—Valley of Ajalon—Kirjath-jearim—First Sight of Olivet and Jerusalem.. 191

XVII.—THE HOLY CITY—OLIVET—CALVARY.

Jaffa Gate—Mount Zion—Hotel—Pool of Hezekiah—House-top View—Walk to Olivet—The Kedron—View of Jerusalem—Panorama—Paths of Jesus—House of Pilate—Temple Area—Via Dolorosa—Calvary—Church of the Holy Sepulchre—Tomb of Jesus..202

XVIII.—A WALK ABOUT ZION—BETHANY.

A Synagogue—Wailing-Place—Relics of a Great Arch—Jews' Quarter—Lepers—Armenian Convent—Tomb of David—American Cemetery—Lower Pool of Gihon—Valley of Hinnom—En-Rogel—Valley of Jehoshaphat—Pool of Siloam—Tombs—Golden Gate—English Church—Walk to Bethany—Tomb of Lazarus—Passage over Olivet—Preaching on Mount Zion..........................213

XIX.—POOLS OF SOLOMON—HILL COUNTRY—HEBRON.

Hill of Evil Council—Cultivated Fields—Well of the Wise Men—Plain of Rephaim—Convent of Elijah—Sight of Bethlehem—Tomb of Rachel—Pools of Solomon—Fountain Sealed—Contrast—"Hill Country of Judea"—Tekoa—Haunts of David—Beth-zur—Valley of Eschol—Hebron—Camping-Ground—Cave of Machpelah—Tent-Life.. .225

XX.—HOME OF THE PATRIARCHS—BETHLEHEM—MAR SABA.

Breakfast—Hebron—Abraham's Oak—Grape Slips—Old Aqueduct—Vale of Etam—Bethlehem—Church of the Nativity—Stable and Manger—Convent of Santa Saba..238

XXI.—THE DEAD SEA AND THE JORDAN.

Our Bedawin Guard—Approach to the Dead Sea—En-gedi—Robbers—Lake Scenery—Sea of Death—Cities of the Plain—A Bath—River Jordan—Nebo—Death of Moses—Prophets of the Jordan—Baptism of Christ—Bathing of the Pilgrims...247

XXII.—JERICHO TO JERUSALEM.

Gilgal—Brook Cherith—Roman Jericho—City of Palm Trees—Quarantania—Apples of Sodom—Fountain of Elisha—Scripture Sites—Adummim—Foot-steps of Jesus—Place of Thieves—Mustapha—Bethany......................................260

XXIII.—CITY OF THE GREAT KING—GETHSEMANE.

Jerusalem—Upper Pool of Gihon—Tombs of the Kings—Quarry under the City—Tomb of the Virgin—Gethsemane—Aged Olive-Trees—Tearful Emotions—Prayer-Meeting in the Garden—Impressions—Pool of Bethesda............270

XXIV.—BENJAMIN—GIBEON—GIBEAH—BETHEL.

Mount Scopus—Last View of the Holy City—Heights of Benjamin—Nob—Mizpeh—Gibeon—Sun Standing Still—Gibeah—Rizpah's Grief—Ramah—Beeroth—Bible Topography—Bethel and its Associations—Abraham and Lot—Battle of Ai—Rimmon—Ophra 280

CONTENTS.

XXV.—EPHRAIM—SHILOH—PLAIN OF MOREH—JACOB'S WELL.

Fertility Amidst Rocky Desolation—Yebrud—Fountain of Robbers—Picturesque Scenes—Shiloh—Lebonah—Arab Horses—Plain of Mukhna—Armed Natives—Salutations—Jacob's Well..293

XXVI.—NABLUS—SHECHEM—MOUNT GERIZIM.

Tomb of Joseph—Vale of Nablus—Reading the Law—Shechem—Olive-Trees—Ascent of Mount Gerizim—Samaritan Temple—A Shrine—View from the Summit—Samaritan Synagogue—An Old Copy of the Pentateuch—Lepers—Scenes by the Way—Shepherds—Bedawin...305

XXVII.—SAMARIA—DOTHAN—PASSES OF MANASSEH.

The "Hill Samaria"—Church of Saint John—Grand Colonnade—Inhabitants—Bible Events—Jeba—Plain of Sanur—Tell Dothain—Pits or Dry Cisterns—Joseph Sold—A Celestial Army—Kubatieh—Jenin............................315

XXVIII.—PLAIN OF ESDRAELON—JEZREEL—SHUNEM—NAIN.

Valley of Megiddo—Verdure—Gilboa—Jezreel—Naboth's Vineyard—Bethshean—Gideon's Army—Battle of Mount Tabor—Bedawin Tents—The Shunamite Woman—Little Hermon—Visit to Nain—Endor—Saul and the Witch.....324

XXIX.—MOUNT TABOR AND THE SEA OF GALILEE.

Ascent of Tabor—First Sight of the Sea of Galilee—Magnificent View—Scene of the Transfiguration—Trial of Baal at Carmel—The New Prophet—Fine Morning—Sons of Ishmael—On the Bank of the Lake—Tiberias—Hot Springs...334

XXX.—PLAIN OF GENNESARETH — CAPERNAUM — SEA OF GALILEE.

Along the Shore—Magdala—"Land of Gennesaret"—Chinnereth—Bethsaida—Capernaum—Home of Jesus—Back to the Tents—Sunday at the Sea of Galilee—Services—Last View of the Lake—Poem.....................................345

XXXI.—MOUNT OF BEATITUDES—CANA—NAZARETH.

Sermon on the Mount—Battle of Hattin—Cana—Vale of Nazareth—Church of the Annunciation—Work-shop of Joseph—Mensa Christi—Girls at the Fountain of the Virgin—Evening in Nazareth—Fine View from the Hill—Footprints of Jesus—Sefurieh—Mt. Carmel—Thunder-storm—Plain of Acre....357

XXXII.—PHŒNICIA—COAST OF TYRE AND SIDON.

Saint Jean d'Acre—Achzib—High Promontory—Alexander's Tent—Ladder of Tyre—Ras el-'Ain—Aqueducts—Tyre, its Present Aspect and Ruins—Paul's Visit—River Leontes—A Curious Story—Roman Relics—Sarepta—The Poor Widow—Footsteps of Jesus—Approach to Sidon—Fruit Gardens—A Christian Family—Sidon to Beirut......:.......................................369

XXXIII.—BEIRUT—SMYRNA—CONSTANTINOPLE—ATHENS—HOME.

Situation of Beirut—Dr. Thomson—Sabbath Service—Farewell to the Holy Land—On the Mediterranean—Cyprus—Rhodes—Patmos—Sights in Smyrna—Mitylene — Ilium — Situation of Constantinople — Saint Sophia—Mosques—Tombs—Seraglio Palace—Bosphorus to Black Sea—Golden Horn—Classic Shores and Islands—Athens; its Scenery and Temples—Mars' Hill—Mount Ætna—Messina—Marseilles—Paris—Homeward Bound....................381

APPENDIX—Visit of the Prince of Wales to the Cave of Machpelah..........393

EUROPE, EGYPT, AND THE HOLY LAND.

I.
The Passage—Ireland—Scotland.

THE Old World! It had been for years my eager desire and hope to see it—to be a pilgrim in its lands historic and sacred, with which are associated the great and thrilling events of the past. I had longed to look upon its mountains, lakes, and rivers, its cities and peoples, its monuments and ruins. At length, by a favoring Providence, the way was prepared, and the preliminaries of the tour arranged. The City of Elms, and dear friends, offering their prayers and benedictions, were left behind; and on a beautiful day at noon I embarked from New York on the steamer *City of Washington*. It was a sad moment, parting with those who had accompanied me to the ship. We watched each other, I on deck and they on the wharf, waving our handkerchiefs, till we could discern each other no longer. Then there were tearful eyes on ship and shore. Such a scene and one's indescribable emotions are not to be forgotten, as the ship begins to move, and bears him away, away, till friends and native land fade from sight. I knew but one of the passengers, the Rev. A. D. Gillette, D. D., of New York, my genial *compagnon du voyage*.

The weather for two days was delightful, though the swell of the sea was considerable from a previous storm. A large majority of the passengers were sea-sick, some of them severely so, scarcely appearing at the table during the voyage. I escaped entirely; and notwithstanding it was a somewhat long and rough passage, I enjoyed it. On the third day out, we met the *Persia*, and exchanged shouts and salutations. The monotony of sea-life is broken in various ways. Now it is calm and clear, and the sun goes down to rest in a bed of molten gold. Then come fogs and rains and gales, and the waves roll and break furiously, while the ship careens and pitches as she struggles on. There is something indescribably grand in the extent and movements of "this great and wide sea." I watch it for hours with constant and delightful thoughts of Him who holds the waters in the hollow of His hand, and whose footsteps are in the great deep. I had longed to see icebergs, and was gratified. Among several, seen at different times, one was gloriously magnificent and beautiful, as it loomed up at some distance, like a splendid architectural pile, with domes and minarets glittering in the setting sun. I was favored also with the sight of several whales sporting and spouting, and partly throwing their huge forms out of the sea. The sight of land was pleasant, as we entered the harbor of St. Johns, Newfoundland, to take the passengers of the *Edinburgh*, wrecked by an iceberg, among whom was a member of my dear flock, who, in the hour of awful peril, was calm in the hope and peace which Jesus gives. This detention, and constant head-winds, made our passage long.

Many agreeable acquaintances were made and conversations held, to be remembered as a perpetual pleasure. The number of passengers was large, and the regulations of the ship admirable. Capt. Petrie was ever cheerful, and unwearied in his efforts to make all comfortable and happy. He read the English Church Service on each of the two Sabbaths, and on the second, two sermons were also preached by Presbyterian and Baptist ministers. On the last evening before the coast of the Emerald Isle greeted our glad sight, we had a very pleasant literary entertainment. Poems were read and recited, speeches made, and songs sung. Instead of proceeding to Liverpool, we, with several others, left the steamer as she touched at Queenstown, on the evening of July 1st. We had been over thirteen days on the sea, and it was grateful to stand again on the solid ground. We were detained but a little by the Custom-house officers, and soon found comfortable quarters at Queen's Hotel.

My first day in Ireland was one of much enjoyment. In the midst of objects strange and novel, excitement ran high, and it was easy to laugh or to weep. The scenery from Queenstown to Cork, and thence to Blarney Castle, is various and enchanting. Hills, valleys, cultivated fields, flowing streams, fine buildings, and old ruins, were surveyed with delighted admiration. This old castle, containing the famous "Blarney Stone," is a grand ruin, covered with ivy, and situated amidst beautiful grounds. We climbed to the top of its tower, and enjoyed the view it presents.

The same afternoon we went by railway to Killarney, in the South of Ireland. Everywhere the fields looked green and rich, bearing good crops, and making a striking contrast with the miserable mud-cabins scattered among them. The next day was Sunday. We walked from the Lake Hotel, about two miles, to the town, over a fine road with a high stone wall and locked gates each side, to the Episcopal church, where we heard from a curate an excellent sermon, evangelical and earnest; but the audience was small. Passing up the principal street after service, we found it full of people, ragged and filthy for the most part, looking as though they had just come out of the wretched huts, matted thickly together, and forming the queerest looking town I had ever seen. I was informed that many of these people were from the region about, and had come to hire out and be hired for the week. We called at the Wesleyan Chapel, and saw the minister, who insisted that one of us should preach in the evening, and the other give an account of the American revival, in which they were greatly interested. Dr. Gillette preached, and I spoke of the revival, more particularly as I had witnessed it in my own city and congregation. Out of a population of nine thousand in this town, there are but one hundred Protestant communicants. The multitudes are ignorant, degraded Papists.

The next day, July 4th, was one of marked interest. A party of a dozen or more Americans, mostly fellow-voyagers across the Atlantic, made the tour of the mountains and lakes of Killarney. We rode several miles on Irish jaunting cars, a vehicle I like much for its ease and convenience. It has but two wheels, and you sit back to back, two or three on a side, looking into the fields each way. One horse will thus easily draw six persons besides the driver, who sits in front. We then walked through the Gap of Dunloe, passing the cottage of Kate Kearney. The scenery, embracing high, conical, bare and rocky hills, and deep vales, with little lakes and lively streams and cascades, is at once wild, beautiful and grand. We were followed by jolly Irish peasant girls, some with bottles of "Mountain Dew," a kind of whiskey, and others with goat's milk, pertinaciously urging us to buy the "punch," and not succeeding they begged as persistently for pennies. At length we reached by a long descent, the head of the lakes, where we took boats, and by strong arms were rowed through a succession of lovely sheets of water, linked together by narrow crystal outlets, and hemmed around by mountainous cliffs and green hills, ever-changing in form, as we glided along a circuit of many miles, till we reached our hotel. Now and then, under some tall cliff, the bugle was sounded, and delightful echoes given. As we passed Eagle's Nest, a bird of Jove soared from the summit of the mountain and swept over our heads. "'Tis the Agle of Indepindence," shouted one of the sturdy oarsmen, and their lusty "hurrahs!" sounded out in honor of the glorious Fourth and of us Americans.

We had made arrangements for a sort of extemporaneous celebration on our return. We had a fine dinner. The American flag was hoisted on a pole; the Declaration of Independence was read; an Ora-

tion and Poem were delivered, the former by William
E. Robinson, Esq., of New York, the latter fell to my
lot; thirteen toasts were proposed, and eloquent and
appropriate speeches made. Dr. Gillette spoke in
behalf of the clergy. The following is one verse of
the Poem:

  O, Country of Freedom!
   What music to-day
  Breaks over thy vastness
   With jubilant sway!
  I hear the glad sound
   Stealing o'er the wide sea,
  And my heart beats response
   To the Song of the Free!

 The celebration, all of which was in good taste and
order, closed with a moderate display of fireworks.
The occasion excited much pleasant interest. The
editor of the County newspaper was present, and
published in his next issue a full account, including
the speeches and poem; and we saw a notice of the
celebration in various papers of the kingdom.

 On the way to Dublin, we stopped at a railway
junction and made an excursion to Limerick, and
spent two hours in walking about that old city and on
the banks of the Shannon. We passed several days
in Dublin, including a Sabbath. It is a fine city, containing many objects of interest. We visited the
Botanical Gardens, Trinity College, on Commencement day, and saw students in their black gowns, and
Professors in their red ones; the Royal Society, containing many ancient relics of Ireland; and Christ's
and St. Patrick's churches, in the latter of which Dean
Swift officiated, and was buried. The Presbyterian

General Assembly of Ireland was in session, and we attended several of its meetings, which were of marked interest, especially the accounts of the great and marvelous religious awakening in progress in the North of Ireland. Some of the ministers said there had been more conversions in two or three weeks in their congregations, than in twenty years before. Some even of the ministers had been converted, confessing that though they had preached the gospel correctly, they had never till now preached it with Jesus in their hearts. Convictions are deep, striking and powerful. Many are prostrated physically, and seem to lie almost unconscious for awhile. These strange bodily manifestations are not encouraged, and are regarded as accidents of a great and glorious work of the Spirit of God. Meetings are held nearly every evening, the churches are crowded, and day meetings are held in the open air. Some of the converts say they were awakened by letters from America. Prayers offered in our revival meetings are no doubt being answered in Ireland. We heard, one evening, an address from Brownlow North, Esq., and formed some pleasant acquaintances with members of the Assembly, and by invitation, dined with Rev. Dr. Kirkpatrick, in whose church they met, and breakfasted with the whole Assembly in the Rotunda, where the ladies provided each morning for about four hundred ministers and delegates. We dined also with a large-hearted Elder, who took us in his family carriage three miles out, to the Roebuck House, his beautiful suburban residence, and allowed us to wander over his richly cultivated gardens and gather as many large and delicious strawberries as we chose.

We were kindly entertained also by the pastor of the Baptist church, who accompanied us to the beautiful region in the County of Wicklow—including a visit to Powerscourt Waterfall, and the Glen of the Downs—and prevailed on us to occupy his pulpit on the Sabbath, and give some sketches of the work of God in the United States. His people were very much interested, and lingered to converse with us after service, and listen to some of the hyms and tunes sung in our revival meetings. We were introduced to several Episcopal clergymen, who are much interested in the revival, and unite with others in prayer-meetings, and we dined with one at his pleasant manse a few miles from Dublin. These cordial and brotherly greetings and kind hospitalities evinced a generous Christian spirit, and were gratefully appreciated.

Belfast, which we next visited, is a thriving, American-like city. On our way thither we passed through Drogheda, where the battle of Boyne was fought, July 1, 1690. The venerable Dr. Cooke, at the head of the Presbyterian ministry in Ireland, having been half a century in the service, kindly conducted us to several immense linen manufactories, the College and Theological Seminary, in which he is a professor, and insisted on our dining at his house. We passed Ballymena on our way to Portrush, and saw several religious meetings in the open air in progress. We had now reached the northern coast of the island, and were in sight of the far-famed Giant's Causeway. A few miles by jaunting car brought us to the spot. But we paused mid-way to survey the grand old ruins of Dunluce Castle, perched on the edge of a cliff hundreds of feet above the sea. It is impossible to give an adequate description of the Giant's Causeway, familiar from childhood in pictures which utterly fail to delineate it. It is a magnificent affair, however, wonderfully bold and unique in its configurations, embracing deep caves, bridge-like abutments, high bluffs and perpendicular columns of basalt and trap.

In our journeys through Ireland we noticed not only ruined castles, but many ancient Round Towers, some of them a hundred and fifty feet high, and in a good state of preservation. They commonly stand alone, and their origin and object appear to be wrapped in mystery. Ireland is more beautiful than I had supposed, and where Protestantism prevails, the people are intelligent and thrifty; but it is all the reverse under Romanism, which is the curse of the country. Another evil is the large land-estates, making the masses all tenants. There are great extremes among the people—the rich and upper class, and the lower class, very poor, with hardly any that may be called a middle class.

There is a marked distinction between Ireland and Scotland. They are different in their scenery, different in the characteristics of the people. Indeed, one is struck with the perceptible change in various respects, as he travels from the center to the North of Ireland. The cabins of the people grow better, their language is more Scottish, the accent broader, and they look better and thriftier in every way. This change is owing to the more general prevalence of

Protestantism in the North. Romanism is a dead weight upon the masses who adhere to it. It crushes the very life of liberty and enterprise out of them. Happy will it be for Ireland when its terrible yoke shall be broken. The present glorious revival is a star of hope and promise.

We had a fine trip by steamer from Portrush to Oban, on the west coast of Scotland. It took us from morning till late at night. We stopped a couple of hours at Islay, a Scottish island. In wandering upon the shore and through a village, we came to the open door of a school-room, and were invited in by the teacher. He called up a class, and exhibited their proficiency in various branches of study. They acquitted themselves well. The school-room was attached to a house of worship. Here, I thought, is a symbol of Scottish character—religion and education united. I do not remember to have seen a school-house in Ireland—none in the rural districts. Another thing: in Scotland you meet with no beggars. In Ireland they are as thick as grasshoppers, and follow and importune you with an almost resistless pertinacity.

We had many a fine view of water and island, of shore and mountain, as we voyaged along through the day. Early the next morning we took another steamer, and went still farther up, through Loch Linnhe and into Loch Levin, passing by old castles and other scenes of picturesque and romantic interest. At Ballahulish we took a coach for a magnificent drive of more than forty miles through the Highlands; and long shall we remember that day. On every hand in endless diversity, rose grand and glorious mountains, crowned with alternate mist and clouds and glorious sun-light, and in one instance with banks of glittering snow. Now the lofty slopes were ragged and rocky, and then they were covered to the very summits with a beautiful grassy verdure, while along the rising and rounded hill-sides large flocks of sheep, and sometimes antlered deer, were feeding. Now a crystal stream like a silver ribbon came gently down the far declivities, and again it bounded along, leaping over a precipice in a splendid waterfall. The Pass of Glencoe is grandly wild. We looked sadly upon the little ruins that mark the spot of a terrible massacre.

The end of our coach ride brings us to the head of the beautiful and mountain-hemmed Loch Lomond. A little steamer takes us quietly over its calm surface, while we observe its romantic surroundings, and gaze upon spots of special or historic interest. We almost expect to see Rob Roy hurrying into his cave. The mist for a moment is lifted from the summit of Ben Lomond, and he appears as if standing tip-toe to look over into the charming lake. We traverse nearly the whole length of the lake, and rest for the night close on its margin. After taking a morning bath in its pure water, we walk to Loch Katrine, smaller, but if possible more beautiful and romantic than Loch Lomond. As we glide over its surface, by Ellen's Isle, and under the shadow of Ben-venue, the charms with which Walter Scott has invested it in the Lady of the Lake, have a living interest. We then pass by coach through the Trossachs, wild, bristling and forest-covered mountains, and along the shores of sweet little lakes, making altogether a rich variety of the most charming and sublime scenery. It would seem that the great and blessed Creator had here taken special pains to awaken in the minds of His creatures an admiration for His handiworks, and a holy aspiration to stand at length by the river of life and the heavenly hills.

We reached Edinburgh by rail the same day, stopping two hours at Stirling. The old castle at the latter place contains many relics of interest—the pulpit and communion-table of John Knox, an almost endless variety of old arms and armor, and various things relating to Mary Queen of Scots, who was here imprisoned. The views from the elevated castle are about as splendid as human eye ever beheld. Battlefields of Wallace and Bruce are in sight. But the wide, green fields, fringed with hedges, the beautifully winding rivers Teith and Forth, the vales and woodland hills, on which the slanting sunbeams fall through the clouds, formed an enchanting scene long to be remembered, and vividly suggestive of the Land Beulah and the Delectable Mountains.

Edinburgh is a wonderfully unique and picturesque city, containing much to interest the traveler. We visited Holyrood Palace and Abbey, and there obtained a good view of the Prince of Wales, as he went out for a walk into the city. He resembles the portraits of Victoria, his mother. In Edinburgh Castle we saw the regalia of Scotland, including the golden and jeweled crown. We went into St. Giles's church, where Knox preached, stood on the spot where he was buried, and went to the house where he lived. In the Advocates' Library we saw a copy of the first edition of the Bible printed with types, and an older copy in manuscript; also Scott's Waverly in manuscript, and a finely preserved mummy, supposed to belong to the house of Pharaoh. There, too, we saw the old Covenant and Confession of Faith, with the original signatures. What a world of varied thoughts such sights awaken!

We made a delightful excursion to Melrose Abbey, wonderful, though in ruins, for the exquisite beauty and finish of its architecture, as well as its grand proportions. Its Gothic arches, great windows, and fine statuary, over which mosses cling and ivies creep so gracefully, seemed like enchantment as

> "The ruddy light of morning bold
> Streamed o'er the ruin gray and old."

We drove to Abbotsford, the splendid residence of Sir Walter Scott, and to Dryburgh Abbey, where he was buried. In the various rooms he once occupied his impress lives in a thousand forms, but a great-grandchild is the only survivor of his family.

On Sunday we regretted the absence of Dr. Guthrie, but heard Dr. Candlish. His manner is peculiar, nervous and twitching; but his sermon was rich and pungent with evangelical truth. I heard also a good discourse from Rev. Mr. Dickie, of the oldest Baptist church in Edinburgh, and enjoyed a pleasant visit at his house. With the family of Mr. T. G. Douglas, formerly of New Haven, Ct., I had a most delightful home during my stay in the city. On our way to England we stopped awhile in Glasgow, a great commercial city, visiting its grand old Cathedral and other objects of interest.

II.
England—Wales—Noted Places.

THE rural scenery of England is garden-like and beautiful. The verdure is rich and velvety, the flowers have bright and sparkling hues, and the fields, divided into small lots by green hedges and ornamental trees, present a picturesque and charming appearance. We were passing through the heart of the island, when the reapers were everywhere harvesting the golden wheat. It was a fine sight, and the crop seemed to be good and large. It is strange to me not to see any Indian corn growing. None is raised here; it would not ripen in this climate.

In passing from Glasgow to Liverpool we had a fine view of the country. We stopped at Beattock, and walked in the evening two or three miles to the little village of Moffat, where there is a celebrated sulphur well, the resort of numerous invalids, whom we saw early the next morning, making their way to the fountain to drink of the nauseous but healing water. At Carlisle we left the train again, and wandering over the city, visited its old Cathedral. We passed through Penrith and Lancaster, observing a venerable feudal castle at the former place. We reached Liverpool in the evening, and were directed to the Crooked Billet Hotel.

Next we made a pleasant excursion into Wales, as far as Caernarvon, stopping a little time at the interesting old town of Chester, and walking on its ancient wall. Beautiful and striking scenery—mountain and river, sea and island—greeted us all the way. Conway and Caernarvon have their splendid old castles. The Tubular Railway Bridge over the Menai Straits, near Bangor, is a wonderful triumph of skill. Caernarvon is a place of much interest. Its castle is a most magnificent ruin. Its massive and lofty walls, surmounted with towers, enclose an area of about three acres. We ascended to the top of the highest tower, and entered the little room where Edward II. was born, the first Saxon Prince of Wales. From a high hill back of the town we saw the Snowdon mountains, and Snowdon itself, rising in bold and shadowy grandeur a few miles from us. We chanced to meet a deacon of the Baptist church. He conducted us to the plain chapel where the eloquent Christmas Evans preached for some years, and where he sat under his ministry. Glorious "specimens of Welch preaching" those walls have often heard. The Welch language and peculiar costume of the old women, especially with their black fur or silk stovepipe hats, are still in vogue.

We visited St. George's Hall, and other public buildings in Liverpool. We had the pleasure of hearing on the Sabbath, and also of enjoying pleasant social interviews with, Rev. Hugh Stowell Brown, for fourteen years pastor of one of the Baptist churches, and the most popular preacher in the place. His house of worship is being enlarged, so as to furnish sittings for 2,200 people. The large hall where we heard him was entirely filled. He is preaching a course of sermons on the Gospel by John. His text, that morning, was—" Ye have not chosen me, but I have chosen you, and ordained you, that ye should go and bring forth fruit, and that your fruit should remain." He first considered the *fact* that Christ's disciples are chosen or selected by Him, and secondly, the *purpose* for which they are chosen. It was an excellent sermon, sound, clear, practical. Mr. Brown is an easy, fluent speaker, adapting himself to the comprehension of the masses. He is the son of a clergyman of the Established Church, and his age, I think, is thirty-six. He is not tall, but solid in form, is in robust health and vigor, and of manly appearance. May he long hold forth the word of life with power and success.

A letter of introduction gave us a very pleasant interview with Rev. Dr. Raffles, now in the fiftieth year of his ministry. He received us with the greatest cordiality and affability. I had made a suggestion of going to the place where his immediate predecessor, the youthful and eloquent Thomas Spencer, was drowned. Dr. Raffles showed us a manuscript notebook, in which Spencer had recorded his texts from the time he began to preach. He spoke of the recent American edition of his Life of Spencer, and of the handsome style in which Messrs. Sheldon & Co. had issued it. The day of this interview we went to London, and the first news we heard from home, was the death of KINGMAN NOTT, so like that of Spencer. It was a sad shock and heavy grief to us, for we knew

BUNYAN'S COTTAGE AT ELSTOW

our young brother well, and loved him, how much! Other well known brethren in the ministry had finished their work also—in so short a time had death plucked a goodly cluster.

Our next excursion was to several deeply interesting places once hallowed by the presence and deeds of the great and good. First we went to Bedford, leaving London early in the morning, July 27th. As we entered the town, and were crossing the bridge over the Ouse, with what intense interest we gazed on the spot where stood the jail in which Bunyan was a prisoner so long, and where the immortal allegory had its birth! The little river flows on as when he saw it from his grated window, but not a vestige of the jail remains. "It was at that corner of the street," said our guide, as we passed along, "that Bunyan heard the pious women talking of religion." This was before his conversion. We went to the house of worship, a large and substantial one, which occupies the site of that in which Bunyan preached. In the vestry we sat in a chair once owned and used by him, and for which a large sum of money has been repeatedly offered and refused. We saw some relics of his also, particularly a little cabinet or tool box, now kept by the pastor of the church, Rev. Mr. Jukes. A pleasant drive brought us to Elstow, and to the cottage in which the glorious tinker was born. We stood within the walls that were once his home. There he mended pots and pans, and there, doubtless, he wrote some of his delightful books. We gave the good lady of the cottage, who kindly received us, a shilling or so for her trouble, and she gave us some nice plum-pudding, just taken smoking from the pot. I plucked a leaf from a grape-vine clambering up the side of the cottage, and enclosed it in my next letter, that it might be looked upon by dear eyes at home.

Another short drive brought us to Cardington, the beautiful residence of the immortal John Howard, and from which he exiled himself that he might labor amid peril and pestilence, for the benefit of wretched prison inmates. He was both a true philanthropist and hero and will be held in everlasting remembrance. We, entered the house in which he lived, and walked under stately trees which he planted amid those charming grounds. The place is now occupied by a member of Parliament.

The same day found us at Kettering, a name and place forever to be associated with the history of modern missions—hallowed, too, as the scene of Andrew Fuller's pastoral labors, and the spot where his precious dust reposes. It is a small, pleasant town, occupying a gradual slope. We made our way to the Baptist chapel. A good woman opened its door, and when she found we were Baptist ministers from America, she warmly grasped our hands, saying she must give us the right hand of fellowship. "Do you remember Andrew Fuller?" "O yes, I was a little girl in the gallery yonder, and recollect his preaching well." More than forty years have passed since those lips, touched with sacred fire and heavenly wisdom, were sealed in death; yet the place seems instinct with his presence. The same room and pews, the same pulpit and communion table, that witnessed his ministrations, remain. A marble tablet to his memory graces the wall. We stand in his pulpit, ready to take off our shoes, and long and pray for the mighty soul of piety that lived and wrought in him. Our feelings are deepened as we go a few steps and linger at his tomb. O rare and excellent man of God! well didst thou do thy blessed work, and thy rest is glorious! We entered the parsonage where Fuller lived and died, and were kindly received by Mrs. Mursell, wife of the present pastor, who was absent.

Up that street, yonder, the great and good Dr. John Gill, the learned commentator, was born. A little farther down the slope, and in reaching the place we pass the chapel of the Rev. Mr. Toller, the friend of Robert Hall, is the memorable spot where the Baptist Missionary Society was formed in 1792, the first of those great modern movements for the world's evangelization. We are kindly admitted to the room, and as we stand there, the reverend forms of those saintly and large-hearted men are imaged to our view. We go to the rear of the dwelling, and see the beautiful lawn where the jubilee was celebrated in 1842. A son of Mr. Toller, the Independent minister referred to above, constrained us to go to his house, where we were entertained by himself and his very interesting family in the most cordial and hospitable manner. He showed us many rare letters and autographs, and the biographical sketch of his father in manuscript, just as Robert Hall wrote it.

Northampton is not far off. We visited it the next morning. Here the Rylands lived and labored, and here Mr. J. E. Ryland still lives. He is the author, editor, or translator of several important works, among them the Life and Letters of John Foster. We had the pleasure of a few moments in his society. From the Baptist chapel where the Rylands preached, we went to that of the heavenly Doddridge, entered his vestry and his pulpit, lifting up our hearts to God for rich measures of the grace that dwelt in him. We saw the pew occupied by Col. Gardiner. The chair, table, and little mirror which Doddridge used are still in the vestry. Here the Rise and Progress was written.

Our next pilgrimage was to Olney, the residence of William Cowper. We found access to his dwelling, and to the little summer-house in his garden, where he wrote "The Task," and many of his hymns. We sang there, perhaps in the very place where they were written, those heavenly lines:

"There is a fountain filled with blood,
Drawn from Immanuel's veins,
And sinners plunged beneath that flood,
Lose all their guilty stains."

Here, too, the excellent John Newton preached and wrote, contributing his portion of the "Olney Hymns." Thomas Scott, the commentator, labored here also. We entered the old church, that has often echoed to their voices.

These two days will long be remembered. Our pleasure was heightened by the company of the Rev. Dr. Stow and Rev. W. C. Child, of Boston. They returned to London, and we proceeded to Coventry, and then to Kenilworth and Warwick, whose grand old ivy-colored castles we wandered through, and afterwards made a pilgrimage to Stratford-on-Avon. Its principal attraction is a common dwelling, with this inscription over the door: "In this house the immortal Shakespeare was born." The room in which the great poet first saw the light is entirely covered with the names of visitors. He was buried in the old church in the town, and its fine organ was being played when we entered it. A bust of the poet stands near his grave. Along side are the tombstones of his wife and daughter. I was interested in the lines upon the latter:

> "Witty above her sex, but that's not all,
> Wise to salvation was good Mistress Hall;
> Something of Shakespeare was in that, but this
> Wholly of Him with whom she's now in bliss."

Leamington, where we took a coach for Stratford, is a fine town, and in some respects the Saratoga of England, having a spring, whose water, though inferior in taste, is yet in effect much like that of the Congress Spring. Multitudes resort to it.

We went by railway to Oxford, a place renowned from the days of King Alfred to the present. Here Richard Cœur-de-Lion was born, and Wickliffe was master of a college. The city has various attractions, but the University is the absorbing one. We got weary in trying to see the various college buildings and grounds. They are very numerous. Some of the edifices are very old, and full of historical interest, and some of the grounds are beautifully laid out and decorated. Some fine walks are shaded by grand old elms. But the elms of England are inferior to our own. Their boughs are not so branching and stately, so Gothic and graceful as ours. They look more like ash trees. We found the spot, marked by a stone cross in the middle of a street, where the martyr Bishops, Cranmer, Latimer and Ridley were burnt. Not far off, a fine monument has been erected to their memory. We returned again to London.

A subsequent visit to Southampton, and interesting excursions from that place, are among the pleasant memories of England. Southampton itself has attractions as a fine and flourishing city. A Thursday evening service at the Baptist chapel, furnished occasion for a brief interview with the pastor, Rev. J. A. Spurgeon, a brother of the celebrated London preacher. He has popular gifts, and a large and growing congregation. Salisbury is easily reached by rail. I visited its splendid Cathedral, and took a drive over the plain —where shepherds are still found with their flocks— to the curious old Druid temple at Stonehenge. It is an ancient ruin, consisting of huge, rough stone shafts, mostly in an upright position, and arranged in concentric circles. Another long day on the charming Isle of Wight was full of lively interest. We reached Ryde by steam, and then enjoyed, amidst lovely and romantic scenery, pleasant drives to Newport—to Carisbrook Castle, a historical and splendid ruin—to Arreton, passing near where the "Young Cottager" lived, visiting the old church, and lingering at the hallowed grave of the "Dairyman's Daughter," in the rear of it. Returning to the steamer at Cowes, we passed near the Osborn House, the beautiful summer residence of the Queen.

III.

London—Bunhill Fields—Preachers.

LONDON is a kind of world in itself. Think of three millions of people in one city! What do they all do? How do they live? Where do they sleep? Ah! how many phases of human life, in all its contrasts of good and evil, of comfort and misery, does this great metropolis present! LONDON! the very sound of it is suggestive of sonorous confusion and indefinite amplitude, and other things indescribable. It is a good place for one to feel humble, and how like a very atom he is in the world. He may drop into the dust, or float away in the air, and who cares? But to the Christian, how precious is the doctrine of God's special providence! He regards with particular care and infinite love the least and feeblest of His trusting children. He who telleth the number of the stars, and calleth them all by their names—O, is it not a blessed thought that He is my Refuge, and underneath me are the Everlasting Arms!

I can only allude to some of the sights and scenes of London and vicinity. St. Paul's Cathedral is a magnificent structure. I ascended to the ball, the highest accessible point, 406 feet from the ground, and enjoyed a splendid view of the city and country about. Westminster Abbey, with its historical associations and monuments of sleeping dead, kings, nobles and poets, is replete with interest. The Tower of London, terrible in its connection with imprisonments, sufferings and violent deaths, one visits with a sense of awe. The British Museum and the Crystal Palace are so ample in their dimensions, and contain such a wonderful variety of things, antique and modern, that one is bewildered and astonished. Hampton Court, the ancient home of Church and State dignitaries, and Windsor Castle, the residence of the royal family, in all their appointments and surroundings, their furniture and paintings are on a scale of magnificence that must be seen to be comprehended. The entrance to the former and its flower-gardens, and the view of the country around the latter, are charming beyond description.

The Houses of Parliament are splendid. We saw the members sitting on their benches facing each other, and with their hats on, and listened to a few indifferent speeches. The lions were not roused. The Zoölogical Gardens are very extensive and the specimens of beast, bird and fish numerous. The Thames Tunnel is more curious than useful. Madame Tussaud's exhibition of wax figures and curiosities is very attractive. Richmond Hill and the Parks of London are worthy of special notice.

But no place interested me more than Bunhill Fields Cemetery. There is the tomb of John Bunyan. I hastened to it. No path is so well trodden as that which leads to the grave of the Tinker of Elstow. O, it is a sacred spot! and as I stood by that substantial, oblong monument, I tearfully longed for more of the Christ-like spirit that gave such a depth and richness and heavenly glow to the piety of the Immortal Allegorist. The simple inscription is—"Mr. JOHN BUNYAN, Author of the Pilgrim's Progress, Obt. 31st August, 1688, Æ. 60." The following verses were inspired by the visit, and a part of them were written while I was sitting on the pedestal of

BUNYAN'S TOMB.

Thou prince of dreamers! I have found
   The place of thy last sleeping,
And grateful tread this hallowed ground,
   With mingled joy and weeping.

Dear Bunyan! long I've loved thy name
   More than my words can measure,
And long shall pilgrims hold thy fame
   A sweet and precious treasure.

Thou wast a burning, shining light
   In thy blest sphere of duty,
Though then unknown a star so bright,
   So rich in heavenly beauty.

God raised thee from thy lowly place,
   Thou plain, untutored thinker;
And gave thee, ah! what gifts of grace,
   O wondrous Elstow tinker!

Thy heart and tongue His Spirit fired,
   When from His foe, He gained thee:
To preach His truth, He called, inspired,
   Commissioned and ordained thee.

What crowds beneath thy earnest voice—
   Thy zeal to save them burning—
Were made to weep, believe, rejoice,
   From sin to Jesus turning!

Satan or man—ay, both, no doubt,
   With mischievous endeavor,
Put thee in jail, to thus put out
   Thy kindled flame forever.

Celestial genius would not die,
   Through years of long confining,
Whilst thou, with comfort from the sky,
   Wast cheerful, unrepining.

Methinks within thy dungeon's gloom
   A light divine had risen,
To make it Glory's ante-room,
   Though still thy Bedford prison.

How clearly there the heavenly path
   Rose on thy spirit's vision,
That from the city doomed to wrath,
   Leads to the blest Elysian.

Then passed before thee in thy dream
   A happy band and saintly;
Thy pictures make them real seem,
   Though oft a little quaintly.

I love to trace their pathway o'er,
   And hear their joyful singing,
Till, through the stream, they reach the shore
   Where angel-harps are ringing.

Keep, Bunhill Fields, his precious dust,
   Housed in thy rare collection—
How fair he'll shine among the just
   In the great resurrection!

Immortal dreamer! slumbering here,
   How sweet thy Pilgrim's story;
On thy blest tomb I drop a tear,
   And envy thee in glory.

> A jewel-studded crown—how bright!
> To thy dear head is given:
> May I be found with thee in light,
> A pilgrim safe in heaven.

That cemetery is full of precious dust. It is a necropolis of dissenting ministers. I stood by the graves of Watts, Owen, Gill, Rippon, Hart, Ivemy, and the mother of John Wesley, whose grave and that of Adam Clarke I found across the street in the rear of a Methodist chapel.

Not far from Bunhill Fields is the district of old Smithfield, which every one familiar with the New England Primer, will recollect as the place where John Rogers, the martyr, was burnt at the stake. I tried to identify the exact spot, but no one knew precisely where it was, only it was somewhere in that little open space. In crossing and re-crossing it I probably stood on the very place where the good man resigned his soul to the chariot of fire.

A word about some of the London preachers. The last Sunday in July I heard Mr. Spurgeon at the great Music Hall in Surrey Gardens. I went early and got a good seat. For more than an hour the people came thronging in, till the immense building was entirely filled. Mr. Spurgeon entered at a quarter to eleven, and as he ascends the pulpit you recognize him at once from his portraits, though he looks rather better than the best of them. He glances over the vast assembly, which is now hushed to silence, bows his head a moment on the pulpit cushion, and then gives out the hymn, commencing,

> "There is a fountain filled with blood."

He reads a part of it with a full, clear voice, which rings in rich, mellow tones through every part of the Hall. He then tells them to sing with heart and voice, reading each verse before it is sung. A leader in front of the pulpit names the tune. A short, earnest prayer follows. Then he reads the fourth chapter of Hebrews, making striking and delightful comments as he passes from verse to verse. At the closing verse he says, "We are called upon to approach the throne of grace; let us therefore all rise and sing one stanza before prayer—

> "Come, my soul, thy suit prepare,
> Jesus loves to answer prayer;
> He himself has bid thee pray,
> Rise and ask without delay."

The assembly rise and sing it. A longer prayer follows, in which various classes and the wants of the world are remembered. He then announces the hymn and reads it, and it is sung as before—

> "Rock of Ages! shelter me."

He says he hopes all will sing; and whoever sings this hymn with the heart, is not far from the kingdom of God. Coming to the last verse, he says, "Sing the next four lines very solemnly." He reads them with a subdued voice, and the congregation sing them as he requests, with good effect, but very properly let their voices out fully on the two closing lines. He then announces his text: Matt. xi. 29—"I am meek and lowly in heart." He presented the meek and lowly character of Christ as a reason why sinners should come to Him. He preached an hour, and all listened with deep and silent attention, and often a tear dropped here and there from many a moistened eye. Numbers stood through the whole service, as did the preacher himself, not once taking his seat after he entered the pulpit. His manner of conducting the service is an element of his success. He seems like a general at the head of an army, marshaling his hosts and inspiring every heart. He sings with the congregation, whose many voices swell the volume of praise to heaven with thrilling effect. Immediately after the sermon, or a notice given, he dismissed the assembly with the benediction. Mr. Spurgeon preached just as I expected he would, and as you would expect him to, after reading one of his sermons. He is simple, direct, earnest, fluent, and has a clear and commanding voice. I heard him the next Thursday evening in his own chapel, and saw him baptize thirteen converts. I saw him in his vestry after service, and was very cordially received and invited to visit him at his house the next day. I spoke of the interest manifested toward him and his sermons in the United States. He seemed gratified, and gave me a handsome book, with his autograph, for a member of my family. I heard him preach again the next Sunday morning on Blind Bartimeus with the same deep interest. His new and magnificent Tabernacle is in process of erection. May God long spare him to preach in it, with no diminution of the power and success that are now associated with his labors.

I heard Dr. Cumming preach a good practical sermon from the text, "Neither be partaker of other men's sins." He is a good-looking man, of medium size, not over fifty, apparently, with a quiet, interesting manner of speaking. He read and expounded a part of the seventh chapter of Revelation, remarking that more people went out of London every Sabbath on excursions of pleasure, than were found in all the churches and chapels in the city; and out of a population of three millions, there were but one hundred and fifty thousand communicants in the churches of all evangelical denominations. Still he believed, in the end, vastly more of the human race would be saved than lost. He thought the Hebrew, Greek, and English languages, would be spoken in heaven among the many "tongues." His house of worship was full. I also heard an able discourse from Rev. Newman Hall, pastor of Surrey Chapel, where Rowland Hill preached. I was very much pleased with Rev. Baptist W. Noel. I did not hear him preach, but dined with him at his invitation in company with Dr. Gillette. He is a perfect Christian gentleman, delighting in conversation pertaining to the kingdom of Christ. Happening into the chapel of Rev. William Landels, at Regent's Park, one evening, we found him baptizing fourteen converts, in the presence of a large congregation; that is, if a baptistery on a level with the floor, and in the *rear* of a large pulpit, can be said to be in the presence of the congregation. He invited us to breakfast with him, and we had a delightful interview at the house of Mr. Lush, an eminent barrister, whose lovely family made us doubly welcome. Subsequently I heard Mr. Landels preach a most excellent and impressive sermon.

His church is in a flourishing state; so is that of

Mr. Brock, where I attended a communion service. Both these chapels were erected or purchased mainly by the munificence of Sir Morton Peto, a member of Parliament, and one of Mr. Brock's deacons.

The singing in all the churches I have attended, is congregational. It is sometimes good, and again quite indifferent. It is best where an organ and choir lead the congregation. I attended a number of prayer meetings in Ireland, Scotland, and England, and found them far less interesting than such meetings are with us. Generally only a very few persons took part, and they were called upon or previously spoken to by the leader. In no instance did I find a meeting in which any brother present was free to take a part, or invited to do so. The prayers and remarks were often tediously long. I do not think the English or Scotch preaching equal in excellence or power to that in our country. The ministers do not work as hard; they are not so anxious and careful. There are marked exceptions, but much of their preaching is like the week-evening lectures of our pastors; expository, unstudied and common place. Most of the houses of worship seem awkwardly constructed and uncomfortable, having straight-backed pews, wide and high galleries, and lofty, tub-like pulpits. Some of the churches have a communion service every Lord's-day. As far as I was able to mingle with the ministers and brethren, I found them truly spiritual and earnest Christians.

IV.

France—Belgium—Holland—The Rhine.

A GREAT fete was about to transpire in Paris, and we hastened across the Channel in a little steamer from Newhaven to Dieppe. It was a smooth, pleasant passage, and the full moon was just rising on a glorious evening, as we landed. After some delay in the examination of baggage and passports, we took the railway, and in three or four hours reached the old city of Rouen, where we stopped for the night. It was a delightful ride, and the green hills and valleys and cultivated fields were beautiful in the moonlight. But now, among a people who spoke a different language, I seemed farther than ever from home. By a little exertion I was able to recall some of the French I once learned, and so got along tolerably well. We spent half a day in Rouen with much pleasure, visiting its old cathedral and fine churches, witnessing a beautiful marriage ceremony in one of the latter, and ascending to the top of the tower of the former, four hundred and sixty feet high, where we had a fine view of the city and country. Joan of Arc was here imprisoned and executed. A fine statue of her stands on the spot where she was burnt. A few hours' ride brought us to Paris. And what shall I say of this gay and gorgeous capital? A lady remarked that it is the best place in the world to forget God in; and the multitudes seem to be improving it for that purpose.

The birth-day of the great Napoleon was celebrated on the fifteenth of August, as a grand holiday, by games and plays, and in the evening by illuminations and fire-works, too extensive, beautiful and magnificent to be described. I never expect to see again such a vast multitude of people together until the final day. The present Emperor made it the occasion of exhibiting to the Parisians, and thousands of others, his immense army, fresh from the recent victorious battle-fields of Italy; and also to show his army the splendors of the French capital, and the exuberant greetings of a people who delight in magnificent pageants and military glory. On the previous day, he brought his army into the city, taking Sunday as the day when the people would have leisure to witness the grand parade. This splendid pageant embraced nearly eighty thousand horsemen and footmen in uniform, and with their arms and implements of war. The Emperor rode at their head as they passed through the principal streets, and then reviewed them in the Place Vendome, in the presence of the Empress and other dignitaries, and countless multitudes of people. Every street, balcony, and window affording a sight of the procession, was crowded; and thousands of seats had been prepared in the Place Vendome, around the column and statue of Napoleon I., which seemed to be looking down on the brilliant spectacle. Indications of the recent bloody battles were observed. Now and then would be seen platoons of soldiers, without muskets or swords, some of them walking with crutches, and others with their limbs bandaged or in slings. Again, only a few of a certain company or regiment would pass together. Their associates had perished on the field. Ah! how many thousands, hurried to eternity amid the horrors of war, were thus missing from those ranks! Frequently a tattered flag, taken from the enemy in battle, was borne along by its captors, amid shouts of the throng and showers of bouquets, thrown from the windows. Austrian cannon, also, the prize of the victors, were drawn in the procession. The whole line, often twenty deep, was between four and five hours in passing a given point.

What striking contrasts, unobserved, unthought of by the multitude, often meet the All-seeing Eye! A minister of the gospel found it difficult to work his way through the crowd and military lines, that he might reach a quiet sanctuary, and preach the word of life to a few who had assembled to worship God. It was my privilege to be one of that few in the American Chapel, where, in the absence of the pastor, my friend and Christian brother, Rev. Dr. Heacock, of Buffalo, preached a most excellent sermon from the words of Jesus, "Let not your heart be troubled: ye believe in God; believe also in me." He spoke of the troubles arising from our nature or fallen state, and those caused by sin; and presented Christ, and faith in Christ, as the only and certain cure.

It is painful to think how few of all the throng and dwellers in this gay city, know Christ by a simple, evangelical, experimental faith. There are splendid churches here, as the Notre Dame and Madeleine, and priests, and services, and ceremonies, such as they are; but they seem to be all outward, and showy, and hollow. There are pictures and images, and burning candles, and gaudy robes, and various manipulations of priests at the altar, and genuflections of the people, with crossings and countings of beads; but scarcely anything that a Protestant regards as intelligent New Testament religion. No gospel truth is preached with simplicity and power; no prayers from full, penitent and pleading hearts seem to be offered. This unendurable flummery of religion meets you everywhere on the Continent—in the cathedrals and churches, in processions through the streets, elevating the host, carrying an image of the Virgin and Child, bearing banners inscribed to saints and prayers to them for mercy, with men holding lanterns and long candles, litttle boys singing as they march, and girls swinging festoons of artificial flowers, while persons of both sexes kneel in the street, or cross themselves as the procession passes. No wonder that the more intelligent are infidels, and that the Sabbath is desecrated by pursuers of gain or pleasure, when nothing better is presented to meet the religious wants of man's nature.

The French are a volatile, unthinking people, living for to-day. They love to be out of doors, chatting with everybody about everything, for which their language is well suited. They scarcely seem to have any homes or family firesides, but live at cafés and restaurants, often eating and drinking on the sidewalks, and sleep, I know not where. Still, they are a very polite and apparently decorous people. They are anxious to oblige you, graciously answering your questions, and going out of their way to direct you.

I cannot dwell on the objects of interest in Paris. The Boulevards, the garden of the Tuileries, and Champs Elyseés, have been often described. The Louvre gallery of paintings contains some exquisite pictures. Pere le Chaise has its attractions as a cemetery. The tomb of the great Napoleon, not yet finished, is a magnificent structure. A view of the city and country from the top of Notre Dame, and of the Triumphal Arch, are not soon to be forgotten. A half hour's ride by railway takes you to Versailles, through the groves of Boulogne, and near the Palace of St. Cloud. But who can describe the Palace of Versailles, and its wonderfully beautiful grounds, groves, walks, statues, lakes and fountains? Its picture-gallery must be one of the largest in the world. You must travel six miles to go through all the rooms crowded with paintings and statuary. You have in these works of art a pictorial history of France, as they are arranged in chronological order. Many of the paintings are large and splendid; but the eye is pained with such an endless succession of battle-scenes, and longs for landscapes and angels of peace. We wandered through every apartment; and the silent language of many a portrait and picture and marble bust seemed to be, Where are the kings who planned and embellished this gorgeous palace?

In going from Paris to Brussels, one passes through a region of no marked interest until Belgium is reached. You pass villages, forests and cultivated fields. In the last, about as many women as men are at work. This is seen wherever you go on the Continent, and to some extent in England. Belgium is one of the most beautiful countries I have seen. It is generally level, and along nearly all its roads and canals, on either side, a fine row of thrifty, grown up trees meets the eye most pleasantly, and affords a charming shade to the traveler. Such rows of trees frequently divide fields, taking the place of hedges in England and fences in our country. You hardly see a fence or a wall, except around a city, in Europe. Brussels, "Belgium's capital," sung by the author of Childe Harold, as he introduces his vivid description of the battle of Waterloo, is in its public buildings, shops, parks, and general aspect, a lively, interesting, gay city, a sort of *petit* Paris. Several places of interest attract the attention of the traveler. The Museum contains some fine paintings by Rubens and Vandyck. A spirited equestrian statue of the crusader, Godfrey of Bouillon, stands in the Place Royale. The room where the abdication of Charles V. took place is pointed out; and in the market-place, in front of the Hotel de Ville, the Counts Egmont and Horn were beheaded by the order of the cruel Alva, who looked from a window on the bloody scene. The great hall, or ball-room, where, on the evening before the battle of Waterloo,

"There was a sound of revelry by night,"

has been converted into a hospital. On entering the church of St. Gudule, one is struck by its beautifully painted windows, one of which, said to be the finest in Europe, long detains you in admiration of its exquisite coloring. Scarcely less interesting are the carved figures of the pulpit, representing the expulsion from Eden. Eve has plucked the apple, and is offering it to Adam, who has a look of surprise and horror, while an angel with a sword is descending, and Death is stealthily approaching.

What a pity that such a country should be so thoroughly Romish in its religion!—that all the struggles of the past, and aspects of the present, should seem to culminate in the prevalence of the strong old delusion! King Leopold, however, is a Protestant; and it is remarkable that he should be universally popular with all classes. We had the gratification of seeing him. As he passed us in his carriage, we uncovered our heads, and he gracefully bowed to us. He is a fine-looking old man; and we were the more interested in seeing him, as he was the husband of the lamented Princess Charlotte, heir to the crown of England, and on whose death Robert Hall preached one of the most eloquent discourses that ever fell from human lips.

An excursion of twelve miles by coach brings you

"—— the place of skulls,
The grave of France, the deadly Waterloo."

It is an undulating plain of cultivated fields; and yet, as an English officer, who was in the battle, acting as your guide, points out the positions of the contending armies, and their various movements, how easily the imagination reproduces the arrayed and bannered hosts, with all the terrible scenes of that memorable day! The great leaders have gone to the grave; and of the survivors of the battle, but few remain: such are the victories of one mightier than human conquerors!

Between Brussels and Antwerp is Mechlin, distinguished for the manufacture of lace. The tourist lingers at Antwerp, which offers some rare attractions. The city is finely situated for commerce on the banks of the Scheldt, and many ships from distant parts of the world are found at its magnificent docks, built under the direction of Napoleon. The old high houses, tapering up to pinnacle forms, have a quaint appearance; and there is a sort of imitation of them in the grotesque straw bonnets of the elder women, and the heavy but pointed wooden shoes worn by the common people. The churches here are embellished to a high degree. The Cathedral of Notre Dame is five hundred feet in length, and its spire, of great architectural beauty, is four hundred and sixty-six feet high. One will not soon lose the recollection of his extensive view from that giddy height, though the name he scratches under the little canopy may be noticed by few, and recognized by none. But the chief attraction is in the interior of the building. There is Rubens' great picture of the Descent from the Cross. You linger long before it in silent meditation, and thoughts of the wonderful skill of the artist are transferred to the overpowering scene he so vividly presents. His delineation of the dead Christ surpasses anything I have seen. The interior of the church of St. Jaques is profusely rich in ornamental statuary, and contains also some fine paintings. Many marble carvings, some from designs of Rubens, are wonderfully elaborate and exquisite. Rubens was buried in this church, and his tomb, with a beautiful picture of his family painted by himself, and hanging on the wall above it, is a great attraction.

We made an excursion through Holland, our principal stopping-places being Rotterdam and Amsterdam. These cities are much alike, and without special interest. They are mostly built upon piles, and are cut up by numerous canals; and as you look through a street, you see many of the houses leaning as if they would some time fall over. In the former city is a statue of Erasmus, and the house where he lived is found after a little searching. The people have a custom of fastening mirrors outside of their windows, that from within they may observe what is transpiring in the street. The women delight in brazen or gilt helmet-like ornaments glittering through their caps, and cropping out at their temples in large spiral wires or rings. Perhaps they think they are pretty. We passed through Delft and Leyden, places of great historical interest in their connection with the Pilgrim Fathers, and the struggles of religious liberty. Holland presents a singular appearance. Its ungainly windmills are sufficiently numerous for an army of pugnacious Don Quixotes. Holland mostly lies lower than the sea, which is kept off by dykes. You look over the fields in almost any direction, and sails of vessels meet your eye; they are threading the various canals running through the country. Passing through Utrecht and Dusseldorf, we reached Cologne, in Prussia, where we were to take a steamer up the Rhine.

From Cologne, however, we first made an excursion to Aix-la-Chapelle, an old town commenced by the

Romans, and noted in modern times as the place where various Congresses have met to settle treaties of peace between belligerent nations. Here Charlemagne is supposed to have been born, and here he died in 814. His tomb is in the Cathedral, a building which he designed after the form of the church of the Holy Sepulchre at Jerusalem, and intended as his burial-place. A century or two after his death, the tomb was opened, and his remains removed. He was found seated upon a marble throne or chair, in his imperial robes, his scepter in his hand, and his crown upon his fleshless brow. The marble chair, and two or three bones, including a skull, said to be those of Charlemagne, are shown to the visitor. His crown is also shown; a priest placed it on our heads. Here, too, is a marble sarcophagus, said to be that of Augustus Cæsar. It is elaborately carved, and bears unmistakable evidence of Roman origin. It was given to this church by one of the early Popes.

But the good-natured priest showed things more marvelous than these. I refer to sacred relics, among which are a piece of the original cross, a nail that fastened one of the hands of Jesus to it, a piece of the sponge wet with vinegar, one of the thorns of the crown, a portion of the napkin that covered the Saviour's head at his burial, and a lock of the Virgin's hair! These relics are kept in richly elaborated cases of gold, set with precious stones. It was somewhat amusing to us heretics to hear such things described as really being what they were said to be, and with a confident air of truthfulness; but the priest got his fee, and we our first lesson of the kind. Other relics, enclosed in splendid cases, and among them the robe worn by the Virgin at the Nativity, and the swaddling clothes in which Jesus was wrapped, are shown only once in seven years. It is said that more than 180,000 pilgrims came to see them in 1853. Next year they will be exhibited again. How great is the power of religious superstition!

We associate with Cologne an agreeable odor; but walk through the streets of that city, and you are greeted with perfumes quite the reverse. Its Cathedral is one of the most beautiful specimens of Gothic architecture in the world. Immense sums have been lavished upon it, and it is yet incomplete.

A sail up the Rhine is delightful. At Bonn, a fine town, with its University where the husband of Queen Victoria studied, the beautiful scenery begins. There the banks grow more bold, rising sometimes to considerable mountains. Their slopes are often terraced quite to the summit, and covered with thrifty vines bearing the white and purple clusters. You frequently pass places of historical interest, old towers, ruined castles, and modern chateaux of much beauty. The spot where the scenery is the most bold and charming, is that so pleasantly described in the following lines from "Childe Harold."

> The castled crag of Drachenfels
> Frowns o'er the wide and winding Rhine,
> Whose breast of waters broadly swells
> Between the banks which bear the vine,
> And hills all rich with blossomed trees,
> And fields which promise corn and wine,
> And scattered cities crowning these,
> Whose far white walls along them shine,

Have strewed a scene, which I should see
With double joy, wert thou with me!

And peasant girls, with deep blue eyes,
And hands which offer early flowers,
Walk smiling o'er that paradise;
Above, the frequent feudal towers
Through green leaves lift their walls of gray,
And many a rock which steeply lowers,
And noble arch in proud decay,
Look o'er this vale of vintage-bowers;
But one thing want these banks of Rhine—
Thy gentle hand to clasp in mine!

The river nobly foams and flows,
The charm of this enchanted ground,
And all its thousand turns disclose
Some fresher beauty varying round.
The haughtiest breast its wish might bound
Through life to dwell delighted here;
Nor could on earth a spot be found
To nature and to me so dear,
Could thy dear eyes, in following mine,
Still sweeten more these banks of Rhine!

The closing couplet of each of these stanzas had to me a significance rendered intense from the fact that the day I was on the Rhine, was one of the pleasantest anniversaries that loving hearts can cherish.

We left the river at Mayence, a city which claims the honor of being the place where the art of printing was invented by Gutenberg, a fine statue of whom stands in one of the public squares. From thence, passing through luxuriant vineyards and fruit orchards, we proceeded to Frankfort-on-the-Maine. This capital of Germany is a very attractive town, well worth a visit of the tourist. Luther lived here for a time. Goethe was born here, and it being the anniversary of his birth, his name, on the exterior of the house where that event took place, was wreathed around with flowers. An imposing and admirable statue of him graces a public square; and near it is a triple statue of Gutenberg, Faust, and Shoeffer, with other emblematic figures, making one of the most striking and interesting specimens of sculpture I have seen. The Town House, a building of the fifteenth century, and used as the Electors' Room and Hall of the Senate, contains fine portraits of all the Emperors, from the time of Charlemagne to 1806. Among other paintings there, also, is a beautiful one of the Judgment of Solomon. We spent a Sabbath here, and attended worship at the English church. The congregation was small, and the minister drawled out the service in a wretched manner. His sermon was a miserable apology for preaching.

From Frankfort, we went by rail to Heidelberg, a very pleasant town romantically situated on the river Neckar, and under the shadows of lofty hills, on the slope of one of which are the ruins of one of the finest old feudal castles in Europe. Some of its apartments are in a good state of preservation. A gallery of paintings and relics was well worth a visit. There I saw good portraits of Luther, Melancthon and others. But what interested me most was the identical gold ring which Luther placed upon the finger of his bride at the time of their marriage. A little relic, but how suggestive! The University of Heidelberg has some five hundred students, several of them Americans. I had a letter of introduction to one of the Professors, but calling at his residence, I found he was out of town, it being vacation.

A visit to Baden-Baden, a famous watering place, convinces one that vicious practices are vigorously pursued there with unblushing boldness. An immense and beautiful hall is mostly devoted to the purposes of gambling. Crowds gather around the tables and many stake their money and lose or win, the losers of course out-numbering the winners. Yet the hope of such dishonest gain encourages the vice. You are surprised to see females vieing with the men in this wicked practice. The sins of the place are in strange contrast with its natural beauties. It is a charming village, nestled among hills and pleasant groves where it is a delight to wander. The waters of its mineral springs, bubbling hot from the earth, are used both for drinking and bathing. We visited the fine apartments of the Grand Duke in the New Castle, and beneath it entered some gloomy subterranean dungeons where according to tradition, persons were once confined and put to death by various methods of torture and execution, such as we have read of in connection with Romish Inquisitions. The dismal rooms are well adapted to such purposes, and there were some evidences of the horrid reality. What startling disclosures are in reserve for the last day!

Strasbourg, on the borders of France, is visited by those who are desirous of witnessing the performance of a remarkable clock in its Cathedral. It is truly a wonderful piece of mechanism. I cannot detail all its operations which I saw at twelve o'clock. A cherub on one side of the dial struck the hour with a hammer; another, on the opposite side, reversed an hourglass which he held in his hands; over the dial, figures of the twelve Apostles came out successively and bowed to a figure of the Saviour, who stretched out his hand to them as giving a benediction to each as he passed. Higher up, a cock flapped his wings, stretched up his neck, opened his mouth and crowed, doing it thrice at short intervals; below the dial, a boy pointed his finger at the day of the month; a figure of the moon showed its present phase; solar time and apparent time were indicated; and a curious part of the mechanism exhibited all the ecclesiastical days of the year. The Cathedral itself is large and worthy of attention. Its beautiful spire is, I believe, the tallest in Europe, being four hundred and seventy-two feet high. The view from that elevation, including the Black Forest of Germany, will be a remembered picture.

V.

Switzerland—A Tour in the Alps.

A MONTH in Switzerland has afforded me good opportunity to see something of its striking natural scenery, its sublime mountains and charming lakes, and to mingle somewhat with its people. These have been weeks of intense excitement and unspeakable delight. On the tops of mountains, in the green valleys, or sailing over lakes, the eye has everywhere met rapt visions, and the heart swelled with ecstacy amid scenes never to be forgotten. Under the low roof of a rude cottage, conversing with its inmates, or in the eternal solitudes of high Alpine passes, the pleasure of the journey has never failed. I have always admired grand mountains. I like to climb their rugged slopes, and look abroad from their glorious summits. The air is pure and bracing; the exercise is vigorous and health-inspiring. Heaven seems to be near, and the presence of God is sensibly felt amid His stupendous creations. I had long hoped some time to traverse Alpine ranges, to visit the home of the glacier and the avalanche, and gaze on the snow-crowned brow of Mont Blanc. And now the favored time had come; and with the mighty feeling of reality, I have often found myself repeating these apt and well-known lines of Byron:

―――― Above me are the Alps,
　The palaces of Nature, whose vast walls
Have pinnacled in clouds their snowy scalps,
　And throned eternity in icy halls
　Of cold sublimity, where forms and falls
The avalanche—the thunderbolt of snow!
　All that expands the spirit, yet appalls,
　Gather around these summits, as to show
How earth may pierce to heaven, and leave vain man below.

From Strasbourg we went to Basle, reaching there the border of Switzerland. Another day's journey and we were at Geneva. This was made partly by rail and partly by steamers. On this route were railway carriages—they never call them cars in England, or on the Continent—constructed after the American style, a pleasant change from the small, coach-like apartments where half the passengers must ride backwards. You enter the English and European rail-carriages at side-doors, and are locked in. Your baggage is first weighed and checked, on showing your ticket. There are three classes, and the fares, except in the third, are much higher than with us. This is a delightful journey, leading through the charming lakes of Bienne and Neuchatel. The valleys are green and fertile, the slopes of the hills are vine-clad, and the distant mountains are glorious. On the right, is the Jura range, and on the left, the abrupt ridges and snow-glittering peaks of the kingly Alps. Occasional glimpses of Mont Blanc, at a distance of sixty miles, thrill you with delight. Lake Leman's clear and blue waters you love to gaze upon. On arriving at your hotel in Geneva, you receive a package of letters from home, and for awhile you forget all this grand scenery in dear communion with loved ones far away!

Geneva is finely situated at the lower end of the lake, where, dividing the town, the Rhone resumes its rapid flow. A pleasant walk of half an hour on its banks brings you to its junction with the Arve. This "meeting of the waters" is a place of much interest. The Rhone is transparent—the Arve turbid. The two currents meet, but for a considerable distance their waters utterly refuse to mingle. At length, the resistance gives way, and the turbid portion tinctures the whole stream. A moral is easily drawn.

* On Sunday I was anxious to see and hear Dr. Merle D'Aubigne, but learned that he was out of town. I had the satisfaction, however, of hearing Dr. Malan. He is a venerable, saintly-looking man, with hoary locks, beaming eyes. and a benevolent expression that fascinates you at once. I understood little of the sermon, as he preaches in French; but his whole manner, the tones of his voice, his gestures, and his evident sweet Christian spirit, impressed me deeply. He came to us as he descended from the pulpit, and invited us to his room, where we had a brief but delightful interview with him. It is a pity there are so few of his spirit of piety in the city where John Calvin preached and wrote his great works.

On the 6th of September, our party of seven, a clergyman from Massachusetts, his wife and sister, a teacher from Rhode Island, a lawyer from California, a New York pastor and myself, left Geneva for a tour among the Alps. The weather was delightful, and all were in fine spirits. We chartered carriages for Cha mouny, over fifty miles distant, and to whose beautiful vale a somewhat long day's journey brought us. It lies at the very foot of the monarch-mountain, and in entrancing view of magnificent glaciers. Much of the way was amid scenery wild and bold enough to excite the dullest mind to lively and profound admiration. We rode along the valley of the Arve, roaring as it rushed on its way, while now on the one hand, and then on the other, lofty mountains rose so precipitous as almost to overhang our path, and in their naked grandeur, exposing the dip and foldings of their strata, while at brief intervals silvery cascades came dancing down at our feet. At one time we entered a narrow gorge between vast wall-like rocky heights, that seemed the very gateway of the Alps, and strongly reminded me of the famous Notch of our own White Mountains. An hour's stop at St. Martin, gave us an opportunity to walk to a bridge in the vicinity, where a vision burst upon us, so glorious and entrancing as to leave its impress indelibly upon our minds. Mont Blanc was before us in all his kingly proportions and perpetual investiture of snow and ice. Full twelve miles distant, yet so immense and pearly brilliant, as the sunlight fell upon his snowy robes, he seemed to lie within less than an hour's walk.

It was past nine o'clock when we reached Chamouny, the latter part of the way being almost a continual ascent. But the moon, peering now and then above the mountain-tops, shone beautifully in a clear sky. A window of my chamber at our hotel afforded a fine view of Mont Blanc, and looking from it, I saw the moon resting, as it were, for a moment, like a silver diadem, on his lofty brow. Beautiful sight! and so absorbed was I with that matchless mountain so etherial, heavenly and awe-inspiring, that at earliest dawn I was awake and gazing upon it, and repeating that glorious poem, Coleridge's Hymn before Sunrise in the vale of Chamouny.

> "Hast thou a charm to stay the Morning Star
> In his steep course ? So long he seems to pause
> On thy bald, awful head, O sovran Blanc!"

Our ascent to the Flegere, opposite Mont Blanc, and more than 6,000 feet above the sea level, gave us a superb view of the grand monarch of mountains, and the range in which he stands, together with the Mer de Glace, the Glacier du Bossons, and other beautiful and glorious ice-torrents that flow slowly down the lofty slopes and congeal in the deep ravines, and have the appearance of mighty cataracts suddenly frozen stiff and stopped in their course. The next ascent was on the Mont Blanc side of the vale, to a point, the summit of Montanvert, higher than the previous one, and from whence we descended a high bank to the Mer de Glace, which was spread out before us in all its glory. We could look for many miles along that icy sea, winding from its source in everlasting snow, to its termination in a green and sunny vale, and whose great motionless billows met the eye in long succession, and glittered in emerald splendor. We walked across its broad uneven surface, the guides assisting the ladies, and directing the course of all. Frequent fissures or rents in the ice were observed, and little wells, in which water stood or trickled down to the depths below. A guide remarked that he had dropped a line into some of these crevices to the depth of 300 feet. The whole mass moves very gradually, melting away at the bottom, and pressed down by the weight of snow above. Close to the margin of this ice-river grow beautiful flowers, a sweet summer fringe on the wintery garment of eternal frost. This, and many other glaciers I have seen in the Alps—gloriously flowing from their sublime sources, as one would imagine the "pure river of water of life proceeding out of the throne of God" to flow—have often reminded me of a grand passage in Coleridge's Hymn:

> Ye ice-falls! ye that from the mountain's brow,
> Adown enormous ravines slope amain—
> Torrents, methinks, that heard a mighty Voice,
> And stopped at once amid their maddest plunge;
> Motionless torrents! Silent cataracts!
> Who made you glorious as the gates of heaven
> Beneath the keen full moon? Who bade the sun
> Clothe you with rainbows? Who, with living flowers
> Of loveliest blue, spread garlands at your feet?
> God! let the torrents, like a shout of nations,
> Answer! and let the ice-plains echo, God!

At Chamouny we met several Americans, and among them, Prof. and Mrs. Stowe and daughter, of Andover, Mass. The day before we left, two or three courageous travelers began the perilous and expensive ascent of Mont Blanc.

Our way to Martigny was by the pass of Tete Noir; and its scenery, in variety, beauty, wildness and grandeur, is beyond my ability to describe. As our path gradually ascended, Mont Blanc seemed to follow us as some great presence looming up in awful majesty. Our mule-path now wound along the shelving edge of tremendous precipices, with snow-capped mountain summits far above us, and deep, abysmal ravines far beneath us, while across our track crystal cascades bounded to the rushing stream below. Then a splendid glacier, skirted by a pine grove, would burst upon our view; then a naked mountain-pile of rocks would literally overhang our path, which, for a short distance, had to be tunneled through the bold and precipitous ledge; then a little island-like prominence would rise from the deep gorge surrounding it, and on which would stand a cottage or two, with a few patches of cultivated soil; then in some nook within an amphitheater of mountains, would be nestled a cluster of rude dwelling-houses, seeming to repose in the isolation of a silent and death-like seclusion. On the one hand a splendid waterfall would greet us, and on the other, some marvel of rock, or bridge, or chasm, or perilous bend in our path. Thus we passed on, hour after hour, till we reached the summit of Forclaz; and then, by a long zig-zag descent, amid shadowing trees, we reached Martigny after dark.

The following day we made a considerable journey, partly by char, or carriage, and partly on mules, to that most interesting spot in these Alpine solitudes, the Hospice of Grand St. Bernard. It is one of the highest passes in these sublime mountains, its elevation being more than eight thousand feet, or half the whole height of Mont Blanc. Before we reached it, "the shades of night were falling fast," and patches of snow and ice lay around us, while the entire region, utterly destitute of vegetation, presented an aspect of chilling bleakness and dread desolation. On arriving at the Hospice, the sight of such a building in such a place—a substantial stone edifice, with comfortable rooms and beds, a good supper, and a fire in the parlor—was very grateful. We were kindly received and entertained by the resident monks, who lead a self-denying life in that desolate place for the good of others. Often hundreds of travelers are fed and lodged daily, and no charges are made. It is customary, however, for those who are able, to leave a liberal sum for their entertainment. But the great majority are poor people, and they give nothing. Valuable presents have been sent to the Hospice by those who have visited it. Recently a lady sent a piano. Who has not heard of the dogs of St. Bernard, and their exploits in rescuing travelers benighted and overtaken by terrible storms of snow! I saw half a dozen of these noble-looking, sagacious and useful animals. There is a chapel of considerable size connected with the main building, and as it was Sunday, we attended awhile the service, which consisted of the usual forms of the Romish Church. About two hundred persons were present. A chime of bells which awoke us at five in the morning, calling to early mass, sounded very pleasantly in that awfully desolate region. There is quite a library at the Hospice, and various old Roman relics, including coins and implements of war found on this spot, which was once the site of a fortress. The Hospice was founded in the tenth century by Bernard, who appears to have been

THE HOSPICE OF ST. BERNARD.

a pious, benevolent man, and was subsequently canonized. Napoleon, with great difficulty, took his army over this pass just before the battle of Marengo. I should have alluded to the *Morgue*, or receptacle for the remains of strangers who have died at the Hospice, or perished in mountain storms and avalanches. It is a low building, near the main edifice; and as you look in through a grated door or window, you see standing all around the room, or leaning against its walls, grim, ghastly and withered corpses staring at you in the twilight gloom of the place. The floor, also, is covered with skulls and other human bones. These remains are placed here, that they may be identified by friends; and if not claimed, they seem to be allowed to remain, as in such a high atmosphere they wither away without being offensive. Still, one does not wish to look at such a spectacle but once. It is amusing to look over the register of visitors, and read the various sentiments and bits of rhyme which many have recorded with their names. The hospitality of the monks elicits a good share of praise. I left these lines:

> As pilgrims found, in days of old,
>   The great rock-shade refreshing, sweet,
> So travelers now, from wintery cold,
>   Find St. Bernard a blest retreat.

On returning to Martigny, I was sorry to part with Rev. Dr. Gillette, my highly esteemed and agreeable traveling associate from the time we left New York in June last. His course thence was homeward. May he have a pleasant and safe journey!

Our next tour was up the valley of the Rhone to

the Baths of Leuk, all the way by carriage. The last nine miles, after turning to the left, and entering another valley, through which we ascended to the verge of the Gemmi pass, were traversed under the pure light of a full moon, and amid scenery remarkable for its wildness and variety. The beautiful road rapidly rises by constant zigzags, and is often on the verge of a ravine frightfully deep and precipitous, while perpendicular mountain walls stand in high and awful grandeur above. At one place, we cross the rushing and roaring stream by a stone-arched bridge more than four hundred feet above the water. The mighty Alpine summits, back of the valley we had left, crowned with perpetual snow, and glittering in the soft moonbeams; and the far tops of the majestic rocky battlements before and around us, fringed with a snow-border, frilled and flashing in lunar radiance, were sufficient to raise to the highest pitch our excitement and admiration.

The Baths of Leuk are a curiosity. The water is slightly saline, and comes up almost boiling hot from volcanic springs. Attached to the hotel where we stopped, is a wing containing a large room, in which are two contiguous bathing tanks, each sufficient for twenty or more persons to bathe together. They adopt this social method on account of the length of time spent in the bath, which after a few days is *eight* hours daily, four in the morning and four in the afternoon. I rose early to witness the first act in the daily drama. On entering the room, I saw nearly a dozen males in one department, and about as many females in the other, all up to their chins in water, and all clad in loose woolen robes. Some were entertaining themselves in playing checkers on pieces of floating boards, and others reading books and papers, or drinking coffee, floating in the same way. Invalids are brought a considerable distance, and over these precipitous passes, that they may enjoy the benefit of the baths.

As we arrived at the village the previous night, we were particularly struck with the vast castellated mountain-walls, hemming in the place, and rising perpendicularly over two thousand feet. And now in ascending the Gemmi pass, we found to our astonishment that the way wound up this lofty precipice It is a fine foot or bridle path, going zigzag up, up, one point of the road lying directly above another, and circling declivities where the way is sometimes cut in solid rock, a sort of groove in the immense perpendicular wall. One could often stand on the verge of the path, and drop a plum-line sixteen hundred feet before it would touch below. In such a transit, you are entirely safe *in the path ;* but a single step over it, and you are lost! There is a magnificent view from the summit. Snow-crowned mountains and Gothic peaks are seen, stretching away in long ridges, exposing the sources and beds of their glaciers, while green and fertile valleys, dotted over with humble Swiss cottages, repose in striking contrast beneath. The descent on the other side of the Gemmi to Kandersteg is mostly gradual, and through a region of rocky barrenness.

A pleasant ride of a few hours the next day brings you to the beautiful town of Thun, lying at the foot of the lake of the same name. Its adjacent grounds and country seats, or villas, are the most charming I have seen in Switzerland. A delightful sail of an hour and a half in a little steamer, and you reach the head of the lake, and a mile further lies Interlachen, another finely-situated town, between two lakes, as its name indicates, and at the time we were there honored with the presence of the widow of Nicholas, late Emperor of Russia. The lakes of Switzerland are as lovely and romantic as its mountains are grand and stupendous. They are beautifully bordered with bold bluffs, or green slopes covered with vineyards. Their waters are blue and transparent as crystal. Who, in wandering among such scenes does not feel his heart swelling in grateful adoration of Him who " girdeth the mountains with strength," bids the water gush from the rocks to flow abroad in fertilizing rivers, and spreads out the clear lakes to reflect the heavens?

VI.

The Swiss—Alpine Journeys—Germany.

ONE loves to linger among the mountains and valleys of Switzerland, where the magnificent forms of nature appear in such boldness, beauty and power. The grandeur and glory that crown these exhibitions of the Divine majesty and might, almost lead us to forget the humble dwellers amidst their shadows. The Swiss are a quiet, somewhat intelligent, and apparently happy people. They are necessarily shut up in small villages or hamlets in the valleys; and to make the most of the little arable soil they have, they often terrace the mountain slopes far up, and plant little patches of grain or potatoes in sunny spots amid the rocks. Their pasture grounds are quite extensive, and are well covered with cattle and goats, which graze on the steep declivities; and as most of them have bells dangling from their necks, the silence of those great solitudes is thus constantly broken. These bells have a peculiarly sweet melody, and those of the churches also, all of which have one, and many have a chime, and they are quite frequently rung. To keep their cattle through the long winter, they gather all the hay possible, mowing steep hill-sides where it is difficult to stand. I saw them in many places gathering their second crop, which was often quite scanty, yet carefully saved. The women apparently do more of this out-door work than the men. They learn to swing the scythe with grace and strength. I saw many of them digging potatoes with huge forks shaped and used like hoes. As it is difficult to get about with vehicles drawn by cattle or horses on their steep hillsides, most of their harvestings are carried in on the backs of men and women. They have a deep huge basket or rack which they strap to their shoulders, and it is astonishing to see the immense loads they will thus carry, even over long distances. In taking their hay from the meadow to the barn, you scarcely see the person who carries it, only a great haystack seeming to walk of itself.

Some of the Swiss cottages are beautiful, and quite ornamented in various ways, and sometimes you will see inscriptions or verses on their fronts, carved or painted. But generally the houses are very plain, often built of hewn logs, and roofed with flat stones, or coarse shingles held in their places by frequent rows of large stones. It may be that these stones are necessary to protect the roof and the house itself from the terrific winter tempests that no doubt often sweep howling through the valleys. The dwelling house and the barn are frequently under the same roof; and for protection against storms and avalanches, all the buildings of a village stand sometimes as closely together as possible. Enter an ordinary cottage, and you will not find it over-neat in its appearance, or that of its inmates. The latter, however, are quite polite and sociable. And this feature of politeness is universal in Europe. I wish it was more so in America.

Even the little boys gracefully take off their hats and bow. It is pleasant to say *Bonjour* to one you meet, and receive such a pleasant return of the salutation.

All sorts of vegetables seem to grow luxuriantly in Switzerland. Potatoes are raised in abundance, and some Indian corn. The first Indian corn I saw was in Germany, near Frankfort. In coming from our country, where it is so common, one constantly notes its absence, in traveling over the British islands and most of the Continent. The people in Europe have a way of planting large fields, not with one, but various kinds of grain or vegetables, each in long narrow strips, a rod wide, perhaps, growing side by side, and giving the field at a little distance, with its different colors, the appearance of a striped carpet. Apples, pears, peaches, plums, and especially grapes, are abundant. In Switzerland you everywhere find excellent honey, and I might add milk; it is "a land flowing with" them.

The Sabbath seems to be better observed by the Swiss than by other Europeans. It was delightful to hear the sweet Sabbath bells pealing through the vales, and to notice a general abstinence from work, and see the peasantry neatly clad, making their way to the house of God. What early associations, and dear thoughts of home it awakened! I could see again the old meeting-house of my childhood, the family pew, and the earnest man of God, with silver hairs, in the little high pulpit. I could see, too, my own beloved people assembling in their wonted sanctuary, and in spirit be with them. Some of the Cantons of Switzerland are Protestant, and in them everything wears a better appearance. Whether their Protestantism is evangelical and spiritual, I had no means of definite knowledge. Romanism all over Europe reveals itself constantly in images of stone, wood, or paint, on churches, dwellings, shops, by the wayside and in the fields. You everywhere see crosses, crucifixes and images of the Virgin and Child. They are supposed to be a protection against pestilence in the cities, dangers on the rivers, and blights in the fields. It is really painful, and often disgusting, to witness such evidences of superstition.

In resuming the narrative of my Alpine journeys, I begin at Interlachen, where it was left. A short carriage drive, passing an old castle where "Manfred" is said to have lived, brought us to Lauterbrunnen, where the valley narrows to a deep mountain gorge. Here is the Staubbach Fall, or Dust Stream, a beautiful sight. A small stream falls over a perpendicular precipice about nine hundred feet; but the water turns to spray long before it reaches the bottom, and in that form falls on the rocks, where it gathers itself into a stream again. Here we begin the ascent of the Wengern Alp, the ladies on horses, the rest of us on foot. As we rise rapidly, the Jungfrau, snow-clad in virgin whiteness, presents a majestic and glorious form to our view. As we reach a still more elevated position on the southern slope, and near the summit of the Wengern Alp, we seem to be under the very shadow of the Jungfrau, and separated from it only by a narrow gorge. Before reaching this point, we had heard sounds like the heavy roar of distant artillery, and knew at once that they were from avalanches out of sight. From the immense beds of snow and ice on this sky-piercing mountain, they frequently form and fall. We were anxious to be gratified with the sight of one at least. Presently a volley-like sound broke upon our ears, and looking up the slope of the Jungfrau, we saw an immense mass of crushed and tumbling ice and snow thundering down to the vale beneath—a sight not soon to be forgotten. A short time after, we saw another, and heard the distant roar and long reverberations of others beyond our view. At a distance, these avalanches look small comparatively, but are really of sufficient size and force to sweep away whole forests, and villages if found in their track. In these ascents, we frequently find a peasant, who, for a few centimes, is anxious to blow his long wooden "Alpine horn," that we may enjoy its numerous and delicate echoes. It commenced raining soon after we began to descend, and the magnificent summits above us were all enveloped in clouds. We reached the beautiful village of Grindelwald early in the evening. Here we were detained a day by unpleasant weather. Two immense glaciers, from vast fields of ice and snow above, come down the ravines between three immense and wildly-grand mountains that here abruptly terminate the valley on the south, in which Grindelwald is nestled. One of these glaciers descends to a point below the level of the village. I found time between the intervals of rain to walk to this glacier and get upon its icy crest, by climbing a little way up the Mettenberg or middle mountain. The names of the other mountains are Eigher, on the right, and Wetterhorn on the left.

From my position on the glacier, I had a most charming view of the village, while the three giant mountains seemed more rugged and awfully sublime, contemplated under their very shadows.

We next made the pass of the Great Scheideck, all taking horses but myself. Having the physical strength which is invigorated by the effort, I prefer walking over these grand mountains, with my thick-soled shoes, and Alpenstock, or baton, pointed with iron at one end, and tipped with the chamois-horn at the other. After climbing one of the most difficult and lofty summits, and where the views are scarcely surpassed in their bold and stupendous magnificence, we found ourselves, and all about us, enveloped in a storm of rain and snow. Occasionally the clouds would part, and disclose a mountain-summit or spire-like peak that seemed to hang from the sky, and so near to us as almost to lean over our path. In our descent, we passed some fine waterfalls, and one near Reichenbach really splendid, and though of greater volume, reminded me at once of the Minnehaha in Minnesota. We reached Myringen after journeying eight or nine hours, and were glad to find a comfortable hotel and a good fire.

At this point, all of our party, except Rev. Mr. Child and myself, took a nearer course to Lucerne, while we were anxious for further mountain excursions. Parting, with good wishes for each other's health and pleasure, we took our pedestrian way toward the Grimsel, our guide carrying what little baggage we had with us. Soon we entered a beautiful and nearly circular valley about half a mile in diameter, and completely hemmed in by mountain walls, the only outlet, breaking the lofty barriers, being a narrow rift* in the rocks for a little stream to flow through. The soil is rich, perfectly level, and was, no doubt, once the bed of a lake. We passed numerous peasants, who seemed to be happy, working in the open air. In stopping to play with some little children, their mother made us understand that their father was killed by an avalanche last winter. Our guide told us he was near him at the time, and when we arrived at the place, he pointed out the precise spot where the sad event occurred. It was a desolate region near the Hospice of the Grimsel. Our path was through a region up the valley of the Aar, wild and desolate, the precipitous sides of the lofty granite mountains having a peculiarly smooth and worn appearance, as if raging torrents or mighty glaciers had rolled or ground over them for ages. Prof. Agassiz, I believe, accounts for their slippery look in this way. He has traversed these regions, and his name we observed, cut in one of these smooth rocks by the path. The imagination often goes back to the time when these "mountains were brought forth," and tries to picture the wild commotions and the terrific displays of nature's elements and forces amid the awful solitudes of that far-off epoch. At Handek we saw one of the finest waterfalls in Europe. Two streams, coming from different directions, flow over an immense precipice in separate columns at the top, but unite their waters into one foaming torrent about halfway down the falls. By a gradual ascent of some twenty miles, with snow-clad summits around us, we reached the Grimsel Hospice, situated some 7000 feet above the sea, in about as desolate and dreary a place as can be imagined.

The next morning, after ascending a thousand feet higher, we began to descend. Snow and ice were all about us, and we encountered several men out breaking a path in the fresh-fallen or drifted snow. Amid the grand views of this region, we soon got sight of the Rhone Glacier, one of the finest in all the Alps. The Rhone takes its rise here, and surely no river could have a sublimer birth-plaae or more gorgeous cradle. We drank at the place where it issues from a cavern in the glacier, and leaped over the infant stream; and then climbing upon the glacier, we walked full three miles on its rough icy surface, often jumping over crevices of immense depth. Far above us, where the ice-torrent flows over from unseen sources beyond, it looks as one standing below Niagara might imagine that to look, if it were suddenly frozen and stopped in its course. Leaving the glacier, we made a long ascent amid pasture-slopes, covered with cattle and goats, till we reached the Furca, a summit affording magnificent Alpine views in all directions. Descending in the valley of the Reuss, and passing the St. Gothard on our right, we arrived, early in the evening at Andermatt, situated on the St. Gothard pass to Italy.

We had a fine drive from Andermatt to Lake Lucerne. The way led down the valley of the roaring Reuss, and amid scenery, for wild picturesqueness and astonishing sublimity, equal to anything I have seen. This particularly applies to a place called *the Devil's*

Bridge, where the lofty and bare mountain-walls, rising from the vale, almost touch each other, scarcely giving room for the river to pass, which here makes several deep plunges down the fearful rocks. The carriage road for three hundred feet is tunneled through a portion of the mountain. Avalanches frequently thunder down into this valley, and the road in one place, for a considerable distance, is walled in and over, to protect it from them. Little niches by the way are made in the rocks or mountain-slope, into which travelers can run from a threatening avalanche.

About two miles before we reach the lake, we pass through Altorf, the home of William Tell. A chapel marks his birth-place. In the public square is a statue of him and his boy, indicating the spot where he shot the apple from his head. Soon after taking the steamer at Fluelen, we pass, on the right bank, a little chapel ornamented with frescoes, where Tell sprang ashore, on escaping from a boat in which Gessler held him a prisoner. Another chapel, as you pass from Lake Lucerne to Lake Zug, commemorates the spot where Tell, concealed in the forest, shot his tyrant foe. Near Tell's birth-place we crossed a stream, in which he is said to have been drowned in endeavoring to rescue a child from the water. How interesting to visit these localities, and to look upon scenes in nature long ago familiar to the eye of the Swiss patriot, of whom we had read in our childhood!

Passing some two-thirds of the way down the calm blue surface of this rock-framed mirror of nature, the most romantic of all the Swiss group of lakes, we reach Weggis, a little village on the right bank, and at the foot of the Rigi, a sort of isolated mountain, about the height of our Mt. Washington, and perhaps ascended by more persons than any other Alpine summit attracts. Views from its top are wide and various, and its sunsets and sunrises are said often to be glorious as the gates of heaven. We had reserved this mountain to the last, and anticipated much in its ascent. It was now a beautiful day, and we lost no time, it being already three o'clock in the afternoon, in climbing up its steep nine-mile path, which I accomplished on foot under a hot sun, and reached the summit in a drowning perspiration, half an hour before sunset, when the golden orb popped behind a dense dark cloud, and so went down. Though we lost the sunset, we enjoyed a panorama of unparalleled beauty and grandeur, embracing endless snow-crowned Alps in the distance, upon whose thousand glaciers we could look, and at our feet lay a circle of enchanting lakes, mirroring the mountains beneath their deep blue surface, and fringed around with cities, villages, and luxuriant vineyards. Such a scene and moment are daguerreotyped forever on the memory. We met the rest of our party on the Rigi, and hoped for a good sunrise. But the starlight of evening gave place to a rain-storm and furious wind that fairly shook the mountain, and made our hotel tremble like a leaf. It was long after sunrise before the storm abated, and the clouds that enveloped us withdrew. Visitors there are liable to such disappointments, and happy is he who can enjoy even a tempest as I did. A luckless tourist has thus recorded his experience:

> "Nine weary uphill miles we sped,
>   The setting sun to see;
> Sulky and grim he went to bed,
>   Sulky and grim went we.
> Seven sleepless hours we tossed, and then,
>   The rising sun to see,
> Sulky and grim we rose again,
>   Sulky and grim rose he."

It was quite late before I rose that morning. I had taken but one suit of clothes and a little extra linen for my pedestrian tours in the Alps. I found to my surprise that my outside garments, drenched with perspiration in ascending the Rigi, had not seemed to dry at all through the night, and as there was no bell in the room, I waited for some one to appear. At length a chambermaid popped her head through the door, but vanished instantly. An hour after, one of our party came to inquire for me. He called a servant and had my clothes taken to the kitchen. They came back in an hour, but alas, only one side of them had felt the fire. They were sent down again, and it was full another hour, before I could appear at breakfast, which answered for dinner as well.

We descended that afternoon, and soon reached Lucerne by steamer, Mount Pilatus looming up grandly on our left. There is an old tradition that Pilate, banished from Judea to Gaul, wandered conscience-stricken, till he ended his life by throwing himself into a lake on the top of this mountain, and hence its name.

Lucerne is an interesting town, having an old high wall in its rear, and a splendid monument to the

Swiss Guards at Paris, in 1792, in the form of a dying lion endeavoring to preserve an armorial shield. It was modeled by Thorwaldsen, and the figure, twenty-eight feet long, is cut in a large wall of solid rock. Two long bridges over the Reuss are ornamented under the roof by a series of paintings, one representing historical scenes, and the other the Dance of Death. We took the pleasant route to Zurich, partly by lakes and partly by diligences, and found it a very lively Paris-like little town, in the midst of a vine-growing country. Some of our party went to Berne, and others of us to Constance, which we reached by railway to Romanshorn, and the remaining distance by steamer, on the beautiful Lake of Constance. It is an old dilapidated town, with few inhabitants compared with its former number. We were specially interested in the memorials it contains of John Huss. In the Minster or cathedral, we stood on the very stone in the floor where he stood when his sentence was delivered to him. We found the house where he lodged, and went to the field in the suburbs, where he was burned at the stake in 1415, and Jerome, of Prague, two years after. We visited the old Dominican Convent where Huss was imprisoned. It is now put to the better use of printing calico. We also entered the *Kaufhaus*, or old hall, where the great Council met by which the two martyrs were condemned, and two infamous popes deposed and another elected. Its sessions continued several years, and it embraced delegates, ecclesiastical and civil, from all Christendom. We saw the chairs occupied by the Emperor and the Pope on that occasion, and also the body of the car in which John Huss was drawn to execution. When called upon to recant, his reply was, "I cannot break my word to my God." He met his fate with a fortitude that moved the hearts of his executioners and enemies. It is interesting to look upon these old buildings that have stood so long, and were the theater of events that transpired before America was known. The great and imposing Council soon passed away, but the old hall remains; and he whom they condemned as a heretic to death, becomes a sainted martyr, and a shining light forever, while scarcely a name of their own is preserved from oblivion.

A few hours' sail down the Rhine brings us to Schaffhausen, passing by the way on our left the beautiful Chateau or country residence of Hortense, the daughter of Josephine and mother of the present French Emperor, who lived a number of years at this place.

A pleasant drive of three or four miles, amid luxuriant vineyards, whose white and purple clusters tempt the eye, takes us to the Falls of the Rhine, one of the largest and most celebrated on the Continent, reminding me of the Falls of St. Anthony. We considered ourselves well paid for the excursion to see them. Having a desire to see Munich and Vienna, I changed my purpose to return to Geneva, and so at Schaffhausen I left my agreeable associate in travel and proceeded toward Bavaria alone. Nearly all of one day was spent in returning to Constance, and crossing the Lake to Lindau. It was a beautiful day, and the lake lay like a dream in a soft haze, so surrounding it and blending water, land and sky, as hardly to leave the lines of separation visible, while a glorious sunset tinted the glassy surface with golden hues. This was a rare picture, inimitable by painter or poet, but which the soul's eye admires and retains that it may feast on the etherial vision.

The railway to Augsburg, 150 miles, leads through a fertile and well cultivated country, undulating at first like New-England, and afterwards level. In the distance the Swiss and Tyrolese Alps, in their crowns of snow, are prominent objects. The buildings in Augsburg have an appearance of ancient and decayed splendor. Some of their fronts are frescoed, and in the principal streets several bronze fountains, erected in the sixteenth century attract attention. The cathedral is a large edifice, in the Byzantine style, and besides pictures and statuary, contains a model of the Agony in the Garden—an Angel offering a cup to Christ, and the three Apostles asleep among palms. Adjoining is the Palace where the Augsburg Confession was presented to Charles V., in 1635. The Kaufhaus, in the Italian style, has some good paintings and finely-carved ceilings. On entering the St. Ulrish and Alfra church, I found a priest exhibiting to three other priests apparently the remains or gorgeously appareled skeleton of St. Alfra, and some other relics, as bones of saints, which the priests touched with their beads, except one, who touched them with his finger, and put his finger to his tongue. What virtue or power to work miracles they thus received, remains for future experience to decide. The hotel of the Three Moors, where I stopped, is more than five hundred years old, and contains a room where the Emperor Charles V. was entertained by Count Fugger, whose mansion it once was. There is nothing of special interest in the two hours' trip by rail to Munich; but Munich itself is full of interest.

VII.
Bavaria—Austria—Italy—Venice.

Munich, the beautiful capital of Bavaria, is a place of many and varied attractions. It has a level situation on the "Iser rolling rapidly," and its general aspect is very pleasant. It is, perhaps, the most beautiful city in the German States. Its streets are generally broad and clean, its buildings neat and tasteful, and some of its suburbs charming. Then it is a great center of art, and, to a considerable extent, of science and literature. Liebig resides here, who has done more to advance Organic Chemistry than any other man. Here Steinheil lives, who is regarded by many as almost dividing with Prof. Morse the honor of inventing the Telegraph. Here is a flourishing University, presenting a fine array of buildings. The Royal Library is a magnificent edifice, and contains over 900,000 volumes, and has room for 2,000,000. It is the largest library, with one exception, in the world. The principal buildings, devoted to paintings and sculptures, are each over five hundred feet long, and are beautiful in design and finish, and some of them are outwardly adorned with fine frescoes and statuary. The old Pinacothek contains a multitude of pictures by several of the old masters, as Raphael, Titian, Murillo and Rubens. The new Pinacothek has a splendid collection of modern paintings. The Deluge, a large picture not quite finished when the artist died, long detains the observer; but he will linger still longer, and in profounder admiration, before the Destruction of Jerusalem, by Kaulbach, a Munich artist, and ranked as the greatest of living painters. Visiting his studio one day, I had the pleasure of seeing him. This, his masterpiece, is wonderful for the grouping and expression of its figures, and the exquisite finish of the whole. The Glyptothek is full of fine statuary, ancient and modern. Besides these, there are many other galleries of art in the city. King Ludwig, notorious for his relations to Lola Montez, spent vast sums to adorn his capital. Perhaps the finest bronze statues in the world are cast here. I had the pleasure of seeing one of Henry Clay, just finished, and ere this on its way to New Orleans, in one of whose squares it is to stand. It is a perfect and lifelike representation of the great Kentucky orator and statesman, as he often appeared in addressing the United States Senate. Fine models of Washington, (equestrian,) Jefferson, and Patrick Henry, were waiting to take the enduring form of brass. In a pleasant suburb, and fronting the splendid Hall of Fame, stands a colossal statue of Bavaria, a bronze female figure and lion. It stands on a pedestal of marble forty feet high, and the figure itself is sixty feet high. By a spiral staircase within, I ascended to the head, in which I was able to stand erect.

Some of the churches of Munich are rich in architectural and pictorial embellishments. Such are the Basilica, or church of St. Boniface, the Ludwig-Kirche, and a Gothic church in the suburbs, whose painted windows are a marvel of beautiful coloring. There is but one Protestant church in the city. It is a fine, large, almost circular edifice, capable of seating about two thousand; and it was well filled on the Sabbath I attended service, the congregation not differing in appearance, dress, and attention, from one in New-York or New-England. The singing is congregational and good. The sermon is delivered without manuscript, and without gestures, in a calm, yet somewhat earnest manner. The Queen of Bavaria, who is a Protestant, occupied her pew, and seemed to join devoutly in the services. Her husband, King Maximilian II., is a Romanist.

In the midst of the Cemetery, in which there are some fine monuments, stands a large building containing various apartments. Looking through the glass windows, or doors rather, I saw several corpses in open coffins, and neatly arrayed in ordinary attire. Wires connected with bells, were attached to their right hands, so that in case life were not extinct, and the apparently dead should revive, the bells might be rung, and aid summoned. A municipal regulation requires that all, with few exceptions, who die in the city, shall be brought to this dead-house, and remain about twenty-four hours.

Having been annoyed for some time with twinges of rheumatism, a physician in Munich recommended the Russian bath. It needs a brave man to endure it the second time. You are ushered into a close seven-by-nine room, filled with medicated vapor as hot as it is possible to bear. You lie down on a bench and dissolve, panting for breath. Soon your attendant comes in and rubs you with a brush, pounds you with his hand and beats you with a bundle of boughs. After fifteen minutes you are taken to another room, and for some time stand under a cold and most profuse shower, raining upon you like icicles, intermingled with slaps from your attendant. Then you are directed to plunge head and ears into the open tank before you, and stay under water as long as you can hold your breath, making two or three such dives. Now you go back to the little dark room of hot vapor; and the whole triple process is gone over three times, taking an hour or more. I have a sort of passion for bathing, and even enjoyed this, finding it so beneficial that I imprudently took another too soon, and immediately started on my journey. The second bath was terribly severe, and that little hot room seemed a perfect purgatory.

In taking leave of Munich, I must express my great obligation to our excellent Consul, Prof. A. Ten Brook, for his many, kind and valuable attentions, and my thanks to Mr. G. W. Petit, a young and genial artist from Philadelphia, who accompanied me through various galleries of art, and to other objects of interest. It is pleasant to meet former friends, and make new ones in a distant land.

From such observations as I have been able to make in city and country, the Germans appear to be a generally intelligent people, who take life easily and patiently, and derive from it not a little enjoyment. They are industrious, moderate in their movements, and social in a high degree. They are devotedly attached to their beer and pipe. The glasses or mugs of beer that some of them will drink in the course of a day, is perfectly astonishing. Stopping at a country inn for tea, quite a crowd was gathered before it, singing songs, and indulging in their favorite beverage. I was ushered into a room where there was quite a party of ladies and gentlemen seated round a table in social conversation, each taking repeated draughts of beer from their glass mugs; and I was surprised to see how often they were emptied and refilled, the women in this respect fully equaling the men. They have a custom of touching glass to glass before they drink. What the Germans eat, especially the common people, costs but little. Living is cheap and so is labor. A man or woman who works by the day or month, does not get half the wages paid in our country.

I did not go to Vienna, as I purposed, but took a shorter way to Italy through that part of Austria called the Tyrol. I made an excursion, however, to Salzburg, situated on a tributary of the Danube, and quite distinguished for its surrounding romantic scenery. A sort of natural, mountain-like wall, partly environs it; and a fine old castle, standing on a high eminence in its midst, reminds one of Edinburgh. But it has other attractions. Here Mozart, whose soul seemed the essence of music, was born, and here is his tomb. I easily found the house where he lived, and repeatedly looked in admiration upon the splendid bronze statue of him, which adorns one of the public squares. There is a beauty in the face and expression, and whole figure, indeed, which charms you. I found, also, in St. Peter's church, a fine monument of Michael Haydn, a composer of eminence, and brother of the author of the "Creation." Another church has a sweet chime of bells, playing twelve tunes, one each month, and some of them are Mozart's beautiful compositions. But I have a sad recollection of Salzburg, as the place where I passed the most miserably wretched night of my life. The journey thither had been the loneliest of all, and the second night after my arrival I was taken suddenly and severely ill, experiencing also a complete nervous prostration, the effect of the bath at Munich, two days before. Besides, I was entirely alone, could converse intelligently with no one, and very likely there was not another Protestant in the place. How I longed to see a friend! I left in the morning, but it was weeks before I fully recovered.

From Salzburg to Kufstein and Innsbruck, the course, partly by diligence and partly by railway, lies along cultivated fields, pleasant lakes, and majestic mountains, the spurs of the Alps. On a high point in Kufstein stands an old fortress, now used as a prison. I wandered with a guide through a long subterranean passage, and came out into a room where there was a well two hundred and fifty feet deep, cut through a solid rock, and supplied with water from the river Inns flowing near. The well was made by two criminals imprisoned for life, who undertook the task on condition of being liberated when it should be finished. They completed it in seventeen years of incessant labor. A noted criminal from Hungary is now confined there. For twenty years, with the aid of confederates, he had carried on a system of robbery and plunder. His course was to ascertain who had money, and by some means extort or secure it. He never committed highway robbery, nor allowed his associates to do it. Nor did he murder his victims. He shot two of his associates dead, however, when he detected them in the act of highway robbery. He was accustomed to go from place to place when he pleased, and escaped detection till partially betrayed by some of his confederates.

Innsbruck is the capital of Tyrol, and lies under the shadow of lofty Alpine summits, crowned with snow. The palace of the Arch-Duke, and the Cathedral, are imposing edifices. In the center of the latter, an elaborately sculptured marble monument of the Emperor Maximilian is surrounded by black statues of old kings, queens, knights and crusaders, clad in their quaint drapery and ancient armor. It is a singular taste that places such things in a church.

Beyond this chain of mountains lies Italy, with its clear skies and sunny shores, which seem to beckon me thither. What various associations of historical, classical, and even sacred interest cluster there! What vicissitudes its people have experienced! What struggles for liberty, amid crushing despotisms, they have made! Soldiers and priests—Austria is full of them—they swarm in Italy—the curse and blight of the people. From the recent battle-fields, thousands of wounded soldiers have been brought over the mountains, and distributed among the different towns, to be taken care of by them. It was stated at Innsbruck, that as many as *thirty thousand* had been there, or through there. The people were quite dissatisfied with this burden, and some were free to condemn the late war as unwise, and to express the opinion that the Emperor of Austria would be better occupied in endeavoring to develop the resources of his country than in trying to enforce his authority upon a people who hate it.

By a tedious diligence conveyance of eighty miles, partly by night, over the Tyrolese Alps, by the Brenner Pass, an old Roman road, and amid scenery often wild, bold or picturesque, Botzen, a thriving town in the valley of the Adige, is reached; and then a ride of some hours by railway, brings one to the town of Verona. In the meantime you go through the village of Trient, where the famous Council of Trent was held. We are now fairly in Italy, and ancient Roman ruins greet us. The great attraction of Verona is its old Amphitheater, a building somewhat like the Coliseum, at Rome, but in a better state of preservation. It was erected about the beginning of the Christian era, and the stone seats for the many thousands of spectators, and balconies for the nobles, and the opposite entrances for the wild beasts and the gladiators, remain as they were at first. In entering the vast edifice, and walking up its more than forty tiers of seats, rising and enlarging one above another, and looking down upon the arena, once the scene of wild and terrible conflicts, the imagination could easily reproduce those exciting and fearful spectacles, and see among the doomed gladiators, perchance, some of the early martyrs of our holy faith, whose released spirits ascended to heaven amid the wild shouts of the unpitying crowd. The tomb of Shakspeare's Juliet is said to be at Verona.

A railroad brings you to Venice, which once could only be entered by boat, as is intimated in the lines of Rogers:

> There is a glorious city in the sea.
> The sea is in the broad, the narrow streets,
> Ebbing and flowing; and the salt seaweed
> Clings to the marble of her palaces.
> No track of men, no footsteps to and fro,
> Lead to her gates. The path lies o'er the sea.
> Invincible; and from the land we went,
> As to a floating city—steering in,
> And gliding up her streets as in a dream.

A unique and wonderful city is Venice, the Queen of the Adriatic, and having her foundations in the sea. Her principal streets are canals; her omnibusses and carriages are gondolas. You hear no tramp of horses' feet—no sound of rolling wheels. The only horses in the city are four of bronze, over the porch of St. Mark's Cathedral, and they are about two thousand years old. The city is remarkable for its varied history, and former wealth and power; for its numerous and splendid palaces, now tinged with decay; for the multitude of its churches, adorned with rich statuary and paintings; for its galleries of art, and other and varied attractions. The masterpieces of Titian and Tintoretto are here. The tomb of the former, in one of the churches, and opposite to it that of Canova, are admirable specimens of sculpture. St. Mark's Square is the great and brilliant center where everybody goes, for promenade and for shopping. In the evening a thousand lights shine upon you from jeweled windows, and the walls of palaces radiant with images of art and beauty. You pass crowds chatting while they sip their beverage at Cafés; and you hear Italian songs sung and violins played, as organ-grinders discourse their music, hoping to get a few soldies or kreutzers from the crowd. Before you is St. Mark's Cathedral, blossoming with domes, minarets, and statues, and wonderful for the various mosaics on its outer and inner walls. There, too, is the Doge's Palace, with its different halls, and beyond it the Bridge of Sighs, leading to the dungeons of the prison. But Venice cannot be adequately described. The former splendor of the city, and the great events that have there transpired, crowd upon one's thoughts, while all that you now behold of the place seems like the tomb of its ancient glory. Excursions by gondola to islands in the vicinity are pleasant. A gondolier, standing at the stern of his curious-looking boat, with a single oar, wafts you gracefully and rapidly along. At Murano you enter the extensive glass-works, where beads for the world are made. You are greatly interested in the processes of their manufacture, and bring away some specimens. You take a longer excursion to Lido, and walk across it, and are now beyond the Lagune of Venice, and wandering on the beach of the Adriatic, picking up shells, and listening to the unceasing music of its rolling surfs. As you glide back over the smooth waters, and under a transparent sky, Venice seems to rise out of the sea before you, and the charming view you now obtain of it will remain daguerreotyped on your memory as a perpetual pleasure.

There is a fascination about Venice that makes one leave it with reluctance. Its situation in the sea is picturesque and unique; its palaces seem like fading enchantments; its various life-phases, ever on exhibition in St. Mark's Square, are a magnet of attraction; the dream-like excursions by gondola along the narrow passages or in the Grand Canal under the Rialto, one likes to repeat; the glorious panorama of city, sea and shore, and distant Alps, from the top of the Campanile, or Cathedral tower, is a vision of beauty; and even the flocks of tame pigeons always flying over your head, or alighting at your feet, in St. Mark's Piazza, win your kindly regard. I had the pleasure of meeting in Venice Rev. Mr. Child and party, including Mr. W S. Greene, whom I had left on the borders of Switzerland three weeks before.

At length the slow railway toward Milan bore us away. Stopping over a train, we spent a few hours at Padua, one of the oldest towns in Northern Italy, and founded as Virgil says, by Antenor, whose tomb we found at a street corner, and bearing an inscription in Greek. Within the walls of an old arena, where various exhitions were once witnessed by excited thousands, we found growing trees of considerable size. We looked into a gloomy old hall called the Palazzo della Ragione. It is of immense size and its roof is said to be the largest unsupported by pillars, in the world. Dingy and mystical paintings hang all around it and at one end, in front of a bust of Livy, stands a colossal wooden horse, constructed about four hundred years ago. At the other end is a block of black granite, and a kind of altar, where insolvent debtors cleared themselves by their exposures to shame. The interior of the church of St. Antonio is gorgeously decorated with sculptures and paintings. The tomb of the saint is in the church, and a number of persons were clinging to it on their knees, or pressing up to touch it, as if they expected saving virtue from the contact. Passing a confessional box in another part of the church, we saw a young girl pouring her confession into the ear of a priest. Striking clocks were first made in Padua. Here for a time, at least, Petrarch, Livy and Galileo had their homes. The last was ten years Professor in the University, and from the old Observatory, still standing, he often surveyed the heavens, and doubtless made some of those discoveries that thrilled the world.

Not long after resuming our journey, we passed through a part of Montebello, where a battle in the recent war was fought; and further along the road, we got a view of the field of Solferino, the scene of the terrible and decisive conflict on the 24th of June, 1859. Returning by this place on the 24th of Oct., just four months after the battle, our train received quite a number of wounded Austrian officers, apparently, brought into the cars on couches, and having only sufficiently recovered to be able thus to proceed toward their homes.

VIII.

Milan—Mantua—Bologna—Florence—Pisa.

It was late in the evening, and raining, when we reached Milan. By the dim light of the street lamps we got a glimpse of its magnificent Cathedral as we passed to our hotel. The next morning found us early at its open square, surveying that marvel of architectural beauty and splendor. It surpasses all other cathedrals we have seen. It is of white marble, grand in design, and most elaborate in finish. Its niches are filled with statues, and its forest of minarets is covered and crowned with them, to the number of thousands. You survey the imposing edifice with wonder, and on entering it, you are astonished to find equal magnificence and decoration; and you conclude that in the Milan Cathedral the sacred architecture of ages culminates, and that here is the exuberant flowering of all ecclesiastical endeavor to impress or captivate the outward sense. Other objects of interest at Milan are several of its churches, that of St. Ambrose being very old—a row of ancient columns of a Roman temple, standing in the center of the city, yet in isolated desolation—the grand Arch of Peace, commenced by Napoleon I.—and the celebrated painting, by Leonardo da Vinci, of the Last Supper. It was painted on the wall of a refectory of an old monastery, and is much injured and defaced by the plaster peeling off, and the attempts of inferior artists to restore it. But you still see in it the work of a master. The head of the Saviour, the best preserved, is wonderful in its combination of majesty and meekness, and of divine authority and human sympathy. The expression of that serene, heavenly face is inimitable. The features of the Apostles and of Judas, are in admirable harmony with the scene represented.

Returning to Verona on the way to Mantua, as the train was leaving one of the stations in the evening, there was quite a smart jerking of the cars, and an outcry toward the rear of the train, as if some accident had occurred, and the engineer was desired to stop. But the train went on, amidst much agitation of the passengers. In the carriage where I sat all were Italians but one, and greatly excited. I remained calm, and a pleasant old lady, screaming "Salvendo! salvendo!" came and sat beside me, and could hardly get quiet till she procured of some one— her son perhaps—a little black crucifix, about six inches long, which she unrolled from a piece of paper, and showed to me with evident satisfaction, and then put it in her bosom. I pointed upward, as if to say, We should trust in God. Before this, in endeavoring to converse with me, she had learned that I was an American.

No one would visit Mantua for anything beautiful in or around the town itself. Its situation is low, and amidst marshes and stagnant pools. But when we think of it as the birth-place of Virgil, and for a time, at least, his residence, who that has read the Æneid would not be interested in seeing Mantua, and wandering in its precincts, where the immortal bard had his rural haunts and home! A splendid marble shaft to his memory, erected by order of Napoleon I., stands in a green and flowery spot in the town. We were greatly pleased with this, for we could find nothing else, save a street bearing the name of the great poet, to remind us that we were near the place of his birth.

A day by diligence took us on through the heart of the country to Parma, crossing on the way the rivers Mincio, Oglio and Po. The last, at Casal Maggiore, where we crossed it in a ricketty old ferry-boat, manned by brigandish-looking fellows, is quite a broad stream, with a rapid current. From Parma we went by railway to Bologna, and were reminded, as we passed through Modena, of the story of Ginevra. We were detained nearly two days in Bologna before we could secure seats in the diligence to Florence. We visited several of its churches and galleries of art. The painting by Raphael of Cecilia entranced by the music of angels, is very fine. The leaning towers, of which we had not heard before, are quite a curiosity. Much to our regret, we just missed seeing the noble patriot, Garibaldi, who had left the place and the hotel where we stopped only a few hours before our arrival.

It was a long and tedious ride to Florence. We left Bologna at three o'clock in the morning, and soon a rain-storm commenced, and continued through the day. Mountain streams often rushed over our path. We crossed the Apennines, but they were mostly enveloped in clouds, and the view on every hand was obstructed. It was too early for breakfast when we started, and the drivers, in order to reach the railway in season for the last train to Florence, could not stop long enough for a lunch to be obtained; so we took our first meal that day, after nine o'clock in the evening, at the Hotel New York in Florence.

I was somewhat disappointed in the rural aspects of Italy. It is not that beautiful country my imagination had pictured it. The season, it is true, was unfavorable for seeing it to the best advantage. We could not expect, at the last of October, to observe the freshness of spring, the bloom of summer, or the ripened harvests of early autumn. Much of the country had a dingy and wretched appearance, like the poor peasants and pertinacious beggars you everywhere meet. The villages and larger towns scarcely look better. There are some pretty cottages and fine villas, but most of the houses have a forbidding and untidy appearance. The people, however, seem capable of better things than they possess. They have been long crushed with Romanism and oppression. But they are now in a state of considerable political excitement. In all the large towns, the streets were full of people, who seemed to be engaged in conversation about their civil affairs. Placards were everywhere posted up, declaring that Victor Emanuel is their king. They will not be satisfied with anything less than the freedom which Sardinia enjoys. They are almost unanimous against the return of the Grand-Dukes; and should Austria attempt to reinstate them, there would be war at once. Venetia would revolt without delay, if she felt able to throw off the Austrian domination. We heard the complaint at Venice—Why should we have these soldiers, who cannot speak our language, quartered upon us? Many thousands have left that Province for the freer atmosphere of adjoining States. The Pope, doubtless, fears that his temporal power will soon pass from him; and with the loss of that, the Papal Church must necessarily be weakened. Italy at present is a sort of seething cauldron, and what the issues will be, it is difficult to foretell. May her star ascend!

On our first entrance into Italy, we saw fields of Indian corn and yellow pumpkins, reminding us of similar sights in New-England. Mulberry, chestnut, pear and apple trees, are plenteous; and about Florence there are olives, figs and pomegranates, with their pendant fruits. The climate is much milder than in the same latitude with us. Roses are now blooming in open gardens. Chestnuts are found everywhere, in the market and on the table. They are very much larger than ours, and are usually eaten roasted. You see women all along the streets, with their charcoal fire and pan of roasting chestnuts. They are quite a large item in the food of the peasants. The lower classes throughout Europe do much of their house or shop work, their cooking, and eating and drinking, out of doors.

Florence has a variety of attractions. The streets, with a few exceptions, are narrow and unpleasant. Its buildings, generally, are not elegant. The muddy Arno divides the city. Its environs are beautiful. One may walk or ride for hours in the Boboli Gardens or the Cascine, with delight. Evergreens and statues adorn the paths. In the Pitti Palace you find paintings that have a world-wide fame. The beautiful creations of Raphael, especially, including his celebrated Madonna della Seggiola, long detain you in rapt admiration. The tables of mosaic are wonderful specimens of that art, carried to such perfection here. The Uffizi Gallery is scarcely less attractive. Many of its pictures and statues are known the world over Here is the famous Venus de Medici, so exquisite and graceful. It is intensely interesting to survey these works of the old masters and of more recent artists. The dome of the Cathedral is more ample than that of St. Peter's at Rome, and was greatly admired by Michael Angelo. Two of the bronze doors of the Baptistery, covered with exquisite bas-reliefs, occupied the artist forty years. The church of Santa Croce, the Westminster Abbey of Florence, contains the remains of Michael Angelo, Galileo, Machiavelli, and others, with their massive marble monuments, adorned with rich and emblematic sculptures. A fine cenotaph of Dante, who lived in Florence, but died in Ravenna, stands with them. The church of San Lorenzo, and the Medicean Chapel connected with it, contain the remains, tombs and cenotaphs of the celebrated Medici family. The chapel alone cost $17,000,000 and is yet unfinished. Its interior walls are of variegated marbles and precious stones, and its dome is covered with splendid frescoes. It is a monument of folly.

We passed an hour very pleasantly in the studio of our countryman, Hiram Powers. We found him exceedingly agreeable and entertaining; and the specimens from his chisel, including a bust of Franklin and Proserpine, and a full length figure, California, which he kindly showed us, are certainly among the finest sculptures we have ever seen.

It is pleasant to turn away from decorated churches, where unintelligible mummeries are being constantly repeated, and enter a humbler place of Protestant worship, and listen to the simple preaching of the Gospel of Christ. There are two such places of worship in this city, at both of which we attended on the Sabbath. One is an English Episcopal church, and the other a Scotch Presbyterian. They both have excellent evangelical chaplains. Happy will it be for Italy when the day shall come that the Gospel, in its purity and power, is preached to her people, and practiced in their lives. Heaven speed that day, and it seems to be at hand.

While taking tea with the Scotch Presbyterian minister, the Rev. J. R. McDougal, at his invitation and residence, he gave an interesting account of an evangelical religious movement now in progress in Florence, and extending to adjacent localities. In the Revolution in 1848, some copies of the Bible came into circulation, and were eagerly read by persons who had obtained the idea that the progress of liberty was identified with that book. A number were thus made wise unto salvation, and they took measures to diffuse the truth more widely. Among these was the Madai family, whose imprisonment excited so much interest in our country. That family lived in apartments adjoining the one in which I obtained these facts. Converts increased, and Bibles were multiplied. The priests were alarmed, and the civil authority was invoked to stop the movement. Numbers were arrested and imprisoned for propagating the evangelical faith. On one occasion, the authorities found a large number of Bibles, and apprehended them and put them in prison. The people, hearing of this, were curious to know what sort of a book it was that was thus treated. They flocked to the prison to see copies of it; and the keeper, perceiving an opportunity to turn the matter to his own account, sold a good many copies to those who were anxious to buy the singular prisoner. So the Word of God was not bound, but had free course, and was glorified in securing further triumphs. From that day to this, the good work has been extending. Regular religious meetings are held, in a quiet way, in various places, conducted by converted Italians, much in the manner of our conference meetings, with reading of the Word of God, prayer and singing. Bibles, tracts, and religious books, are circulated. I have seen several of these publications, and among them a translation of the "Philosophy of the Plan of Salvation," a work which thoughtful Italians read with much interest. Every year some are arrested and imprisoned, but the number of such cases is diminishing, and true converts are increasing. This is certainly an interesting and hopeful movement.

I made several delightful excursions among the environs of Florence, and to the summits of the hills that look down upon the beautiful vale of the Arno, in which it is situated. Fiesole is about five miles to the north, a city older than the Tuscan capital, and a thousand feet above it. Portions of old Roman ruins are still visible. But I was vastly more pleased with an excursion in the opposite direction, to a high eminence, surmounted with a tower, called Galileo's Observatory. Part of the building was over a broad, fine road, between lofty cypresses, interspersed with oak and larch, and which leads to an imperial palace, where, a few nights before, a grand ball had been given by the city authorities and attended by about three thousand guests. Strangers were not numerous, and the times rather dull in Florence; and this ball was, no doubt, mainly designed for the benefit of the shopkeepers, who furnished the materials of dress and display. Even kings and emperors are often obliged to resort to similar expedients, to allay the complaints and retain the favor of their subjects.

From the top of Galileo's Tower one gets an entrancing view of the city and adjacent country. The valley for many miles, with the winding course of the Arno, is spread out like a map. Ranges of Apennine hills on the east hide Vallambrosa from view. We went to the villa of Galileo, near by, where that philosopher lived and died, and where Milton, during his visit to Italy, held interviews with him. From this Observatory, it is said, Galileo made those discoveries, in regard to the moon, to which Milton, in the Paradise Lost, alludes, when saying that the shield of Satan

> "Hung o'er his shoulders like the moon, whose orb
> Through optic glass the Tuscan artist views
> At evening from the top of Fiesole,
> Or in Valdarno, to descry new lands,
> Rivers or mountains, in her spotty globe."

Entering the Baptistery one day, which is a large octagon or circular edifice, near the Cathedral, I wit-

FLORENCE FROM THE SOUTHEAST.

nessed the ceremony of baptizing an infant. The little, well attired subject, who had evidently not yet seen two Sabbaths, was brought into the building by a woman, accompanied by a young man, when two priests made their appearance, and these seemed to be all the persons any way concerned in the matter. One of the priests took the child, while the other stood by, holding a huge lighted wax candle, three or four feet long. The officiating priest breathed in the baby's face, and made the sign of the cross on its forehead and breast, and gave it to the arms of the young man, and proceeded to read something from a book, while the other priest frequently responded, Amen. This over, the first priest took from a little box a pinch of salt, and put it into the mouth of the child. Then they all went to the font, the young man repeating something as he carried the infant. The officiating priest now touched his own tongue, and then the baby's face, with his finger. Then pulling back the child's cap, he held the little creature upright over the font, crossed it, rubbed some oil on its neck and forehead, and bending its head downward, he dipped up a dish of water, and poured it liberally on its head. This caused the child to cry, and that was the end of the ceremony.

Returning one evening from a pleasant social circle of Americans, for the most part, I encountered on one of the the numerous bridges of the Arno, a singular funeral procession. The coffin, on a bier, and draped in black, was borne on the shoulders of several men, strangely appareled in long dark robes and ghastly-looking masks. They were preceded and followed by a number of others in similar costume, and carrying elevated torches.

Florence improves upon acquaintance. I first entered it at evening, in a violent rain, and for a week or two the weather was anything but pleasant or mild, making everything seem cheerless, and my first impressions not very agreeable. But when the weather became settled, the skies delightfully clear, and the air pure and invigorating, things wore a new and more pleasing face. New and congenial acquaintances were formed, and repeated visits to the wonderful creations of art and genius rendered my stay in the city increasingly attractive; while the streets and buildings assumed an improved appearance, and the muddy Arno sometimes really had a transparent aspect, especially under a glorious Italian sunset, or the glitter of a thousand lamps that line its borders at night.

Travel brings pleasures and benefits, and a kind of education, that can be acquired in no other way Opportunities are constantly afforded for observing the grand and beautiful works, both of nature and art, as well as for studying the character and habits of different peoples. No day need pass without something of good or profit seen, learned, or experienced. Even the annoyances that one meets constantly—the discomforts and perplexities of journeying where passports, custom-houses, and various hungry officials detain and tax you; the swarm of beggars, including the lame, the blind, and the diseased, as well as the destitute and the lazy, who beset you like a pack of ravenous wolves; the ignorance and degradation that surround you; the blind and puerile superstitions of the people, amid magnificent temples apparently devoted to God's service; the great poverty of lands rich in natural capabilities and varied beauties—all these things make you grateful for the land of your birth, and lead you to prize more highly its people, its government, its religion, and all its good institutions.

Here, and in fact throughout Italy, great contrasts are continually meeting the eye. Go into the galleries of painting and sculpture, enter many of the cathedrals, churches, palaces, and other public or private buildings, and often as you walk along some street or open piazza, you behold beautiful and astonishing creations of art and skill—pictures and statues that have a world-wide fame, and in the contemplation of which you are lost in admiration and delight; and then as you turn away from these, and look upon the realities of life around you, you see sad and disgusting evidences of mental darkness, wretchedness, and low, groveling tastes and habits. Go out into the country, and you are struck often with the beauty and richness of valleys, hill-sides, and table-lands; you see numerous evergreen trees, cultivated and trained in gardens, whose walks, arches, bowers, and fountains are like the enchantments of Aladdin's Lamp; you see a flourishing growth of olives, oranges, figs and pomegranates; and though on the verge of winter, and in sight of snow on mountain peaks in the horizon, whose cool breath you feel, you are greeted by the way with beautiful hedges of roses, in bud and bloom, as they adorn the grounds of some villa, or hang over the high walls by the road-side. And while some of the more pretending villas, or humbler cottages, please you with their beauty and neatness, you will not fail to observe many a filthy and miserable habitation, with inmates to correspond; ragged women at work in the fields; donkeys and cows yoked together, with plows, carts and other agricultural implements of rude and awkward construction. Hands in the city are making tables and jewelry of exquisite mosaics that cause you to wonder at the perfection of human ingenuity; and hands in the country are using various utensils of tillage so clumsy and ungainly that a Yankee would hardly deem them fit for fire-wood or old iron.

On the afternoon of the 25th of November, we left Florence for Pisa, where we arrived by railway, just at evening, and from an elevated window of our hotel, first got a glimpse of the Leaning Tower. Familiar from childhood with the pictures and accounts of that remarkable structure, could it be that my eyes were now really beholding it? In the morning we hastened to the spot where it stands in connection with three other objects of unusual interest—the Baptistery, the Campo Santa, and the Cathedral. The Baptistery, erected in the twelfth century is a beautiful building of white marble, circular and dome-like, relieved in the exterior by fine Corinthian columns. The interior is mostly marble also, and exquisitely finished. In the center is a large font, fourteen feet in its longest diameter, adapted and probably used for the immersion of candidates for baptism. The large room rising into the high dome, afforded delightful echoes; and when a few of us sang a part of the hymn,—

"My heavenly home is bright and fair,
Nor pain nor death shall enter there"—

the fullness and prolongation of the sounds were organ-like and charming. The Campo Santa is a cemetery, an immense oblong structure, with cloisters extending around it, and the open space within filled with earth, to the amount of fifty-three ship loads, brought from Calvary. There are numerous monuments in the cloisters, and some striking frescoes. One of the latter, representing the Last Judgment, has a touch of satire, as well as truth, no doubt; for the artist has mixed kings and queens and monks with the wicked. The Cathedral is spacious and splendid. "The doors are of bronze, the roof is of carved and gilded wood, the floor of marble white and yellow; statues of exquisite workmanship adorn the walls, while a dim light spreads through the painted windows, and clothes with a mellowing softness, the stupendous columns." But I was interested most of all in the Campanile or Leaning Tower. It is a beautiful marble structure, fifty-three feet in diameter at the base, and about one hundred and eighty feet high, inclining toward the south more than thirteen feet from the perpendicular. My first view of the Mediterranean was from its top; and what thoughts such a sight awakens? The waters of that sea lave the shores of Palestine, and are linked with the stirring events of ancient and modern history. A prophet was once cast into it, and an apostle wrecked upon it.

At Leghorn, a considerable commercial town, we took steamer for Civita Vecchia, the port of the Papal

States, where we arrived in about twelve hours; and after many annoyances and taxes of patience and purse, we were on the railway for Rome. A ride of three hours through an uninteresting country, brought us in sight of the domes and towers of the eternal city!

IX.

Rome—Its Churches—The Vatican—Tivoli.

Rome! How interesting the place! How suggestive the word! What a train of associations it awakens! The records of the past are unrolled; great characters in history stand before us; and events that filled the world with their grandeur and significance seem to be transpiring again. Who has not desired to see Rome! What student of classical literature, what lover of eloquence and poetry, what admirer of art, and mental power in its various exhibitions, has not longed to visit Rome, and wander amid the ruins of its former greatness and glory?—to look upon the Seven Hills where the city of the Cæsars was enthroned—to walk beneath the massive arches where they led their triumphant processions—to muse amid the broken columns of the Forum, where Cicero and other orators swayed assembled throngs—to linger under the shadow of the Coliseum, and think of the exciting scenes it once witnessed—and to trace the footsteps of the great Apostle to the Gentiles, who, prisoner though he was, wielded an influence under God that was felt through the city, and pervaded even the Imperial Palace! Who has not had a curiosity at least to look upon the sources of that mighty religious organism and power, that have so long exercised a tremendous influence on human destiny, and still retain so much of their old energy, superstition and sway? The dream of years has at length been realized, and what only was known by the hearing of the ear, is now familiarized by the seeing of the eye. On the 28th of November, I entered the gate of the so-called Eternal City. But how, in these brief and hasty way-notes, can I adequately describe what I have observed of ancient and modern Rome?

There are about as many churches in Rome as there are days in a year. The majority of them are very ordinary structures; and sometimes, when the exterior is quite plain and even forbidding, you will find the interior elaborately ornate and gorgeous. There is but one Gothic church in Rome, and very few of these edifices have painted windows. The principal materials of ornamentation are marbles of various colors, and other rare stones, statuary, paintings, silver and gilding. You will sometimes find nearly the whole interior of a church, its floor, its columns, its walls, its altars and chapels, gleaming with polished and exquisitely carved and finished marbles of almost every hue. The niches are filled with statues and pictures—monuments of Popes, Cardinals, Bishops and Saints, and paintings of Scripture scenes, in which dignitaries of the Church are often strangely blended; while crucifixes and Madonnas everywhere abound. Frequently most horrid scenes of martyrdom, agony and blood are represented. Everything that can affect the senses, and through them move the passions, finds a place in these ecclesiastical decorations and emblems.

One of the first churches the stranger visits, is that

great and wonderful edifice, St. Peter's, whose magnificent dome reflects the unrivaled genius of Michael Angelo. Its construction occupied centuries, and the most renowned architects lavished their skill upon it. A great part of the incredible amount of money expended upon it, was realized from the sale of indulgences. In going to St. Peter's, a friend pointed out the house where Raphael, the prince of painters, lived. It is in a narrow, mean and dirty street, and the house itself is only worthy of its location. Looking up its dingy front, I saw a clothes-line, well laden with nether and other garments, hanging along its windows, and partially intercepting the view. After crossing the muddy Tiber by the Bridge of St. Angelo, amid colossal marble statues, with the immense circular Tomb of Hadrian, now a fortress and prison, rising before you, and passing some distance along a narrow, filthy street, lined with huckster-shops, you come to the large, open, oval Piazza of St. Peter's. On either hand is a magnificent range of colonnades or porticoes, with four rows of massive round pillars, over sixty feet high, while along the top are standing some two hundred statues, which the imagination might easily transform into celestial visitants come to watch the trains of earthly worshipers. Before you is a large Egyptian obelisk, and on each side, beautiful fountains throwing their crystal jets and spray into the air, and which often have a halo of rainbows about them. Beyond these, rises the imposing facade of the great edifice, and crowned with gigantic statues of the twelve Apostles. This view excites your profound admiration, and though the enclosure embraces about ten acres, there is such harmony of outline and proportion, that it does not seem half so large.

You enter this church, as you do others at Rome, by lifting a heavy leather curtain, and then your eyes meet a sight, for vastness and majesty, richness and grandeur, afforded by no other religious temple in the world. Amplitude and height, massiveness and splendor, characterize the interior. Look up into the sublime dome, and you do not wonder that Michael Angelo called it "a firmament of marble." The pictures are all in mosaic, and are finely wrought. Amidst all this display of rich ornamentation, you see much that you deem neither agreeable nor in good taste. A double flight of stairs leads down to the reputed tomb of Peter, above and around which over a hundred lights are constantly burning. Near by, elevated a few feet above the floor of the church, is a black statue of the Apostle, before which you see persons come and kneel, and rise and kiss the great toe of the projecting foot, which is considerably shortened by this unceasing labial attrition.

On my next visit to St. Peter's, I ascended to the roof, which is quite a plateau, or place containing dwellings and families living there; and then to the base of the dome, and then to near its crown, from whence you look down the frightful distance to the floor of the church, where men and women, and processions of priests seem but creeping pigmies. Finally I went to the very top, and squeezed through the narrow entrance into the ball! Fine views of the city and the Campagna might have been had, but for the smallness of the apertures opening to the world without.

The interior of the church of St. Paul, outside the walls of the city, is in some respects quite equal, if not superior, to that of St. Peter's. The splendid monolithic columns, the rich altars of malachite, the costly portraits in mosaic of the successive Popes, and other exquisite pictures, excite your wondering gaze. The St. John Lateran, is scarcely inferior in the rich and costly finish of its architecture and embellishment. Its cloisters contain relics which an attending priest is ready to exhibit. He shows the stone well-curb, by which Jesus conversed with the Samaritan woman; the two halves of a column rent at our Lord's crucifixion; the porphyry table on which His raiment was divided; and that also on which He and His disciples partook of the Last Supper. He shows a stone slab, too, with a hole in it, and says that a priest once, doubting the Real Presence, dropped the wafer, and it went miraculously through the table! So, I suppose, he was cured of his unbelief. Near this church is a building, called the Baptistery, in the center of which is a porphyry font, sufficiently large for immersion, in which Constantine was baptized, as it is said.

In this vicinity is the church of the Holy Staircase. The Santa Scala, or Staircase, consists of twenty-eight marble steps, covered with boards, and said to belong to the house of Pilate; and not only that, but they are affirmed to be the very stairs on which our Lord descended from the Judgment Hall. Hence great virtue is attached to them, and to go up them on one's knees, and pay a fee for it, produces great blessings to the devotee here and hereafter. So an attending priest assured us, though we did not make the trial. Others, however, were continually plodding up, and kissing the stairs as they proceeded. It was on these stairs, I think, that Luther's eyes were measurably opened to see the absurdities of Romanism.

It is quite common in Catholic countries to erect a church over some spot that, by tradition or otherwise, is regarded as sacred. St. Peter's occupies the site where the Apostle, whose name it bears, is said to have been buried, though there is no reliable evidence that he was ever in Rome at all. The splendid Basilica of St. Paul stands without the walls in a low and unhealthy location, that it may cover the place where the Apostle to the Gentiles is supposed to have had his sepulchre. A church on the Corso—St. Maria in Via Latta—is regarded as occupying the site of Paul's hired house, where he lived two years in the charge of a soldier. You are guided to dark rooms under the church, and are shown portions of the old house where the Apostle lived; and the priest points to a spring or well which he says was miraculously provided, curb and all, so that Paul could there baptize his converts. A church has been built over the old Mamertine Prison, in whose dark dungeons tradition says Peter and Paul were confined. It is not unlikely that the latter was taken from this place to his martyrdom, having first written here the glorious words to Timothy: "I am now ready to be offered, and the time of my departure is at hand. I have fought a good fight, I have finished my course, I have kept the faith; henceforth there is laid up for me a crown of righteousness, which the Lord, the righteous Judge, shall give me at that day, and not to me only, but unto all them also that love his appearing." We may readily believe that here Jugurtha was starved to death, and the companions of Catiline strangled. Here, also, in the floor of the prison, we were shown a miraculous fountain, and on the wall a rough bas-relief of Peter baptizing the jailer. I suppose it would not be difficult to find other springs, by making similar excavations at the foot of the same Capitoline Hill. The church of St. Pietro in Vincoli was built to preserve the chain with which Peter was bound at Jerusalem. I was interested in this church, not on account of this relic, but from the fact that here Hildebrand was crowned Pope, with the title of Gregory VII. in 1073. Here, also, is a magnificent statue of Moses, by Michael Angelo, in which the majesty and meekness of Israel's lawgiver are wonderfully blended. I went to the church of St. Onofrio, on the Janiculum, to see the last resting-place of Tasso, the immortal author of Jerusalem Delivered. The poet died in Rome in 1595, at the age of 51. Recently a very richly-carved monument in marble has been erected to his memory. In the church of the Capuchins is Guido's Archangel standing on the neck of Lucifer, a remarkable painting. The Lucifer is said to be a likeness of a Cardinal, afterwards Pope Innocent X., whose criticisms had displeased the artist. The grave of Cardinal Barberini, by whom this church was built, is marked by this simple and singular inscription: *Hic jacet pulvis, cinis et nihil.* Under the church are four rooms, used as a cemetery, the earth in them having been brought from

Jerusalem. They present the most singular and unique appearance imaginable. They are all filled with human skeletons and bones, arranged with a taste and skill, for beautiful forms and figures, that would do honor to an artist. The ceilings and walls are covered with bones, so placed as to resemble the most beautiful ornaments in plaster. There are festoons of these bones, and the chandeliers hanging from the ceilings are made of them. Some entire skeletons have drapery on them, and on some of the skulls I noticed the names of the persons to whom they belonged, and the dates of their birth and death. When a monk dies, he is buried in the oldest grave, from which the skeleton is exhumed, clothed, and placed in one of the rooms, where a previous skeleton stood or lay, but is now removed, and its bones piled up or distributed in the curious manner described.

Who has not heard of the Vatican, if he has not heard its thunders? It is an irregular pile or collection of buildings, adjoining St. Peter's on the right, and embracing some thousands of rooms and halls. Squads of French soldiers are continually standing around the entrance, and one generally finds a large number of them paraded or being drilled in the square of St. Peter's. Several long and broad staircases lead to the halls and museums of the Vatican, where are gathered and preserved an immense number of works of art. The sculpture galleries are very extensive, and you range through them in delighted admiration of the ancient, interesting, and beautiful or grand productions of the chisel. You linger long before such statues as the Laocoon and Apollo Belvedere, and wonder at the genius that could invest marble with such elements of life, passion and power. You see many busts of persons distinguished in historical and classical literature, and are gratified with a truthful representation of their faces and features. Two of the most celebrated pictures in the world are in the Vatican. The Last Judgment by Michael Angelo, covers entirely the farther wall of the Sistine Chapel. The light is not good, and one fails of the profoundest impression this great painting is adapted to produce. I was better pleased with Raphael's inimitable picture of the Transfiguration. It was his last and best work; and before he had quite finished it, he was suddenly cut off by death at the early age of thirty-seven. This glorious painting, bearing the last and fresh traces of his master-hand, was suspended over the couch where the dead body of the illustrious artist lay in state, and at his funeral it was borne in the train immediately preceding his remains. Raphael sleeps in the Pantheon, a grand old temple, built before the Christian era, and in a better state of preservation than any contemporary building in Rome.

The Pope resides in the Vatican, except during four months in the summer, when he occupies the Quirinal, or Pontifical Palace on Monte Cavallo. Our Consul gives Americans permission to visit this palace. It has extensive apartments, many of which are adorned with fine paintings, tapestries and furniture. The adjoining garden is shady with lofty box and cypress, relieved with statues and fountains. In one part of the grounds is an organ played by water, and a large number of hidden pipes, which at the will of an attendant, throw jets of water in all directions, causing the visitors to make a hasty retreat to an open building at hand. The Pope ought to be satisfied with his accommodations; and yet his head must sometimes be uneasy even under the triple crown. From the Vatican to the Castle of St. Angelo, formerly Hadrian's Tomb, but now a strongly fortified and guarded place, there is a walled passage by which, in case of disturbance or danger, the Pope may escape to the castle for safety.

There are numerous palaces in Rome, containing galleries of paintings and sculptures of more or less merit. In the Spada stands the colossal statue of Pompey, at the base of which the great Julius Cæsar was assassinated. On one of its legs is a dark spot, said to have been made with the blood of the renowned victim.

On the 8th of December occurs the Festival of the Immaculate Conception, when the Pope and his Cardinals officiate at the Sistine Chapel in the Vatican. In going up the long flight of stairs leading to the Vatican, I found a couple of waiters to take my overcoat and hat, for which they must be paid a small sum in advance. Perceiving I had on a frock coat, they undertook to pin back the skirts to make it resemble a dress coat; but did it so bunglingly, that though the guard at the door let me in, the ushers inside, casting significant glances at my wardrobe, would not allow me to take a seat with those who were more fortunate in the cut of their coats, but gave me a good standing-place among some priests. A gentleman immediately behind me, and in the same fix, could not get in at all. I suppose the Pope's version of a certain passage is, *God is no respecter of persons, but he is of coat-tails.* The ladies were required to dress in black, and wore only veils on their heads, of the same color.

The Cardinals came one after another to the number of twenty-five or thirty. They ride each in a splendid carriage, with gorgeous and glaring equipage, and three or four attendants bedizened with livery, while they themselves are covered with scarlet and gilt robes, which are held up by two or three persons as they enter the chapel and go to their seats. The Pope enters by a side door in his rich robes and miter, and sits on his throne-like elevation covered with a sort of silver drapery. Two or three persons stand by him continually to take off and put on his big head-covering, and to adjust his robes. He is a pleasant-looking old man, and when he waved his hand in benedictions toward the audience, there was among the faithful a general prostration and crossing themselves. The services were very uninteresting, consisting of the usual turnings and bowings and mummery. One priest made a short address in Italian.

On the 10th I attended the opening of the American College in Rome. This institution is designed for the education of young men from America for the Romish priesthood. A number of such students was present, and among them an African. Good music, a spirited address in Italian by Cardinal Barnabo, burning incense, and elevating the Host, with the usual genuflections, constituted the exercises. The graduates of this college, I suppose, are intended to return to America, to diffuse the leaven of Romanism in our land. We must meet them with our own educated and God-sent ministry, in the propagation of the pure and blessed Gospel of Christ.

On the preceding day, we made a delightful excursion to Tivoli, some eighteen miles nearly east from Rome. We passed the massive tomb of Plautius, and crossed a considerable stream of a milky hue, and filling the air for some distance with a strong odor of sulphur. Tivoli is most romantically situated on a hill of the Alban group, and we passed an extensive olive orchard as we ascended to the village, which in itself has few attractions, its houses being forbidding and filthy. The old Temple of the Sybil, perched on a most commanding site, is a beautiful and interesting ruin. We wandered with great delight among the declivities, the grottos, and along the waterfalls, which constitute the chief charms of the place. We looked at the ruins of the Villa of Mæcenas, who was the patron and entertainer of Horace. Orators, philosophers, and poets, were accustomed to make their homes or haunts amid the localities of Tivoli. On returning we rambled over the extensive ruins of Hadrian's Villa, in a suburb of the village, and wondered at the grandeur of the monarch, when that vast field was covered with the architectural glory with which he invested the place. We returned under a clear mild sky, and the exquisite purple tints of a glorious sunset faded from the Alban and Sabine hills, only to be succeeded by the soft splendors of a full and glorious moon, that made our homeward drive most charming.

X.
Old Rome—Coliseum—Catacombs—Christmas.

NOTHING interests me more than the relics of the past, when the Eternal City was in its palmiest days. It is impossible to convey the impressions they give of the wealth and power of the old Romans. Acres of ruins mark the places where stood some of the grandest structures on which the sun ever shone. The Palace of the Cæsars is a plowed field. Half-buried arches stand out in their grim desolation, and are overgrown with shrubbery and cypress. Where stood the Villa of Mæcenas, the Golden House of Nero, and the Baths of Titus, is a mass of ruins. A part of the halls and chambers have been excavated, and some of the finest sculptures and vases in the Vatican were found in them. You follow a guide with torches into these rooms, and you still see remains of exquisite marbles, mosaics and frescoes. The ruins of the Baths of Caracalla are still more ample and stupendous. Those of Diocletian were remodeled by Michael Angelo and turned into a church, which, out of Rome, would be regarded as a most magnificent edifice, and yet it includes only a portion of the old structure. The cloisters of this church are extensive and fine, and in its court stand some venerable cypress trees planted by Michael Angelo three hundred years ago. In this church we were shown what were said to be the bodies of the martyrs Felicitas and Prosper, with various other relics. The ruins of the Claudian Aqueduct, stretching away over and beyond the Porta Maggiore, are one of the most striking and impressive relics of the old city, which must have been abundantly supplied with water. There are now over a hundred fountains, some of them very elaborate and picturesque in statuary, and other contrivances for throwing columns of water and spray into the air.

Among the most remarkable and interesting objects in Rome, are the ruins of the Forum and the Coliseum. I have made several visits to these localities; but let me sketch an evening ramble amid the shadows of these astonishing relics of a departed age. On a cloudless, moonlight evening, a few of us took a stroll from the Piazza di Spagna to the Corso, and from thence by Trajan's Forum, whose broken pillars of granite and floor of variegated marble, and whose lone, majestic columns, attest the former splendor of the edifice, to the broad stairway of the Capitol, ascending which brought us to the site of the ancient Capitol, occupied by the present edifice, in which are some fine halls of statuary, and where you linger in rapt admiration before the Dying Gladiator. We descended the Capitoline Hill close by the grand Arch of Septimius Severus, and before us, on the right, were the silent and solemn ruins of the Forum. A few columns, here and there, are still standing, in exquisite beauty and finish, as if to remind us of the splendor of the ancient edifice, where Cicero and other orators discoursed so eloquently to vast assemblies of the people. What grandeur then! What desolation now! We enter the *Via Sacra*, where Horace loved to walk, and passing on our left the magnificent arches of the Temple of Peace, we reach the Triumphal Arch of Titus, built to commemorate his conquest of Jerusalem. On one of its inner walls we see bas-reliefs of the golden candlestick, the trumpets, and the ark, which the conqueror snatched from the consuming Temple, and bore as conspicuous spoils in his triumphal procession through Rome. Who can describe the thoughts awakened by such a sight, at such an hour! A little farther on eastward, while grand old broken columns, disclosed by the moonlight, lie along the way, we have the lofty and beautiful Arch of Constantine on our right, and almost directly in front rises, in hoary majesty and sublime decay, yet in overwhelming vastness and grandeur, that kingly ruin and wonder of the world, the Coliseum! As we approach the entrance, a French soldier, as sentinel, salutes us, and permits us to enter. We wander over the arena, amid the shadows of the arches and walls. All is silent and serene. How softly the moonbeams fall on a spot where, nearly eighteen centuries ago, such strange scenes of excitement and death were witnessed by assemblies numbering almost a hundred thousand people! What multitudes of the early Christians were there thrown to the wild beasts, to be torn in pieces amidst the deafening shouts of their unfeeling persecutors! There, how often was the Gladiator

"Butchered to make a Roman holiday!"

As I thought of these scenes, and looked up above

the gray old walls to the sweet moon and serene stars, most delightful thoughts of heaven, where the martyrs are crowned with glory and all the blessed rejoice, possessed my mind, and I observed to a friend, There is one city where there are no ruins, and the temple therein shall never decay; how glorious the privilege of a home and inheritance there, where all is purity and peace! That City is, indeed, Eternal.

It is not difficult to imagine with what pride and satisfaction the Coliseum was regarded when it stood in its unimpaired and sublime magnificence, and how astonished pilgrims, on beholding it, should exclaim—

"While stands the Coliseum, Rome shall stand;
When falls the Coliseum, Rome shall fall;
And when Rome falls—the world."

We returned to our lodgings, musing on human greatness and decay, and with pictures made on the memory that can only fade with life.

Old Rome is not only partially buried by the gradual accumulations on the surface for nearly two thousand years, but beneath these relics there are extensive recesses, stretching away for miles, excavated in the tufa, or soft rock, and crowded with the tombs and remains of the dead. I had visited the tombs of the Scipios and the Catacombs of St. Sebastian, which contain numerous underground passages and chambers; but I was anxious to make further excursions into these wonderful subterranean cemeteries. Through the favor of Rev. Dr. Smith, acting President of the American College, a large party of us were gratified in making a visit to the Catacombs of St. Calixtus. We rode out some miles on the Appian Way—where, some days before, I had made a longer excursion, and was greatly interested in the tombs and relics along that old road, where Roman chariots once wheeled in triumph—and stopped at a gate opening into a garden or field. We entered, and proceeded a few paces, and then, with lighted tapers, a guide, and Dr. Smith to make explanations, we descended a narrow aperture, and for nearly three hours wandered amid those dark chambers of death. How interesting was this journey to a lower world! We sometimes descended, and then ascended—turned now to the right and then to the left—at one time going through long passages just large enough to admit a single person, and presently we would come to a recess or chapel, arched above and supported by pillars cut in the rock, and large enough to hold twenty or thirty persons. Everywhere, on the right hand and left, were burial-places, cut, one above another, in the sides of the passage. Sometimes a niche indicated, by its larger and smaller graves, a family vault. Most of these graves had been opened, by removing the marble slab that covered and sealed them, and contained inscriptions relating to the dead. We saw bones, skulls and skeletons in these graves, and could often read the inscriptions on the broken marble. Sometimes, in the chapels, there were portraits and religious emblems painted on the walls and ceiling, as well as carved on the tomb-stones. Here, doubtless, many thousands of the early Christians, in times of cruel persecution, met for divine worship, and here martyrs and others were buried. It was pleasant to emerge from this region of gloom and death to the refreshing light of a clear day. As we hastened back to the city, the last rays of the setting sun were tinging in purple and gold the adjacent hills and horizon. O how beautiful the light and glory of that world into which the believer emerges when he leaves this state of sin and darkness!

Christmas holidays in Rome! The foreign observer cannot but find it interesting to see how the great festival of Christmas is kept in the Eternal City, where the day was first set apart as a holy day, having been changed by the Church from a heathen to a Christian festival. And one might well conclude, after witnessing the various ceremonies of the occasion, that the heathen element was not yet entirely eliminated. The observances begin the night before Christmas, and services of various sorts, in different churches, are kept up through nearly all the hours of night; but none of them seemed to be of any special interest.

St. Peter's was the great attraction on Christmas Day, which, this year, occurred on Sunday. I went at an early hour, to get a good position for observation, and succeeded, though for the want of a dress coat I was not admitted to seats provided for such as wore the prescribed outer garment, and for ladies arrayed in black and veiled. On entering the vast and glittering structure, the scene presented had more the aspect of a military rendezvous, than a place of Christian worship. Long lines of soldiers, in gay and brilliant uniforms, and thoroughly armed and equipped, their muskets and swords gleaming in the light that streamed from the windows, stood under the magnificent nave and dome, and were being drilled by their proper officers, giving their various commands as on a muster-day. In different parts of the church, priests and other ecclesiastics were perambulating about, in all imaginable forms and colors of dress, from the long, tight, scarecrow-looking robe, to the full and tawdry glitter of crimson and scarlet. Major-domos, or marshals and ushers, were also most fantastically habited, some of them in short clothes and stockings, with big white ruffles, reminding one of the portraits and costumes of Philip II. of Spain, and Sir Walter Raleigh.

At ten o'clock, the soldiery divided into two extended columns, from the door to the high altar, and a bustle about the entrance indicated the approach of the Pope and his retinue of Cardinals and others. Soon His Holiness was brought in, seated on a chair resting on a platform, borne on the shoulders of men. Above him was a rich canopy, while he himself wore his tiara and his gorgeous pontifical garments. Before him went men bearing seven long wax candles burning, while others carried in full view the triple crown; at his side were borne large fan-like things, of ostrich or peacock feathers, indicating that his eyes were upon all, and all eyes upon him; and in his rear was a long procession of Cardinals and Priests, mostly arrayed in scarlet robes. As the pageant moved on towards the altar, the Pope slightly bowing and waving his hand, the military lines by sections and others fell on their knees before him. He was carried to a seat behind the altar where, during the services, he remained part of the time, or when not personally officiating at the altar. The Pope's choir, without the aid of instrumental music, except once when the silver trumpets were blown, sang quite frequently, though not extraordinarily well. Cardinal Antonelli, the Pope's Secretary, and Premier in temporal matters, officiated a part of the time. He is of medium height, and slender, with dark hair and eyes, and with a decided intellectual cast of countenance. The ceremonies over, in which I could discover nothing particularly relevant to the occasion, the Pope and his train left the church in the same manner in which they entered it. The whole, as an exhibition or show, was a grand pageant; but as indicative of the religion of Him who was meek and lowly of heart, it was simply ridiculous.

At various other churches, special ceremonies were observed. At St. Maria Maggiore there was, in a sort of basement room, a miniature representation of the birth of Christ—the manger, oxen, and other surroundings. A portion of the real cradle, or manger, at Bethlehem, was exhibited—so they say—and a picture of the Virgin and Child, said to have been painted by Luke. The church at evening was partially illuminated, and made a fine appearance. At St. John Lateran and at Trinita di Monte, the music was superb. At the latter church, a few nuns, with sweet voices, sang at Vespers almost daily. At a church near the Capitol, there was quite a scenic display through the week. By means of a painted pasteboard and perspective, Bethlehem was represented, the shepherds and their flocks in the fields, and the angel hosts. But the central figure and chief attraction was the celebrated *Bambino*, or figure of the infant Saviour, brilliantly clad, and bedecked with jewels. This Bambino is regarded with great veneration, and is supposed to have great power in healing the sick. It is often sent to the rooms of invalids, and its fees—for it never makes a visit without a fee—are sometimes more in amount than those of any doctor in Rome.

On Saturday, the last day of the year, there was a grand display at the splendid church of the Jesuits. Seats had been provided—in the Romish churches of Europe very little provision is made for people to sit—and at three o'clock in the afternoon the large edifice was well filled. You rarely see Catholic churches filled. They are generally open, and persons are going in and out, kneeling, crossing themselves, and counting their beads, at all hours. The music at this church on this occasion was very fine. There are five different organs in as many galleries, and as they were played one after another, the effect was novel and agreeable. A well-trained choir, with excellent voices, sang admirably. About four o'clock the Pope and his train entered. He walked, preceded by a large military company, and followed by ecclesiastics. The choir sang, and a portion of the congregation responded, or joined in choruses, with good effect. The Pope officiated at the high altar, and the choir sang the grand Te Deum in a manner that was deeply impressive. One could here realize something of the power and fascination which the Catholic religion has over some minds. The gorgeously ornate church, with its fine paintings and statuary, the grand display of the Pope and his retinue, the bowing of the military and others on their knees as he passed, the charming music of organ and voice, the solemn responses, the burning of candles arranged for effect, and "the dim religious light" of the closing day—all were adapted to impress and captivate the senses.

There are, I believe, about ten thousand priests in the city of Rome. One meets them constantly in the in the street—sometimes singly, sometimes in companies or processions. You know them at once by their dress, though each different order has a costume peculiar to itself. Their robes are of all colors and patterns—black, red, brown and white; and while some are close-fitting, others are full and flowing. Most of them, as throughout all Italy, wear low oval-crowned fur hats, with very broad brims, which, in two or three places, are bent up and tied to the crown. Some of the monks and Capuchins go about the streets with their heads entirely bare, and scarcely anything on their feet; while the Cardinals and some other priests are richly, and even gorgeously, appareled. The Cardinals have their splendid carriages and liveried servants. It must, of course, require an enormous tax to support so many priests. The better class of the Roman people, it is said, feel deeply the oppression of the hierarchy. You see the men in their cloaks walking the streets with a sad and downcast look. In the time of the temporary Revolution in 1849, the carriages of the Cardinals were seized and burned; and it is thought, in case of another such outbreak, the Cardinals themselves would not be spared. The people of Rome, as of all Italy, are poor. The standard of wealth is low, and there are few who are even called rich. The common people are very poor, and live from hand to mouth. They are neither industrious nor persevering. Generally, if they can get a job of work, and the pay for it, they will live as long as they can without seeking any further employment. They live very cheaply; and beggars meet you importuningly at every step. You pity the poor creatures, and deplore the state of society, the religion, and the government, which produce such unhappy results. In Rome, you see the extremes towards which the Papal faith ever tends. Its arrogant assumptions and pretended prerogatives exalt and aggrandize a few, while its oppressions, exactions, and blinding influences, keep the many in deplorable ignorance and wretched subservience and beggary. How intelligent Englishmen or Americans can be so far beside themselves, or so ignorant of the rudiments of Scriptural religion, as to become Romanists, I cannot see; and yet it is said a considerable number, especially of the former, every year go over to the old superstition while residing at Rome. It would certainly seem that they must be deficient in brains, Bible knowledge, or common sense; for of all places where Romanism exhibits its glaring deformities, its marked absurdities, and its manifest evil tendencies, Rome itself is the most conspicuous.

In my brief way-notes, many things can only be alluded to in an unsatisfactory manner, while others are entirely passed over. I would like to speak of a visit to the Protestant burying ground, and the graves of Keats, Shelley, and others, and the Tarpeian Rock; to the pyramid of Caius Cestius, and the Mausoleum of Augustus; to the Temples of Minerva and Vesta, and to several picture galleries; but passing over these, and all mention of the shops of jewelry and Roman mosaics and cameos, I will just say a word of some villas and studios which I visited with interest.

In the suburbs of Rome are a few beautiful villas. The gardens of the Villa Albani are delightfully laid out into charming walks, shaded with evergreen shrubbery, and interspersed with fountains and flowers. But the large collection of antique sculpture in the buildings interested me most of all. There were busts of poets, philosophers and heroes, whose likenesses one is much gratified to see. The Villa Borghese is even more extensive in its grounds, halls and statuary. It contains a splendid specimen of modern sculpture—by Canova, I believe—a partially recumbent figure of Pauline Bonaparte, sister of Napoleon I. She married the Prince Borghese, and was a woman of remarkable beauty.

I have a very pleasant recollection of visits to several studios of American artists residing in Rome. At the rooms of Mr. Chapman, of Mr. Terry, and of Mr. Ropes, I saw some admirable pictures. Mr. Chapman is well known in New-York; the other two gentlemen have lived, I believe, in Connecticut.—From the latter State is Mr. Ives, a fine sculptor, in whose studio I saw an excellent bust of Senator Seward, a beautiful Ruth and Rebecca, and a Pandora of exquisite proportions and finish. His Excelsior is also deserving of high praise. At Miss Lander's and Miss Hosmer's studios I also saw beautiful specimens of sculpture. Miss Lander's Evangeline and Virginia Dare are certainly gems of art. Mr. Rogers, model of doors for the Capitol at Washington, struck me as superior to the doors of the Baptistery at Florence, which Michael Angelo deemed worthy to be the gates of Paradise.

I must say a word about Pincian Hill. It is a more conspicuous eminence, and attracts more visitors than either of the ancient Seven Hills. Ascending the long flight of steps from the Piazza di Spagna, around which the shops and hotels have quite an English or American appearance, and turning to the left, you soon reach one of the most charming spots for promenading in Rome. Before you arrive there, if it be late in the afternoon, you pass on the fine street almost as many carriages as it will hold, and numerous pedestrians going to or returning from the summit of the Hill. Among the persons you meet few are natives; here and there you see one in the peculiar costume of the peasantry, with conical hat, embroidered coat or dress, and anything but neat in general appearance; but the multitude thronging the beautiful, garden-like grounds, with shady walks adorned with statuary, and fountains, and flowers, are English, Americans, Russians, and others. A military company in fine uniform, with an excellent band of music, is often found here. The view from this spot is enchanting. In one direction beautiful suburban villas meet your gaze, with the Campagna, and the Alban and Sabine hills beyond; in another you see the Janiculam, St. Peter's, the Vatican, and various windings of the Tiber, as it courses through the city and towards the sea. My first visit to Pincian Hill was near the close of a *fete* day, when it was thronged with gay carriages, and crowded with fashionable pedestrians;

but the most interesting sight was the glorious sunset. It was a lovely day, the sky was clear, and the golden rays fell softly yet brilliantly over domes, towers, and groves of pine and cypress, till something of heaven seemed to be blend with earth. The scene was sweetly suggestive of the glory of the celestial city. It was not often that we had such a sunset or such clear skies while I have been in Italy. About half of the time it has been rainy and disagreeably cold, which, added to the filthy streets of the towns, the dismal dwellings of the people, and the general shiftlessness of almost everything pertaining to man, beast or field, pretty effectually dispelled the poetic charm of Italian loveliness.

> I stand on one of the ancient hills,
>   In the hoary city of Rome,
> And a glorious scene my spirit thrills,
>   As I look away toward home.
>
> 'Tis the setting sun in his brilliant dyes,
>   And what matchless tints are given!
> They seem like the light of celestial skies
>   O'er the jasper walls of Heaven.
>
> How softly on groves of cypress and pine,
>   On domes, turrets and temples old,
> The blending glories linger and shine,
>   And bathe St. Peter's in gold.
>
> On Alban slope and Sabine crown
>   The purpling sunbeams play,
> And drop on the winding Tiber down
>   Like glimmerings of upper day.

XI.
Naples—Pompeii—Vesuvius—Baiæ—Malta.

The knell of another year has struck, and its last month, passed in the imperial city, has fixed its imperishable record on the memory. Now, on a bright morning of the New Year, we take our last look of Rome, grateful for the privilege of visiting a place of such wonderful interest, and yet a feeling of sadness cannot be avoided, as thoughts of the past and present of the city crowd into the mind. Her coming history—what will it be? She will doubtless participate in great and stirring scenes of change and revolution; and some of them may be even now at her gates! At Civita Vecchia, after the usual delay of police regulations, we took a fine French steamer, and had a pleasant run to Naples, which we reached about sunrise the next morning. We had ample time to survey the beautiful harbor and its surroundings, including Mount Vesuvius, while the slow officials were procuring us permission to land.

Naples is a large city, the largest in Italy, and has a fine picturesque situation, but contains little in itself that interests the tourist. The city rises gradually from the beautiful bay, and the Castle of St. Elmo sits like a crown on its highest eminence. A few of the streets are fine, and have an air of business thrift; but for the most part the town is filthy and seems to be filled with a dirty and lazy set of good-for-nothing vagabonds and beggars. One, however, may profitably spend several days in most delightful and exciting excursions in the vicinity of Naples. Our first trips were to Herculaneum and Pompeii.

We greatly enjoyed our visit to these buried and partially excavated cities. A half an hour will suffice for seeing all that can be shown of ancient Herculaneum. It was no doubt a large and splendid city, but owing to the hardness of the volcanic tufa or rock that covers it, very little of it has been unfolded to the light. We descended with candles to that portion of a splendid amphitheater which has been opened, and from which many fine statues have been taken and removed to the Museum in Naples. At some distance from this an excavation of a few houses has been made, but there is nothing there to excite much interest. Quite a bustling town has been built over the remains of this silent city of the dead.

Pompeii, which was overwhelmed by the same remarkable eruption of Mt. Vesuvius in the first century, has been excavated to a considerable extent, and we wandered for nearly a whole day through its deathlike streets and dwellings, and still we left much of it unseen. It is impossible to describe the appearance of this singular city, or to convey adequately an idea of the profound interest awakened at every step. We walked over long, well-paved streets, where the rutmarks made by the Roman chariots were as evident as if they had wheeled along there but yesterday. We entered houses, and their various apartments, as parlors, dining-rooms, bed-rooms, kitchens, and baths, and often saw on their walls various and elegant frescoes, the colors still bright and beautiful, indicating the refinement and wealth of their occupants. We passed into temples, forums, and theaters, and from the columns or fragments of columns and other portions of the buildings still standing, an idea may be formed of the former magnificence of these structures. A piece of statuary here and there is still left where it was found; but most of these works of ancient art have been removed to the Museum in Naples. Often there is enough left in a building to indicate its use. We thus saw bakers' and barbers' shops, noticing in the first the mill and the oven. I was greatly interested in the private dwellings, in the arrangement of the rooms, and the appropriate or peculiar pictures painted on their walls. In a dining-room for instance, there would be pictures of fishes, fowls and game. Often there would be remnants of beautiful mosaics in the floors, and of the marble fountains in the open courts. In some of the cellars the old earthen wine-jars remain standing against the wall just as they did when the great and sudden calamity overwhelmed the city. In the house of Diomede, you see the spot in a basement room where several persons of the family huddled together and perished. An impress of their figures of different heights remains upon the wall, where their skeletons were found. Pictures in some of the houses indicate a low state of morals among the people; and perhaps for their great wickedness, God in his Providence overthrew them, as he did the Cities of the Plain. Along both sides of one of the streets, as you enter the city, are rows of tombs, some of them apparently large family vaults, and were once richly ornamented with various marble sculptures, fragments of which remain. But I cannot linger to particularize. Pompeii was covered with cinders and ashes, which are easily removed; but not half the city has yet been laid open. Trees are growing just above the houses not yet excavated. The tops of the buildings and of the columns are generally gone; and the *stumps* of the city indicate its former greatness, as the stumps in a cleared field show how the stately forest once flourished there.

After my visit to Pompeii, I was anxious to see in the Borbonico Museum at Naples the statuary and other objects of interest found in the buried cities. The collection is exceedingly large, varied and wonderful. I have not anywhere seen so fine and full an array of ancient sculpture. One room contains statues in bronze, and several other rooms are filled with marble figures and busts, many of which are exquisite in proportion and finish. Frescoes from Pompeii, without number, are here preserved. Domestic utensils and implements of husbandry, in copper and iron, as well as all sorts of pottery and some specimens of glassware, fill several large rooms. One is struck with the resemblance of many of them to implements still in use with us. You see there specimens of the jewelry, the bracelets, the finger-rings, and the cameos which the Pompeiian ladies wore. There too is some of the fruit, and a loaf or two of bread, stamped with the maker's name, dried and slightly charred, but otherwise appearing precisely as they did nearly eighteen hundred years ago. You see also the key of the city gate, found in the skeleton hand of the sentinel, who did not desert his post at the coming on of the fiery storm that destroyed the city. The day in the Museum, as the day at Pompeii, was worth many leagues of travel to enjoy, and its sights and impressions can never be effaced from the mind.

Our next excursion was to the remarkable volcano of Vesuvius. A carriage drive of some two or three hours brings us to the foot of the mountain. There the ladies and some of the gentlemen take horses, while others of us walk to the base of the cone, a distance of some five miles, being a gradual ascent, and part of the way over immense fields of lava, folded and twisted into various shapes as it flowed hot down the mountain side. Its black wavy forms resemble, in everything but color, vast glaciers. The region has an awfully bleak and desolate appearance, and one almost shudders at the emblems of terror and power around him. It is no easy matter to ascend the cone. The ladies had to be helped up by the guides, and often stopped to rest. It is very steep, and the loose sand and scoriæ give way under your feet at every step. At length all got up safely and in good spirits; and sitting down by a little fiery fissure on the summit, we had some eggs roasted by volcanic heat. Then we proceeded to the verge of the awful crater, looking down into its smoking and fiery abysses, as gusts of wind occasionally cleared away the sulphurous obstructions to our vision. The fog which had enveloped the mountain during our ascent was now dispelled, and we had glorious views of the grand and desolate scenery around the volcano, and a beautiful panorama of Naples, the bay, and a portion of the Mediterranean Sea and its islands. The descent of the cone was quickly made, and in high glee at the ludicrous manner in which we slid, ran and pitched along. It was impossible to go slowly or gravely. A little below the foot of the cone we turned aside to see a river of red hot lava flowing out of the mountain and down its slope. It was a grand, terrible sight, and for some distance we could hear the grating, crackling sound of the glowing lava current. We all reached our lodgings in safety, with another day of wonder strongly and prominently marked in the calender of life's pilgrimage.

One more excursion remained, and then we were ready for the expected steamer to bear us to the Orient, though we had longings for a sight of the temples of Pæstum, but could hardly find time to see them now. Our last excursion was to Baiæ, the favorite resort of emperors and nobles and literary men in the palmy days of Rome. The Appian Way, from the imperial city passed hither, and extended to Pompeii. Just before we entered the grotto of Possilipo, a long tunnel or underground road, which Seneca likened to a gloomy prison, we stopped at the Tomb of Virgil, a spot of deep interest, though there may be some doubt as to its being the resting place of the remains of the illustrious bard.

We stopped next at Pozzuoli, the modern name for Puteoli, mentioned in the Acts of the Apostles as the place where Paul, Luke, Aristarchus, and others landed, after their long and perilous voyage in the ship whose sign was Castor and Pollux. "The south wind blew," says the sacred narrative, "and we came the next day to Puteoli, where we found brethren, and were desired to tarry with them seven days." I confess I felt a deeper interest in the place on this account, and turned away from the remarkable ruins of the Temple of Jupiter Serapis and the Amphitheater, to look upon the little bay which the great Apostle sailed over, and to try to identify the spot where he must have stepped upon the shore. How pleasantly that week must have passed with the brethren he found here. Alas! I fear he would find none such to welcome him now, should he visit the place at the present time. True, it has its churches and those who call themselves Christians, but how unlike the primitive disciples!

A few miles further along the sea-shore, and turning a little way to the right into the country, we reach the famous lake Avernus, around which much of mythology and mystery gathered in ancient times. There is nothing specially interesting about it now. At its southern side we entered a dark subterranean passage leading over a river that might be another Styx. After proceeding some distance with torches, we turned into a side path, and on the shoulders of demon-looking men we were borne over a water-passage to the cave and bath of the Sybil. Here were chambers walled and arched with brick. We returned, not caring to penetrate any further or to see whether Charon could be found at his post.

The ruins about Baiæ are certainly extensive and interesting, especially the Baths of Nero, where the hot mineral water still flows; the temples of Diana, Mercury, and Venus; the *Piscina Mirabilis*, an immense stone reservoir fed by the Julian Aqueduct, and designed to supply the Roman fleet; and the Prisons of Nero, containing dark underground dungeons which we entered with lights. The greatness and even grandeur of all these ruins indicate the magnificence and splendor that once rested upon these beautiful hills overlooking the sea. But the gay and tumultuous life of the past is succeeded by a dreary and almost silent desolation.

On the tenth of January we left Naples in a French steamer for Malta. We soon passed the romantic bluffs of Sorrento on our left, and the beautiful rocky island of Capri on our right. During the night we were in view of Stromboli, belching forth at intervals its volcanic flames into the darkness. In about twenty hours, passing the straits between Scylla and Charybdis, we reached Messina, a considerable town on the island of Sicily, where we stopped a few hours, but found nothing of special note save dirty streets and a filthy looking people. We passed through the straits of Messina, observing Reggio, a town on the Italian coast, the ancient Rhegium, mentioned in the voyage of Paul, already alluded to, and where he was detained one day. The next morning we arrived at Malta, an island deeply interesting as connected with the voyage and shipwreck of Paul. We spent a few hours in the clean, pleasant, English-like town of Valetta, visiting fine shops and purchasing specimens or lace, and some delicious oranges, and would like to have gone to St. Paul's Bay, and identified if possible, the place of the shipwreck, but the steamer for Alexandria was ready to depart, and we hastened on board. In a little less than four days more on the restless Mediterranean, we came in sight of the towers and minarets of the city founded by the great world-conqueror. On Sunday, at sea, we got permission of the captain, and a few of us, mostly Americans, held a religious service in the cabin, with prayers, singing and a sermon from the text: "If God be for us, who can be against us?" As we came to anchor in the harbor, what thrilling emotions were awakened in view of our proximity to the ancient and historic land of the Pharaohs, the banks of the mysterious Nile, and the shadows of the majestic and hoary Pyramids!

XII.

Egypt—Alexandria—Cairo.

Here I am, in "the land of Egypt," beyond the Mediterranean, the Great Sea of the ancients. Here it lies, the same land now in its general outline and configuration as when Abraham saw it, and the successive Pharaohs and Ptolemys ruled over it. Through it the same river tracks its long course. The same billows break on its lower margin. The same great deserts stretch away from the sides of its narrow valley of perpetual verdure, guarded by the same barren sentinel hills. The same warm sun is over it by day, and the bright stars look down upon it as of old by night. Egypt is no Utopia—no myth. Here she is now, though

> "A stain is on her glory,
> And quenched her ancient light."

My first day in Africa, in Egypt, in Alexandria, remains a curious and vivid picture in the halls of memory. Our steamer had been waiting most of the night outside the harbor for the day-dawn and a pilot. The Egyptians never do things in a hurry. At length, the sun rose gloriously over the minarets and monuments of the city, and we entered the harbor, January 16th. Now a lively and novel scene was presented. Little boats surrounded us, and instantly a swarm of fellows, of all colors and costumes, came climbing up into the ship, anxious to take us and our baggage ashore, and to this or that hotel. Black and white, with every intervening shade, and some with rich, flowing robes, and others with scarcely any robes at all—with turbans and tarbushes—they pressed around us, and in broken English and Arabic, most pertinaciously offered their services. It was difficult to keep out of their clutches. Selecting such as we needed, and making arrangements with a hotel-keeper, we landed in due time, and easily got our baggage through the Custom-House.

From the windows of our omnibus—an innovation upon the kingdom of donkeys and camels, caused by railroads—we saw novel pictures and phases of life. Prominent in the view were those huge, ungainly, but useful and patient animals, rows of camels, swinging along their burdens of human and other freight. Many and marvelously little donkeys were tripping along, under big bundles, much larger than themselves, of men, women, and goat-skins of water filled plumply out even to the nose and toes, each looking in shape like the animal itself. Now we passed a majestic and solemn Turk in full and flowing dress, and now an almost naked Arab or Nubian; then a group of women, carrying heavy burdens on their heads, their faces closely veiled, except their eyes, though their feet and legs were bare; and then, perhaps, a singular-looking figure astride a donkey, which, on a nearer view, proves to be a Turkish female, in a white veil, but almost completely enveloped in enormous folds of black silk. A succession of these new and strange features of life excited and absorbed our

7

attention till we reached our hotel. These appearances were truly Oriental.

After a late breakfast, some of our party of a dozen walked toward the southern part of the city, delighted with a view of the graceful and noble palms, with bananas and acacia trees, that skirt and adorn the city. We came to an eminence covered with short green grass, which we ascended, and then sat down to enjoy the prospect of city, shore and sea. But the city we now looked upon was not really that which Alexander founded, and which so wonderfully flourished under the reigns of the Ptolemys. Of that city, with its grand temples, its famed Museum, and its immense library, nothing remains save, perhaps, two lonely columns. While thus engaged, another of our party came up to us, mounted on a donkey, and just then, others or these animals being brought by the boys who have them in charge, we were soon all having our first experience in donkey-riding, and enjoying it wonderfully. Donkeys are a great "institution" in Egypt. You find them everywhere. But they are scarcely larger than a good-sized sheep; and a man six feet high, and weighing nearly two hundred, is somewhat reluctant at first to ride such a puny beast. He feels as though it might be proper for him to carry the donkey part of the time—his superior bulk, also, and his feet nearly touching the ground, give him a sort of ridiculous appearance. But he soon gets over all this, and is quite surprised at the strength and nimbleness of the donkey, which trots or gallops away with him at an easy and rapid pace. We were so delighted with this kind of riding, that we kept at it for several hours in gleeful excitement. Each donkey is in charge of an Arab boy or man, who runs after you, often urging on the donkey, and whipping him unmercifully. No matter how fast or far you go, the donkey-boy will keep along, ready to show the way, and take charge of the animal when you stop. These boys speak considerable English, and are continually praising their donkeys or themselves. Crowds of them are early at your hotel, calling your name, and urging you to take their donkeys. "Mr. Doctor, take my donkey; he bery good."

Our first excursion was to Cleopatra's Needle, a fine obelisk of red granite, seventy feet high, and nearly eight feet square at its base, and covered with hieroglyphics. It formerly stood at Heliopolis, a few miles from Cairo, and bears the name of the Pharaoh who was contemporary with Moses. The leader of the Israelites doubtless saw it as it stood there. It was removed to Alexandria to ornament the temple of the Cæsars before which it stood, with another similar to it which long since fell, and now lies near by, almost covered with earth. Pompey's Pillar, or more properly, the Column of Diocletian, which stands to the opposite or western side of the city, next claimed our attention. This conspicuous monument is about a hundred feet high, standing on a pedestal, and surmounted by a capital. The main shaft is cylindrical, and consists of a single stone, nearly thirty feet in circumference. Both of these columns stand at a considerable distance south of the present city; the old Alexandria, with its gorgeous temples, palaces and schools, in the midst of which they once stood, having passed away, and left nothing else remaining but mounds of earth and heaps of rubbish. These, too, will at length fall. Around the base of Cleopatra's Needle the salt waves of a high sea break and foam, and it is by their action, and that of the atmosphere, gradually being destroyed. And the pedestal of Pompey's Pillar seems little less than a pile of loose stones, ready to give way to the crushing weight above. From a Bedawin tent, near this monument, where "two women were grinding at a mill," came a cry for *bucksheesh*, a word we shall often hear.

One gets an idea of the greatness and populousness of ancient cities by the extensive tombs or places of sepulture which, as cities of the dead, hewn in rock, and built beneath the surface, have longer escaped the hand of destruction. It was so in Rome; it is so in Alexandria. A short ride from Diocletian's Pillar brought us to the slope of an eminence honeycombed with houses of the dead of long ago. We entered and explored a number, and found the architecture of some of them, combining fine Grecian characteristics with embellishments in fresco, whose colors are still bright and clear. We subsequently visited other catacombs along the sea-shore beyond Cleopatra's Needle. They were like the first, and appeared to be very extensive; but numerous Arabs or Egyptians were digging among them for stone for building materials, or to burn for lime. Thus the tombs prepared with so much care and expense, are ruthlessly broken into, the sanctuaries of the dead invaded, and their bones scattered with the sand and rubbish. Several fine sarcophagi, sculptured in stone, were lying about, half-buried in earth. Somewhere in this city the tomb of the great Alexander was despoiled, and the golden sarcophagus containing his remains was stolen. Such is the sacrilegious cupidity of man. In these catacombs many of the early Christians doubtless found a resting-place, and in times of persecution, fled hither for "freedom to worship God." Perhaps they had heard the gospel from the lips of John whose surname was Mark.

There is nothing attractive about the buildings in Alexandria. Those occupied by Europeans for business or residence have an air of substantiality and comfort, contrasting strongly with the mean and filthy shops and abodes of the natives. Our donkey-riding brought us quite to the northern suburbs of the city, where, overlooking the sea, stands the Palace of the Pasha. We were permitted to ride through the gate guarded by numerous soldiers, and passing along a shady and pleasant garden, whose summer-like aspect had a refreshing appearance, we stopped in front of the palace, and walking over a mosaic pavement, we entered the building. At the head of a flight of stairs, we were required to leave our boots and shoes, and put on slippers which were brought to us. We were then conducted through the various public and private rooms of the palace. They were furnished partly in Turkish and partly in European style, and some of the rooms and chambers were both tasty and elegant. The rich and luxurious divans attracted special attention. One room or hall contained fine portraits of the Pasha, and of Mohammed Ali and his sons. Adjoining the palace, is the *harem*, which we were not permitted to enter. The mosques and churches in Alexandria are quite inferior edifices.

Prominent among the buildings and business of the city are the various bazaars, Turkish and Arab, located along in the same quarter of the city, yet distinct from each other. The shops, which are rude, low buildings, standing close together, are arranged on both sides of very narrow streets, some of which are so narrow as not to allow even of donkey-riding through them. The merchant or shop-keeper sits cross-legged in the center of his little room, where he can reach, without rising, almost every article in his shop. His tarbush or turban on his head, and smoking his long pipe or chibouk, he does not stir or ask you to buy, or seem to care whether you purchase or not. But if you do buy, he will try to get a good price for his wares, much greater than he would expect to get from a native. Long before sundown every shop is closed.

It needed but two days to see everything of special interest in Alexandria. The railway is now completed to Cairo, a distance of one hundred and fifty miles. But a railroad in Egypt is a strange innovation upon all previous methods of locomotion. It is a great convenience, however, and since the overland route to India has become such a thoroughfare, it is a necessity. But it was a singular sight to see swarthy Egyptians in Oriental costume in charge of the train. The carriages or cars were part of them made in England, and part in America, and partake of the characteristics of each. We happened to go with the passengers of an English steamer just arrived, and who were bound to India. The train was a very long one, and we were about seven hours on the way.

It was a day of excitement not soon to be forgotten; for the scenery, and various objects observed by the way, were both novel and interesting. We passed along Lake Mareotis, and one of the branches of the Nile, now with palms on the one hand and fig-trees on the other; now the valley or prairie-like fields stretching off a long distance, covered with wheat, growing in green luxuriance, or interspersed here and there with beans or some other vegetable growth, crowned with blossoms; and in striking contrast with these appeared occasionally most wretched and filthy looking mud villages, and groups of half-naked human beings, of all ages and in every kind of grotesque costume. Some time before we reached Cairo we caught sight of the Pyramids, and felt, in our wondering excitement, like shouting over the grand vision. Old Cheops and its companion, which stood probably in the days of Abraham, and which that patriarch saw, as he went into Egypt—which met the gaze of Moses for many years, and which Jacob and Joseph had often looked upon—monuments which have stood through so much of the world's history, and under whose shadows events so stupendous have transpired—the Pyramids, of which we had heard and read with wonder from our childhood—to actually see them with our own eyes, even at a distance, was surely an era in our lives, and a day long to stand out in marked prominence. Our all-absorbed attention was ere long turned to numerous domes and minarets rising out of groves of palms and sycamores, and soon we were domiciled in the Hotel D'Orient.

Cairo, the Grand, the Magnificent, the Beautiful, the Blessed, as it is called, is a fine specimen of an Oriental city. All varieties of Eastern people, and phases of Eastern life, may here be seen and studied. Look out upon the Ezbekiah, or open square, bordered by venerable shade-trees, green even in mid-winter, in front of the Oriental Hotel, and you will see a lively and chequered scene—a picture of many lights and shades, that will long be remembered. Turbaned men and veiled women, boys with their donkeys to let and little girls accosting you, "Ya, Howagi, bucksheesh," beggars of course; now a Frank carriage rattles off, an Arab always running before the horses, and shouting, "Riggolett!" get out of the way; and just across the road, is a native group or circle, in great merriment, engaged in some litle exhibition of monkey tricks, or a miscellaneous dance. A few steps bring you to the bazaars, where all sorts of knick-knacks are for sale. But look well as you go through the narrow streets which the sunlight never visits; for the buildings so sociably near on the ground, as they rise up story after story, approach still nearer, and in some places almost, or quite, touch each other, where bright eyes are peering through the lattices. Now in passing you are half buried in the huge folds of an old Turk's dress, and you emerge, only to come in collision with a donkey or the legs of its rider; and then you see coming a huge camel, with a mountain of a load on its hilly back, and actually no room is left for you to pass. You begin to think of being generally smashed up, when you discover at the way-side a little niche just deep enough to shelter you, and made on purpose for such an emergency. You turn into another street, and meet a procession of thirty or forty men, women and children; those in front have some rude musical instruments which they beat or blow, and along about the center, you see three females walking together, the middle one quite young and rather gaily attired; she is a bride going to the residence of her husband, who has never yet seen her face. This is a wedding in Cairo.

I visited but two or three mosques, as they seem not to have any very special attractions. The Mosque of the Citadel, however, is one of the finest in Cairo, and is richly ornamented, having splendid chandeliers and stained windows, which the Moslems generally discard. Before entering the square leading to the mosque, we had to exchange our boots and shoes for rag-slippers. In this square is the Well of Joseph, said to have been dug by the ancient Egyptians. Here, too, for this square is within the citadel, the ill-fated Mamelukes were massacred by order of Mohammed Ali, who, under the cover of friendship, enticed them within the walls. Their power was thus brought to a bloody termination. In the mosque were a few of the faithful at prayer. With their faces towards Mecca, they frequently dropped on their knees, and then bowed their faces to the floor, rising to their feet again, and going often through the same forms, uttering at intervals audible words of prayer. The minarets of this mosque are lofty and beautiful, and are seen at a great distance, as it stands on the highest ground in the city. The view also from the ramparts of the citadel is wide and interesting.

The Mosque of Amer is a thousand years old, the oldest, I believe, in Egypt. It occupies a large space of ground in Old Cairo, but has a dilapidated and deserted appearance. There is a tradition that when this building falls the Moslem power will wane. If this be true, the downfall of this strange power is not far distant; for portions of the old building have already tumbled down, and the rest seems rapidly tending to the same prostrate condition. Let it go. Two stone pillars, standing near together on the same pedestal, have been regarded as a sort of test of salvation. If one can pass between them, he may hope to enter the paradise of the faithful; but if he has devoted himself so much to the good things of this life, as not to be able to pass this test, he may not expect entrance to the Prophet's heaven. When I looked at the pillars, or rather the space between them, as our party were passing through, one after another, I thought my own chances were small, with such a test; for a taste of Egypt's flesh-pots, to say nothing of leeks and onions, has rather increased my sizable proportions, so that I found it impossible to squeeze myself through, as did also one other of our large party.

On the afternoon of a Friday, the Moslem Sabbath, we went almost down to Old Cairo to witness the performances of the Dancing Dervishes. We entered a plain room, where a few persons were seated on sheepskins arranged on the floor in a sort of semicircle. Others came in from time to time, till there were about forty in all. Some of them began to chant or sing, sometimes one, and sometimes several, or all together. Some of them knelt, and bowed, and prayed like those described above. But the principal performance consisted in their all standing up in a circle, with a leader in the center, whose motions and sounds they imitated. They all bowed low, and lifted their bodies erect, and continued to bow and raise themselves, and at each lifting of the head, all uttered a deep guttural sound or suppressed howl. Their motions grew more rapid, and their utterances louder as the performance continued. The Egyptians usually shave their heads, but several of these dervishes had very long hair, and after they got well under way in the bowing process, one of the leaders pulled off the tarbushes of such, and then their hair flew over and back in wild and bushy profuseness, adding not a little to the strange and ridiculous picturesqueness of the scene. They continued this performance an hour at a time, till it seemed impossible that they could endure it any longer. They evidently became greatly excited, and one of them actually fell into an epileptic fit with convulsions, and lay for some time insensible on the floor.

A pleasant ride of four or five miles northward along the Nile, and over a fine thoroughfare, lined by shady lebbek-trees, and where we met numerous trains of loaded asses and camels, reminding us of the Ishmaelites entering Egypt with the captive Joseph—brought us to the Shoobra gardens and a palace of the Viceroy. The extensive gardens are threaded by various walks in excellent order, and the numerous orange and lemon-trees, filled with fruit, and the odor of geraniums and full-blown roses, rendered our walk through them very agreeable. How unlike the latter part of January at home! The palace-court in these gardens contains an immense marble fountain or basin, finely sculptured from Carrara marble by Italian artists, who have shown their skill in representing various kinds of fish in bas-relief on the sides of the fountain.

Very different scenery we found a day or two after, in an excursion to the Petrified Forest, six or seven miles east of Cairo. Our way, after leaving the city, and the Tombs of the Caliphs, was over a broad and dreary desert, no tree or dwelling relieving the vast and arid desolation. At length we reached something of an eminence—the border of the Mokattam hills—covered with small, loose and chip-like stones, and our guides told us this was the forest. We had thought of standing or at least prostrate trees, in a state of petrifaction; but scarcely a stone around us would measure a foot in any direction. They were, however, certainly petrifactions of wood, and as such, a curiosity, a few specimens of which we gathered from our examinations.

I made a very pleasant excursion with a friend to the ruins of Heliopolis, or the City of On. It was in a north-easterly direction, on the border of the land of Goshen, and it took our nimble donkeys about two hours to bear us thither. We passed along by green fields of waving wheat and luxuriant clover, with here and there fig-trees, tamarisks and acacias.

Just before reaching the site of the ancient city, we turned into a garden, where was a very old and large sycamore tree, on which many names and dates were cut. There is a tradition that Mary and Joseph, with the infant Jesus, stopped to rest here, in their flight into Egypt. We picked a few leaves from the tree and went on.

We found nothing of Heliopolis but old earthen mounds and a few vestiges of the once splendid Temple of the Sun. There were garden-like patches under cultivation among these artificial hillocks. the Fountain of the Sun is a pool fringed about with shrubbery. But the most conspicuous relic is a fine obelisk, standing in its original position, probably at the entrance of the temple; and there it has stood near four thousand years, being, as is supposed, the oldest of its kind in Egypt. It often met the eye of Joseph, whose father-in-law was a priest of the temple. Moses passed it as he went to his studies. Herodotus speaks of it, and Plato meditated at its base. Lone monument of the mighty Past!

XIII.
Land of Moses—Life on the Nile.

WHILE in Cairo and vicinity, one is impressed with a feeling of deep interest in being in the midst of localities with which is associated so much of Bible history. Abraham and Sarah have been here. I have looked upon hill, vale and river, if not Pyramid, that their eyes once saw. I visited the spot where tradition says the infant Moses was found by Pharaoh's daughter in the ark of bulrushes among the flags of the Nile. It was the margin of the beautiful island of Rhoda, which furnished a charming site for a royal palace. Near by is the Nilometer, an ancient contrivance for marking the daily height and rise of the water in the river. Over this land Joseph ruled as a princely Viceroy. He had a home, perhaps, at On, or Heliopolis, just over there on the borders of Goshen, the land that was subsequently given to his father and his brethren. They grew up in Egypt, a strong and mighty people; but under kings that knew not Joseph, they were sorely oppressed, being compelled to make brick, just as I have seen menials making brick now, of the mud of the river mingled with straw. Here the voice of God was heard speaking to Moses and to Pharaoh, for the deliverance of his captive people. Here that succession of mighty miracles was wrought, which confounded the gods of Egypt, and at length broke the power of the oppressor. Here the angel of death passed over the blood-sprinkled doors of the dwellings of the children of Israel, but entered those of the Egyptians, and laid prostrate and lifeless the first-born in every house. Here was the most wonderful movement the world ever saw—the great exodus and march to the Red Sea, through the long wilderness, and to the promised Canaan. Here, in after years, Jeremiah prophesied and wept. And at length, a fugitive family came hither, Joseph and Mary, from Judea, bringing the Holy Child, born in Bethlehem, but whose life the wicked Herod sought. Beneath a dingy Coptic church in Old Cairo, I looked into a grotto where it is affirmed the Infant Saviour was concealed.

What great events have here transpired! What remarkable personages have here lived, have looked on yonder Mokattam hills, have walked on the banks of this river, and have gone to rest in these tombs of rock and sand! Customs that prevailed three thousand years ago are still continued, and I am often reminded, by what I see, of things recorded in the Bible. Calling one day on the Rev. Mr. Barnet, an American missionary in Cairo, I had the pleasure of seeing there also the Rev. Mr. Lansing, American missionary resident at Alexandria, who, as he came into the room, saw there his old Arabic teacher, and their friendly salutation was falling upon each other's necks, reminding me at once of the meeting here of Joseph with his brethren and father. I enjoyed pleasant interviews with the above faithful missionaries, and was invited to preach for the former, but was prevented from doing so by a temporary illness—a severe attack with high fever—which kept me two or three days in bed. The sympathy and kind attentions of my traveling associates, including the excellent medical care of Dr. J. G. Adams, of New York, are gratefully remembered. During this time an American traveler from Philadelphia died at our hotel. He had lately come from Palestine, and had there contracted the Syrian fever. He had left his wife and children in Geneva to await his return. It was a sad case, and excited much sympathy among all.

At length, after considerable parleying and negociating, our contract and arrangements were made for a trip up the Nile, and a survey of some of the grand and wonderful ruins of Upper Egypt. We made Thebes the limit, distant nearly five hundred miles, reserving the privilege of going further if time would permit. Our dragoman is Achmet Saidi, a shrewd Egyptian, who has taken many Americans up the Nile, and among them Bayard Taylor. He takes us up and back for a stipulated sum, furnishes boats and board, pays all expenses by the way, and allows us a certain number of days for sight-seeing.

On the evening of January 25th, our party of twelve Americans, who had come on together from Naples, took possession of our two Nile boats at Boulak, the landing for Cairo. The next forenoon we began to sail with a favoring breeze, and for two days those grand old monuments, the Pyramids, were in sight, scattered along the west bank of the river, and on the border of the Lybian desert. We reserved our visit to them until our return.

Our pleasant party consists of eight gentlemen and four ladies. Among them are four ministers, three Baptist and one Dutch Reformed, also a Baptist Deacon and a Presbyterian Elder. There are six on each boat, and we have daily worship as in a family, and on Sundays we all get together on one of the boats and have a sermon or a social prayer and conference meeting. These services are occasions of deep and tearful interest, strongly reminding us of similar meetings at home. We live very much as we should at a good hotel, and are free from care, with ample opportunity to read and write, to observe the sights and scenes along the valley, to walk and hunt on shore, and during the days reserved for the purpose, to visit the magnificent old monuments, tombs and temples found near the banks of the river. The weather, with cool mornings, is June-like and delightful. But our progress is often very slow, for the crew have to track or tow the boats when we cannot sail with the wind. We were about three weeks in going to Thebes.

Life on the Nile, in the mild climate, under the clear skies, amidst the green fields, the sandy plains, the barren hills, the strange scenes and wonderful ruins of Egypt, is a life at once dreamy, luxurious and full of interest. The air is dry and sufficiently bracing, and invalids usually find great benefit from a trip on the river. It is the place to possess and enjoy an excellent appetite, judging from our own party. Yet I imagine after five or six weeks, it must become a somewhat tiresome and monotonous experience.

It is certainly interesting to be floating on such a river as the Nile, often alluded to in the Bible, once miraculously turned to blood, and in whose valley, and along whose banks, in long ages past, transpired events so stupendous and astonishing. Flowing down from hidden fountains and snowy summits far away in the unknown regions of Central Africa, its waters roll by day, and murmur in the moonlight, the same as when they reflected the glory of the Pharaohs, more than three thousand years ago. Egypt had a history, grand and thrilling, before books, or parchments, or written languages were known. Much of that history is sealed; some of it is shadowed forth in the curious hieroglyphics that cover those magnificent ruins and monuments that are the wonder of the world. If the Nile could tell us all it has witnessed—if it could sing of the deeds of old, the triumph of arts and arms here—how thrilling would be the story, how sublime the epic! Before the Pentateuch was written, before the Law was given on Mount Sinai, there stood on the banks of the Nile cities, temples and tombs, which, in vastness and magnificence, have never yet been surpassed. How different is the Egypt of to-day from the Egypt of the Pharaohs and the Ptolemys!

In ascending the river, one is struck with the richness and vast capabilities of the soil. The vale is but a few miles in width, bounded by the Lybian desert on the west, and the Arabian on the east, the barren sands, or rocky, desolate bluffs, often approaching quite near to the river margin; while again, the fertile

THE NILE AT OLD CAIRO.

plain, covered with luxuriant crops, extends back for a considerable distance. No soil can be more productive; it needs no artificial enriching; the annual overflow of the river, somewhere from August to October, spreads over it a deposit more valuable than gold. How wonderful this arrangement of Providence, in a country where rain is never or rarely known. If a year pass without this overflowing, great scarcity or a famine is the result.

It is a beautiful sight to look on these extensive fields of wheat, of a deep green color, and a luxuriant growth, the grain, even in mid-winter, two feet high. Large fields, also, of beans, peas, onions, mustard and tobacco, meet the eye, some of them rejoicing in their crowns of bloom. Doura, or Indian corn, is raised in abundance, its tall stalks serving for firewood and building materials.

One of the more common sights attracting the eye of the traveler on the Nile, is the process of irrigation, or methods by which the water of the river is raised up, and distributed over the fields. Near Cairo, and also near Thebes, it is done by water-wheels, to which leathern buckets are attached, which fill as the wheel touches the river, and are emptied into a trough at the top. These wheels are turned by oxen or buffaloes, animals that only slightly resemble the wild buffalo of our country, and yet are quite different, except in size, from the ordinary ox. I first saw them in Rome, and have observed them quite frequently since. Another method of raising water, to a small height, is that where two men stand facing each other, with the trench containing the water to be raised between them, into which they drop a leathern basket or bucket attached to each of their hands by a rope, and as it fills at once, they lift it by stretching the ropes to a horizontal position, and empty it by slackening the rope on the side over which the water is poured. In this way a large quantity of water is easily and quickly raised. But the more common instrument is the *shadoof*, which closely resembles the old-fashioned well-sweep and pole, though much smaller, except the leathern bucket or basket, while the weight is composed of a large piece of dry Nile mud. It usually takes four of these instruments to raise the water from the river to the top of the bank, a distance of thirty or forty feet. One raises it from the river's edge, and pours it into a trench above him, where another shadoof takes it, and so on to the top, each person raising it from eight to ten feet. You see in a day sometimes a hundred of these instruments in operation, while the entire clothing of each man working them would not comprise a yard of cotton cloth.

The water runs off into the fields and artificial channels, which, by being indefinitely multiplied, give it a wide distribution. Any of these little channels, as occasion requires, may be closed or opened by moving the earth with the foot. Hence the allusion in Deut. xi. 10—"For the land, whither thou goest in to possess it, is *not* as the land of Eygpt, from whence ye came out, where thou sowest thy seed, and waterest it with thy *foot*, as a garden of herbs."

The scenery along the Nile is peculiar; the low ranges of hills and bordering deserts, without a solitary tree or spire of grass, contrast strongly with the profuse luxuriance and grateful verdure of the valley, with its occasional clusters of stately and graceful palm trees, which sometimes, also, for a long distance stand in beautiful lines along the river's bank. You look upon these glorious trees, now and then interspersed with the Dom, or branching palm, with delighted and unwearied admiration. Flowers of various kinds may be gathered, and the cotton and castor oil plants are often observed. Pigeons, ducks and wild geese are very abundant. The ibis and pelican are frequently seen, and sometimes crocodiles.

Prominent along the river banks, on slight elevations and generally embowered in groves of palm, are the numerous villages, and towns of the natives. There are no isolated dwellings, and these villages, at a distance, have quite a picturesque appearance. But enter them, and walk through their narrow, dusty streets, and you find them most filthy and repulsive. The buildings or huts are generally made of mud and corn-stalks, often without roof, floor or furniture. The half-naked inhabitants are lying about in the sun or gathering around you with eager curiosity. In the larger towns, where a Governor lives, you see buildings of unburnt brick, and a few covered with white stucco, or plaster.

I have often observed, under these clear skies and still atmosphere, a profound silence brooding over all the landscape. No "busy hum of men," no rustling of leaves, no solemn music of forest, no cascade's song, not a sloping field of wheat moving in the breeze, not a cottage or a fence to arrest the long continuity of vision, or break the deep spell of universal stillness.

The objects that meet your eye look like pictures. Over the level field of observation, you see a few Arabs walking in their long robes, or riding their donkeys and camels, and they stand distinctly and boldly out from a back-ground of cloudless sky. What beautiful heavens are over us by day; what gloriously bright stars and blessed moon at night! Aye, in this far and strange land, those celestial orbs remain the same as when gazed upon in the presence of dear ones at home. Pleasant thought! And He who telleth their numbers, and calleth them all by their names, is here and there, and holding over us the banner of His love.

Sometimes, for two or three days together, a strong wind from the north or northwest, sweeping over the Lybian desert, fills all the air with fine sand, and the appearance of the heavens, with the dust-clouds in the horizon, obscuring the sun, is that of a prevailing storm. You would say there is rain or hail yonder, but it is only a sand storm, unpleasant indeed, and so severe, at times, as to prevent sailing on the river. Occasionally an eddying wind raises a column of sand like a water spout, far up into the air. We had rain in Alexandria, a little in Cairo, and a few drops fell as we were sailing in view of the grand old pyramids near the site of ancient Memphis, but since then we have had absolutely none; and I must confess to a pleasure in witnessing a succession of bright days and glorious risings and settings of the day-king, with delicious moonlight evenings of etherial beauty and splendor.

Besides the great variety of boats one sees on the Nile,

and sometimes hailing the American flag and exchanging salutations with travelers from our own land, a very frequent sight is a group of native women or girls, robed in their single loose garment of blue cotton, coming down to the river, to fill their large earthen jars with the somewhat turbid but delicious water of the Nile. They walk a little way into the river, wash their hands and feet, fill their jars, lift the enormous weight to their heads, where they balance and bear it quite a distance to the village. The women are the burden-bearers in this and all barbarian or Mohammedan countries, and perhaps this is a reason for their general ugliness in feature and expression. There are some exceptions; but I have nowhere seen the beauty which some travelers observe in the Egyptian females. In this respect they are inferior to the men, some of whom have fine forms and features, which their flowing robes and turbans set off to advantage. But one's pity is deeply excited for all classes of these natives, as he sees how miserable are their habitations, how poorly they fare, how filthy their habits are, and how destitute they are of intelligence or comfort. Most of them are the blind adherents of the False Prophet, without any apprehension of the true method of salvation. There are Coptic Christians here and there, descendants of the ancient Eygptians, and better looking than the Arabs, but how much of true religion they possess, I have not the means of knowing. The fellaheen, or natives, seem to be well disposed, inoffensive and indolent. They have little ambition or incentive to better their condition, as their taxes are heavy, and their wages almost nothing.

Our crew number about twelve for each boat. They get higher wages than those who till or irrigate the soil; and yet I am told they each receive but about twelve cents a day and board themselves. They often work night and day, towing and poling the boat, and when it gets aground in sailing, as it often does, they jump into the water up to their arms and apply their backs to the side of the boat and push and grunt it off the sand bar. When there is no wind or a head-wind, they tow the boat with a very long cable to which they attach themselves with a sort of rope harness, singing as they track along the shore: "Hay halee saw." In the scanty clothing they wear they lie down to sleep on the deck, in the hold, or on the sand, if the boat stop by the shore. They are nearly all Mohammedans, and some of them are quite devout, observing the hours of prayer by washing their hands and feet and prostrating themselves on the deck, bowing towards Mecca and praying aloud, not fearing or caring for those about them. Captain Said, the helmsman Hassan, and the boatswain old Abdallah are often at their devotions, and sometimes we hear their voices in prayer before day-dawn. Noticing that our dragoman did not pray, we inquired, "Are you not a Mussulman?" "I am, thank God." "Does not the Koran require you to pray as these others?" "Yes, but I did up my praying for the trip before I left home." Our cook is a Nubian, black as night, and he performs his duties most admirably. Our table-waiter, Mahmoud, is a good natured young Egyptian, and is very

GHAWAZEE, OR DANCING GIRLS.

proud of being able to speak a few words of French. Our crew live in a simple and primitive manner. They have a pile of bread on the rear deck, baked in small loaves or cakes, sufficient to last them two weeks or more. They break up some of it in a wooden bowl, moisten it with water, and then pour over it a thin broth of lentils. They gather around it in a circle on the floor and eat it from the dish with their fingers. They rarely eat anything else except a sort of clover, a few onions, and a little sugar cane, which they pick up along the shore. Diseases of the eyes are exceedingly common, and full half of the males have purposely had the forefinger of the right hand cut off to avoid conscription, as they have a horror of the army. The women are fond of ornaments, and you frequently observe rude bracelets on their arms, rings on their fingers, in their ears, and sometimes in their noses, and if they are able, a wreath of silver coins around their heads.

Stopping a few hours at a considerable town, we found an annual festival of some sort, of fifteen days' continuance, in progress. The bazaars and market places were crowded, and various games, exhibitions, and ceremonies were going on. In several thronged cafes two or three of the Ghawazee, or dancing girls, immodest in dress and manners, were tripping to rude music, for the admiration of the crowd. In the open air, several groups of men were sitting in circles, and some one either chanting or addressing something to them; and I observed one large circle, standing and bowing and howling, precisely like the Dervishes already described.

While passing through one of the bazaars, I met a funeral procession of forty or fifty persons. Several men, carrying rude banners, were followed by a number of children crying; then the corpse in a wooden box, with a shelving roof-like top, borne on the shoulders of men, preceding a considerable company of women loudly wailing with the others.

We reached Thebes on the fifteenth of February, finding the weather oppressively hot during the time that we remained there. A day or two before our arrival, a falling out between the reis or captain and the helmsman, furnished a striking exhibition of angry temper. First they expended their wrath in a stormy deluge of loud words, the venerable and dignified Arab Hassan evidently gaining the victory in argument over the young and sturdy Egyptian Said. Then they rushed upon each other, but were prevented from coming to blows by the interference of others. The vanquished captain in a terrible rage, rent his only garment from top to bottom, sprang ashore, picked up a handful of dust and put it on his head, and lay down on the bank, frothing at the mouth and quivering with passion. It was a fearful manifestation of anger. Hassan returned to his place at the helm, and the boat went on, leaving the reis, who soon recovered from his wrath, and overtaking the boat, quietly resumed his usual position.

XIV.

Thebes—its Temples and Tombs—Down the River.

THEBES must have been the greatest and most magnificent city in Egypt. Almost as old as the flood, situated in a fertile valley, where it expanded to a vast and splendid amphitheater, and adorning both banks of the Nile, it was in extent, wealth, and architectural glory, the flower and crown of ancient civilization. Nearly a thousand years before Christ, Homer sang of its hundred gates, and some of the Sacred Prophets speak of it as being "populous," or containing a "multitude." No one can visit its present unparalleled ruins, or linger among the gorgeous mausoleums of its kings and princes, without being deeply impressed with a sense of its former vastness and grandeur. The contrast suggested by the present Thebes, a miserable representative even of Arab filth and squalidness, is overwhelmingly powerful; and the imagination is continually struggling to restore and repeople the city, and look upon its splendor ere it was devastated by the Persian conqueror. But these mournful relics and the utter desolation of the once imperial metropolis teach most impressive lessons.

> "Thousands of years have rolled along,
> And blasted empires in their pride;
> And witnessed scenes of crime and wrong,
> Till men by nations died.

> Thousands of summer-suns have shone,
> Till earth grew bright beneath their sway,
> Since thou, untenanted and lone,
> Wert rendered to decay."

It was a warm beautiful forenoon when we came in sight of the remains of this ancient and wonderful city. The high hills that guard the valley from the vast deserts on either hand, receded as we approached and exposed an immense plateau now mainly covered with green fields of waving wheat and grass. Soon our eyes caught over the left bank of the river a small portion of the ruins of Karnak, and presently we saw through our glasses, fine views of massive columns seeming to rise up out of the soil, in which indeed they are deeply imbedded. These were a portion of Luxor, and ere long our boat was made fast to the east bank only a few minutes' walk from these stupendous relics. After an early dinner we were wandering among them. Some of the mud cabins in the present village of Thebes are built among and upon the grand old ruins of the temple of Luxor. Magnificent columns, covered with hieroglyphics, and still standing in their original positions, are filled around and half covered with the accumulated dust and filth of ages, while some are entirely obscured by the wretched hovels that cluster about them, and can be seen only by entering these repulsive abodes, amid yelping curs, braying donkeys, cackling fowls, and dirty Arabs. But as you look upon these old pillars of stone, exquisitely chiseled, wander through the halls that yet remain, and survey their vast gateways and colossal statues, you feel that they who built them were men of genius and power. One of the most beautiful objects here is an obelisk of

RUINS OF KARNAK AT THEBES.

red granite, more than three thousand years old, and yet its appearance and its hieroglyphics are still fresh and unimpaired. Another of the same size formerly stood near it, but now it adorns the Place de la Concorde in Paris. It was interesting to see the American flag waving over the Temple of Luxor. In that Temple our Consular Agent, Mustapha Aga, has his home. He is a clever Arab, will treat you with coffee, and be happy to sell you something from his collection of antiques, consisting of mummies, images, and scarabæi, at a good price.

A mile and a half north of Luxor are the ruins of Karnak, the grandest temple in Egypt, if not in the world. I visited it just at evening, enjoying as I returned as gorgeous a sunset as mortal vision could desire. Ah! what varied scenes, what splendid pageants, what ages of glory and decay, that setting sun has witnessed here. It is impossible to describe Karnak. One must see it, or he will have no adequate idea of its astonishing magnitude and beauty. Such an array of massive gates, towers, columns, obelisks, and statues, is a perfect marvel. Think of a temple, including its various halls and apartments, twelve hundred feet long, and about five hundred feet wide, its massive walls rising like palisades, and its immense pillars like forests, with avenues leading to it from each point of the compass, along which, in some instances for miles, were ranged double rows of colossal sphinxes of gray, red, and black granite. The edifice is said to have occupied about seventy-five acres, it having been enlarged from time to time, by different monarchs, each striving to outdo his predcessor. In the grand hall there are still standing over a hundred columns, nine to twelve feet in diameter, and many of them over sixty feet high. All are covered with various hieroglyphical sculptures and paintings, whose colors are still bright after the lapse of nearly forty centuries. In one place you see a group of Jews led captive by an Egyptian king. The characters interpreted agree with the Bible account of Shishak's victory over the King of Judah. A striking verification of the sacred record. Profound and various are one's reflections as he wanders amidst these sublime relics, fallen columns, broken obelisks and shattered sphinxes. What immense processions of people once marched along these avenues, gathered in these halls, and worshipped at the shrine of Amon! What treasures have the votaries of idolatry lavished upon their gods!

Grand as are the temples of Luxor and Karnak, there were others on the opposite or west side of the river, well worthy of belonging to the city of a hundred gates. Passing some two miles over a fertile plain, once a part of Thebes, and you come first to the Temple Palace of Koorneh; farther on is the famous Memnonium; and still beyond is a cluster of magnificent temples called Medenet Haboo. I group all these together, though each deserves a separate description, for they are certainly grand old structures, rich in immense columns and various sculptures and paintings—buildings, " of which the very ruins are tremendous." In the last is a hall which was remodeled and used as a church by the early Christians. We could see traces of their transforming work. Here was a room set apart in a heathen temple for the worship of the living God. Here true disciples of Jesus once offered prayers in His name and sang hymns to His praise. We also, sitting on fragments of its deserted walls, sang sweet Christian melodies, songs of heaven and immortality, as we often did in the old temples and tombs of Egypt.

On the border of the green vale or plain, not far from the temples last alluded to, are two colossal statues, in a sitting posture, about sixty feet high, I believe; one of which, that on the right as you approach from the river, is the renowned Vocal Memnon. It is an immense figure of Remeses, and was reputed to give forth a musical sound at the rising of the sun. It was visited by emperors, philosophers, and poets from distant countries being attracted by its fame. One of our Arab guides climbed up to a secluded spot near its head, where he struck a stone that had a faint and peculiar jingle. This may explain the old and wonderful vocal phenomenon. The statue by its side is nameless. Together they form striking objects on being approached from the river.

At the Memnonium there is a still larger statue of Remeses II. once a single block of Syenite or granite, but now thrown down and broken into several pieces. It is difficult to convey an idea of the vast magnitude of this kingly ruin, or of its imposing majesty, when it stood in the temple and represented the monarch sitting on his throne, his " hands resting on his knees, indicative of the tranquillity which he had returned to enjoy in Egypt after the fatigues of victory." The weight of this statue is estimated at more than eight hundred and eighty-seven tons. Its width across the chest is at least twenty-five feet, and the foot is six feet in breadth. It was no easy matter to climb upon this huge, but finely chiseled and polished Goliath of statuary, prone and broken as it is. If one marvels, as well as he may, at the human power that made, transported, and set up such stupendous monuments, it is scarcely less a matter of wonder how those early invaders could so thoroughly shatter them.

Beyond the objects last described, along a stony and sandy vale, amid bold and bleak hills that seem a kind of barrier to the great Lybian desert, are those ancient and splendid mausoleums, the Tombs of the Kings. They are excavations in the lime-stone hills, and were originally closed, and their entrances concealed. But the curiosity and cupidity of adventurers from time to time found access to them, and disturbed the royal dust and treasure that had reposed for ages in those magnificent chambers. One of these tombs was opened in the time of the Ptolemys, two thousand years ago, and it was then hundreds of years old. Others have been recently discovered. We first entered that opened by Belzoni, who took from it a beautiful alabaster sarcophagus, which is now in the British Museum in London. We descended into this through an entrance about eight feet square, and perhaps fifty feet long. Then we descended several flights of stairs and entered various large halls and smaller chambers at the right and left. The entire length must have been three hundred feet. The whole is cut out of solid though not very hard rock, and the walls and ceiling of the entrance, halls and chambers are all covered with elaborate sculptures and hieroglyphics. There are thousands of images, large and small, of human beings, of animals, birds, reptiles, objects worshiped, Nile boats, processions and various utensils. Some of the figures are painted, and the colors seem still fresh as they are bright. The other tombs we entered were similiar to this. In some we found large granite sarcophagi, but the mummies had all been removed. The apparent freshness of these sculptures and paintings, yet so old, was very remarkable. I noticed in one room that the work was not complete when the tomb was closed. One of the walls was only about half covered with sculptured hieroglyphics. It had all the appearance of a work in present progress, so sharp and well defined was every touch of the artist's instruments. It seemed as if he had left his toil for the day, to resume it to-morrow. And yet those last touches were made near three thousand years ago!

On the other side of the hill we saw several similar tombs, evidently belonging to distinguished families in the days when Thebes was in its prosperity and splendor.

I was anxious to see some tombs containing mummies, and expressed such a wish to the guide. "Follow me," said he. A few of us went with him up the slope of a sand-hill, where we came to a small entrance, just large enough to admit us singly, going backwards in a horizontal position. On getting through this, we could almost stand upright, and with candles to light the darkness, we found ourselves in a room perhaps fifteen feet square, and full of mummies lying promiscuously about, to what depth I know not. We could not take a step without treading on them. We followed the guide through a small aperture into another room, and so on, till we had passed through six or seven of these apartments, all filled with mummies, some of which were partially unrolled, and had a ghastly appearance, their limbs cracking under our feet, as we were obliged to trample over them in our way. We stopped a moment to pull off pieces of mummy-cloth, but were glad to get away from the strange spectacle, and creep through the little orifice to purer air. These pits were doubtless the tombs of the common people. The whole region is a vast necropolis, honey-combed with tombs and caves. In some places parts of mummies, skulls, bones, teeth, and strips of mummy-cloth lie scattered over the ground, and near some rude dwellings I saw evidence that the wretched natives actually use the mummies for fuel. O degenerate Egyptians! But why were your ancestors so careful of their bodies, and so anxious to make them immortal? Did they think the departed spirit in some far future age would return and seek a union with its material form so wonderfully embalmed, enclosed and entombed, and that both would live together again? So it would seem. I procured a fine mummy shawl of linen, in which some daughter of Egyptian royalty may have slept for ages.

Having bid farewell to Karnak, where the tourist lingers last and longest, and cut our name on one of its grand old columns, we turned the prow of our boat northward, and were soon floating down "the River of Egypt." It is emphatically *the* river, and unlike any other, in that it has no tributaries, but flows on as large in Nubia as in Egypt, as full in the far regions of Ethiopia as when it empties itself into the Mediterranean. It was pleasant, at a distance of six thousand miles, to turn our course homeward, though we purposed to visit the Holy Land by the way. Headwinds and sand-storms very much retarded our progress.

We stopped to see the fine temple at Dendera, which is in a tolerably good state of preservation, and among whose sculptures is a figure of Cleopatra with her son Cesarion. At Siout we made an excursion to the ruins of ancient Lycopolis, whose immense sepulchres in the side of a lofty hill, were once the refuge and abode of early Christians. We visited the tombs at Beni Hassan, which are perhaps as old as any in Egypt, dating back to the days of Joseph. Indeed, in one of them there is a representation, as some suppose, of the arrival of Joseph's brethren, or their presentation to Pharaoh. Some of the well-hewn, rocky chambers are from thirty to forty feet square, their walls covered with pictures of the people and their pursuits in that distant period.

Between Kench and Girgeh we were overtaken by a furious sand storm and compelled to tie up to the east bank for a good part of the day. I looked longingly to the summit of the high rocky bluffs rising abruptly, near the shore, and had a curiosity to see what was on the other side. I had seen no higher mountain in Egypt. The elevation must have been nearly two thousand feet. I made the ascent alone, finding it somewhat difficult to climb the almost perpendicular ledges near the top. I was surprised to find no declivity on the other side. The surface was covered with small stones and fossils, having the appearance of a macadamized road, while a vast desert, slightly undulating, stretched away as far as the eye could reach. The view was scarcely obstructed by sand in the air, and the far vision of the Nile and its green valley was a delightful picture that one loves to remember. I walked about a mile on the bold height and descended through a deep gorge to the river. I saw no person, but Achmet assured me it was a dangerous adventure, for robbers might be lurking in the region of my rambles.

Many incidents of sights and scenes by the way might be given. I will mention one or two. Walking through a village, as some of us often did, while the boats lay at the bank, and just as we were leaving, an intelligent looking Nubian beckoned me to enter a building a little way off. I followed him, and another servant went for the rest of our party, who were in advance of me. We found in an open room, with a carpet, a well dressed and fine looking Turk, smoking his chibouk and drinking coffee. He bade us take seats on the divan and in chairs, and we conversed as well as we were able, telling him we were Americans, and where we had traveled. He offered us chibouks, and treated us to coffee. His servants took off their shoes whenever they approached him. It was a pleasant interview.

While passing through the bazaars of Benisouef, I witnessed a remarkable specimen of female rage and wrath. A woman came to a shop, and made some sort of accusation against the man who kept it. She poured upon him a storm of fiery words. As she proceeded, she grew fiercer in her denunciations, her eyes flashing fire, her features all signifying her intense passion; and her invectives of scorn, of satire, of irony, were accompanied with most terribly expressive gesticulations, and fiendish grimaces. She put her fingers to her face, and pulled her features into satanical shapes, to give additional force and point to her tempestuous tirades. A young woman, perhaps her daughter, joined her in a similar spirit and manner against the poor fellow, who, after attempting to withstand the terrible onslaught of accusation and rebuke, was obliged to "subside," and tacitly acknowledge himself overmastered. I never saw such a demonstration of female anger. No stage scene could equal it.

XV.
Memphis—The Pyramids—The Red Sea.

At length we found ourselves floating by the Pyramids and almost in sight of Cairo. It was a bright and beautiful morning when we stopped at the west bank and prepared for a visit to the Pyramids of Sakkara. They stand on the border of the Lybian desert, about six miles from the river, though the distance seems much less. Our nimble donkeys bore us through fine wheat-fields and magnificent palm-groves, now covering the site of ancient Memphis. Old mounds and broken images indicate the place where that great and splendid city once flourished. The Prophet Amos speaks of Memphis, and in Isaiah, Jeremiah and Ezekiel it is called Noph, as Thebes is called No Observing the prostrate and shattered sculptures of gods and men, I was reminded of a Divine prophecy and its literal fulfillment: "I will destroy the idols, and I will cause their images to cease out of Noph." (Ezek. xxx. 13.) The most remarkable statue here is a colossal figure of Remeses II, over forty-two feet in length, not including the pedestal. It lies prostrate on its face, several feet below the surface of the ground, which had been excavated about it. It is somewhat mutilated and broken; the face, however, is perfect and beautiful; an amulet hangs about the neck, and there is a small female figure at the side, probably a daughter of this Pharaoh.

The cluster of Pyramids at Dashour appeared finely several miles at our left, and the largest of these at Memphis now assumed a huge proportion as we came under its shadow. It seems to be almost square at the base, around which the sand has drifted, and it tapers upward in terraces of large rough stones. Achmet, in answer to an inquiry, assured me it was impossible to ascend it; he had never known any one to do it. I nevertheless made the attempt and succeeded in gaining the top, as did one or two others of our party, where the view of barren desert and green valley was broad and beautiful.

The region around these sublime old structures for the dead, abounds in tombs of various kinds. These pits contain not only the mummied remains of human beings, but those also of animals, birds and reptiles, objects of worship or sacred interest among the old Egyptians. But the chief object of attraction here is the tomb of Apis or the Sacred Bull, one of the gods worshiped at Memphis. As each successive bull died, he was embalmed and buried in a splendid granite sarcophagus. We saw, as we wandered in the immense excavation, over twenty of these sarcophagi, exquisitely hewn and polished, and some of them covered with hieroglyphics. I measured several, and found them about equal in size and form. They are thirteen feet in length, eight in breadth and depth, besides the cover which is about two feet thick, and so admirably fitted as to make the whole appear like a solid block ten feet high. The lids of most of them are partially displaced for the removal of the mummied bull. The interior is finely hewn out, leaving the walls about a foot thick. What grand, massive, expensive coffins, and all for senseless beasts, yet worshiped as gods! From the worship of this idol which the Israelites had witnessed here, no doubt sprang the idea of Aaron's Golden Calf at the foot of Sinai. We returned in the afternoon to our boats, and gliding down the river reached the landing opposite Old Cairo at sunset, prepared for an excursion to the grander Pyramids of Ghizeh the next day. But some of us improved the evening in a donkey ride to Cairo, so anxious were we for letters from home and news from the busy world, beyond the pale of which we had seemed to be excluded so long. I had dreamed the night before of getting two letters for myself and two for one of our party at the banker's, and on inquiry there found the dream as truly realized as had been the dreams of Joseph. Egypt must be a good place to dream in.

Another fair morning and a fine ride over the fields brought me face to face with the marvelous Sphinx and at the feet of hoary, old Cheops. A marked day in a tourist's life! As I approached the Great Pyramid, I was somewhat disappointed in its size until I came quite near it, when it seemed at once to expand to a magnitude quite overwhelming. One looks up to the vast pile, silent and spell-bound. A sense of awe comes over him, with a new idea of the power of man and the perpetuity of his works. I could now easily conceive how this stupendous monument might cover full twelve acres of ground. A single side of its square base is more than seven hundred and fifty feet long. Nearly five hundred feet in perpendicular height, its four slopes are very steep and seem to blend in a point at the top. A party half way up appear like birds or squirrels on a church steeple. Each side is a vast stairway of stone layers from a foot and a half to four feet in thickness, each layer being indented a foot or little more, allowing that much for the width of the successive steps. It is somewhat difficult and dangerous to climb over the higher steps, for if one should lose his footing at any considerable height he would likely roll to the bottom with every limb and bone broken. About forty gentlemen and ladies ascended while we were there, but all I believe were assisted by the Arabs except myself. Two of these half-naked and impudent fellows seize their victim by the hand, one on each side, and drag him or her up, begging, flattering and threatening for bucksheesh, though they have already been paid. I determined to go up without their help. I had scarcely begun the ascent when two of them darted before me and bade me stop. I undertook to go around them, and they still hedged my way. I then pushed them aside with my Alpine baton, and went on, but they kept close to my side. I repeatedly assured them that I should not allow them to help me, but they persisted in following me two-thirds of the way to the top, all the while urging the necessity of their assistance and my danger without it. They said my head would swim, my feet would slip, and my strength would fail; and they used some words both in Arabic and broken English by no means complimentary; but all in vain. They seemed surprised at my persistence and defiance, and the ease with which I climbed from step to step, and finally left me to enjoy the glorious ascent alone. The little space at the top, that may be thirty feet square, is covered over with visitors' names. The view is wide and grand, embracing the Lybian desert and the Pyramids on its border, the Nile and its valley, the minarets and citadel at Cairo, and the Mokattam hills. I lingered to read again letters from home, and then descended, jumping from layer to layer, and passed those that were half way down when I started. I found it a more difficult task to creep along the small, dark, steep, and suffocating passages leading to the chambers of the king and the queen in the interior of the Pyramid. These passage-ways and the separate chambers, that of the king being much the larger, are lined with smooth-hewn granite, while the whole exterior of the Pyramid is of limestone, the blocks being handsomely cut and jointed. The King's Chamber contains an empty sarcophagus, where the monarch hoped for undisturbed repose, but his sealed and gloomy sepulchre was long since entered and rifled of its treasures.

Another Pyramid, Cephrenes, almost as large as Cheops, stands near it, and smaller ones are in the vicinity, with numerous tombs and relics of palaces, among which we wandered and mused, lingering last at that marvel of ancient sculpture, the Sphinx. This impressive figure was evidently hewn from the native rock where it still stands. It is in the form of a couchant lion, with a human head looking out upon the fruitful valley of the Nile. The features though mutilated have a benignant expression. It looks like the representation of some old Egyptian divinity, and its colossal form, a hundred and forty feet long, sixty feet high, and the head a hundred feet in circumference, must have deeply impressed the worshiper, as it does the beholder now. The day of this excursion to monuments, some of which perhaps Abraham saw, ended our six weeks of life on the Nile. They were weeks of strange, novel and wonderful interest. It is impossible to describe many events and adventures that gave zest and variety to our daily experience, and in which the humorous and ridiculous were often blended. O rare and unique are the sights and scenes on the Nile. The recollection of those winter weeks will be a perpetual pleasure. The delightful climate, the clear sky and soft moonlight—our hunting excursions on shore; our wanderings in the villages; our donkey-riding to the old temples and monuments; our visions of ancient civilization and of modern life in Egypt; our exuberant spirits unburdened by care; our unwonted relish of table comforts, with augmented health, weight and vigor—all conspired to make the trip one of overflowing delight and unmistakable benefit.

One more excursion I was resolved to make before leaving "the land of Egypt," as it was not safe to enter Palestine through the long desert by Mt. Sinai and Petra as I had desired. I was very anxious to go to the Red Sea, and view the place where the great miracle of the passage was wrought. Only one of our party chose to accompany me. The distance is ninety miles from Cairo by railway. We started early in the in the morning, March 9th, and soon the green border of cultivated land, buildings and trees, all disappeared from view, like receding shores as one goes out to sea. I seemed to be in a desert ocean, not entirely level, but wavy and ridgy, like a rolling prairie. Everywhere the horizon shut down upon this sandy, pebbly waste. Not a building, not a tree or shrub—nothing but the still, awful desert, spread out as far as the eye could reach, under the warm sunlight. Once, before reaching the sea, a few shrubs, huts and Arabs were seen. At length we came into a sort of vale, with a sandy, stony ridge rising on our right, while at some distance before us, a little to the left, we thought we saw the sea, for which we were anxiously looking. The still water and the plainly marked shore appeared to be distinctly in view; but they receded and vanished as we approached, being only a *mirage*, a frequent phenomenon of the desert. But ere long our eyes were gratified with a sight of the Red Sea, first appearing as a narrow strip of dark green water, lying between glittering sandy shores. Beyond it, those arid wastes were a portion of Arabia, of Asia; while at our right, close to the margin of the sea, rose the long, dark mountain range, called Jebel 'Attaka. We had probably passed the site of Migdol; and Suez, to which we had arrived, may occupy the place of Baal-zephon. We were now at the shore of the sea, whose dark green widening waters stretched far away to the south. We found a good English hotel close to the shore.

It was intensely interesting to enter "that great and terrible wilderness," and advance perhaps in the very track of the marshaled and marching Israelites; and as I looked out from a window of my room that evening, and saw the full moon rise beautifully over the sea, I was probably looking upon the very spot where the stupendous miracle was wrought, and the mighty procession passed through the channel of the sea, whose divided waters stood like walls on either hand. Above them there, was the astonishing pillar of fire. On that deep sea, on those sandy shores, on that dark mountain side, its glowing radiance was cast. Right there before me, also, the hosts of Pharaoh perished. A little south of me, as the Hebrew host were by the shore before the passage, Moses in serene majesty stood, spoke words of cheer, and said, echoing the Divine command, Go forward! and stretched his wondrous rod over the sea, whose waters at once began to divide before him.

A few writers think the passage occurred a little further down the sea. I was struck, however, with the topography of the place I have described, as according well with the Divine record. The Israelites, with that mountain barrier at the right of them, the sea directly before them, and also extending up on their left, would be completely hemmed in, as the Egyptians pressed up behind. As may be supposed, I read the inspired account of these transactions there with profound interest.

The next morning, as I was crossing the sea in a boat, the sun rose gloriously over its waters, as it rose on the morning after the passage. I landed on the Arabian side, perhaps at the place where the Israelites landed. A profound stillness rested upon everything. The vast desert stretched away before me. Beside ourselves, not a human being, not an animal was seen. We went on a few miles, over sands mingled with pebbles and shells, gathering a few of the latter, till we came to a slightly elevated place called the Wells of Moses. Here were some brackish springs and pools of water, a few stunted palms and tamarisks, with other vegetable growths, and two or three huts with Arab inhabitants. This is the traditional place where the song of Moses and Miriam was sung. The Bible account says that Israel saw that great work which the Lord did upon the Egyptians, and saw them dead upon the seashore. From the point where I stood, all this could be plainly seen. There doubtless the delivered and rejoicing hosts stood. There Moses with the children of Israel sang his sublime song, and there Miriam with the women responded in triumphant chorus. There, too, looking out upon the same sea and shore, I read aloud from the Bible that glorious song.

"Our slavery is finished, our labor is done;
Our tasks are relinquished, our march is begun:
The arm of the Lord hath divided the sea,
Jehovah has conquered, and Israel is free.

Proud boaster of Egypt! be silent and mourn;
Weep, daughter of Memphis, thy banner is torn;
In the temple of Isis be wailing and woe,
For the mighty are fallen, and princes laid low."

XVI.

Palestine—Joppa to Jerusalem.

The Holy Land! What profound and thrilling associations do these words awaken! The tender memories of childhood rustle like the moving of angel wings—the hallowed lessons received from parental lips and earliest teachers loved and revered, but now at rest, are revived—with many a wondrous story of Patriarch, Prophet and the blessed Lord of Life and Glory. And now, as the land of Egypt recedes while the steamer sails out of the harbor of Alexandria, I am pleasantly and strangely impressed with the nearness of that wonderful territory around which so many interests cluster, and where I have so often been in thought, imagination and sacred revery. O Land of Promise! I have heard of thee with the hearing of the ear, but now, by the favor of Providence, mine eye shall soon see thee, and long cherished visions shall be realized. Our pleasant party of a dozen on the Nile, had arranged, with the exception of two, to make the tour of Palestine together.

On the second morning, March 15th, our steamer anchored off the ancient city of Joppa—now commonly called Jaffa—and the coast of Palestine was in view. We had a comparatively smooth passage, and the ladies with us were flattering themselves, at the start, that they should get through this little trip without sea-sickness; but they were all obliged to pay tribute to Neptune. He has never been able, however, in his most boisterous efforts, to exact anything from me.

About sunrise we were ready to debark; and I was now for the first time to plant my feet on the soil of the Holy Land. We were favored in having a calm sea, for in rough weather, so unsheltered and rocky is the harbor, that a landing cannot be effected. The ships a week before and a week after us, could not stop, and were obliged to carry passengers for Joppa on to Beirût. The little boats that took us ashore glided along between the rocks to greet the city coming down to the water's edge. Situated compactly on a conical or rounded hill, it has a fine appearance, and you see almost the whole city at a glance, as you approach it from the west or northwest. Its grayish brown stone or plastered buildings rise picturesquely one above another, till an old castle-like edifice sits like a crown at the top. But distance lends enchantment to the view. Enter, and you find it like other Oriental towns. The houses are huddled together in strange confusion, as if the builders cared nothing for comeliness or convenience. The streets are narrow, crooked, and filthy; and as we wound up a labyrinthine alley to our hotel, we passed a multitude of horses, camels and donkeys, waiting to carry away pilgrims or goods. Indications of considerable thrift and business are not wanting. Persons are moving about, bearing burdens on their heads; and I noticed that the people are of a lighter complexion,

HOUSE WITH A CHAMBER ON THE ROOF.

HOUSETOP, OR ROOF AND BATTLEMENTS.

more intelligent and better-looking than the Egyptians.

It was pleasant to meet Mr. Saunders, an American missionary from Rhode-Island, who, observing our arrival, had come to invite us to his house. His interesting family gave us a hearty welcome. Ascending to the flat roof of his dwelling, we had a fine view, embracing a broad expanse of the Mediterranean, the sandy shore and plains bordered with olive groves on each side of the city, and in the horizon on the north the ridge of Carmel jutting into the sea. The *house-top* is often referred to in Scripture. The ceilings are generally arched, and the top is leveled and plastered, making a fine airy promenade, and a good place for retirement, as it is usually surrounded by a balustrade or battlement, and frequently has a little room at one corner. Here I thought of Peter going to the house-top to pray, and where he had his trance and vision. Indeed, we could look upon the house-top of a building a little below and south of us, by the sea-side, called the house of Simon the tanner. Thither we soon went, and saw in the court-yard of that house, the well or spring, where they say Simon obtained his water; and there too were some old stone troughs, or vats, used in the process of tanning. Why may not this be the veritable site of Simon's house, where Peter was entertained?

I see yonder where those beautiful oranges came from that we had on our breakfast table. The Jaffa oranges are famous—large, juicy, sweet and delicious. The recollection of them is still refreshing. East and south of the city, stretching out on the border of the great Plain of Sharon, are the most luxuriant fruit gardens and orchards I ever saw. As we went out among them, the air was laden with fragrant and spicy odors. Flowers and fruits covered the trees; and such acres of thrifty orange groves, all golden and pendent with the delicious fruit, I saw nowhere else. It was an enchanting sight. Everywhere these tempting and beautiful oranges are before you, indoors and out. Beyond the gate, for some distance by the wayside, were huge baskets and piles of them for sale; and you could get a dozen of the best for a piaster, (four cents.)

If one wishes to observe what is occurring, let him go to the gate in the afternoon, where a motley crowd is gathered in the open space and around the fine fountain. A great many matters are transacted in the gates of Eastern cities. There the people meet, and as from a newspaper, learn what is going on, talking over the things in which they are interested. The Bible frequently speaks of this. The King and the Court are at the gate. There burdens are imposed or lightened; there the poor are turned aside; and there judgment is established. As Joppa is surrounded by a wall and ditch, and has but this one gate, all these characteristics may be witnessed there.

One of the oldest cities in the world, Joppa, in the distribution of the land, was given to Dan. In Solomon's time, the timber which he bought of Hiram, was floated thither from Tyre, and then carried to Jerusalem. The cedars of Lebanon, for the second temple, were transported in the same way. Here Jonah embarked for Tarshish, in a vain endeavor to avoid going to Nineveh, as the Lord had commanded him. Much of the history of Joppa is written in blood. It has been the scene of terrible strifes and cruel massacres. Jews, Romans, Saracens, Moslems and Christians have fought decisive battles here. Napoleon figured here, too, in no very enviable light. It is said that he ordered hundreds of sick soldiers to be poisoned, and had some four thousand prisoners of war, taken in the capture of the city, shot down in cold blood.

Interesting as Joppa is on other accounts, and especially as the place where the Apostle Peter had the remarkable vision, opening his mind to the great truth of Gentile evangelism, it has a peculiar sacredness, also, as the scene of Dorcas's charitable labors, death, and miraculous restoration. A "woman full of good works and alms-deeds which she did," her death was greatly lamented; and as Peter, who had been sent for at Lydda, came to the upper chamber where her remains lay, "all the widows stood by him weeping, and showing the coats and garments which Dorcas made, while she was with them." But a glorious miracle, wrought at the hands of Peter, and in answer to his prayers, soon changed their mourning into joy. Tabitha again lived to prosecute her benevolent deeds; and her brief story, like that of Mary, who anointed the head of the Lord, embalmed on the page of revelation, lives wherever the Gospel is preached. Character is immortal, and beneficence is beautiful. I am not aware that any house in Joppa is designated as Tabitha's, but a grave and a sarcophagus have been found in a garden, and as there was no positive evidence that they belonged to any one else, they were assigned to her.

It was a beautiful afternoon of a spring day, and memorable as our first in the Holy Land, when we left the old city of Joppa on our way to Jerusalem. The threatening clouds that had hung in the sky in the morning, parted and floated away, and a warm Syrian sun flashed over grove and field. Our path for some time was through luxuriant orange-orchards, and between hedges of rank and lofty cactus—a plant that often grows here to the height of fifteen feet, while its trunks near the ground are sometimes about two feet in diameter. Our baggage had gone on before us on the backs of mules, and we, one after another on horseback, pursued the narrow track often traversed by pilgrims and tourists. There is not a carriage-road in all Palestine; nor did I see a vehicle with wheels in any part of the country. Everything not carried on foot, in the arms, on the head or shoulder, where the women frequently carry children, is borne on the backs of mules, camels, donkeys and horses. One frequently meets a long caravan of camels loaded with sacks of grain or other articles of merchandise.

We were now on the great Plain of Sharon, o whose rose Solomon sang, and it is still blooming with flowers. It extends from Carmel to the south, along the sea, and includes the land of the Philistines. It was pleasant to pass fields of wheat and barley, and see natives here and there cultivating the soil, and appearing more industrious than the fellaheen in Egypt. Their oxen are small, wearing a long rude yoke. Their plow is a very simple and crude instrument; its point or share is iron, but scarcely turns a furrow one way or the other, only slightly breaking up the soil; its beam and single handle are two sticks crossed and fastened together near the point, the one extending forward to the yoke, and the other up and back, where the laborer may "put his hand to the plow," while in the other he carries a goad.

On our right was Philistia; and there dwelt that people from whom the Israelites suffered so much. There were Ekron, Ashdod, Ascalon, Gaza and Gath, inhabited by the worshipers of Dagon.

Ten miles over the plain a little south of east, brought us to Ludd, retaining nearly its ancient name Lod, a city of Benjamin. It is called in the New Testament Lydda. It is now a flourishing village, embowered in fine orchards of olive, pomegranate, fig, mulberry, sycamore and other trees. Its green and fertile fields contrasted strongly with its filthy streets and forbidding houses. It had an eventful history, with various reverses, under the Romans and in the time of the Crusades. It is distinguished as the birthplace and burial place of St. George, the patron saint of England. The ruins of a Gothic church, erected by King Richard, the Lion-Hearted, some of the walls and arches of which are still standing, are quite striking and picturesque.

But Lydda is specially interesting as the place where Peter wrought a miracle in healing Eneas, who had "kept his bed eight years, and was sick of the palsy." It was a glad day for the poor paralytic when he heard from the Apostle's lips the strange announcement, "Jesus Christ maketh thee whole!" and a glad day too for the few disciples there; for then the multitudes of Lydda and Sharon turned to the Lord.

Two or three miles south of Lydda is Ramleh, where we spent the night in a large Latin Convent, and found comfortable accommodations. Our dragoman, Ibrahim, made all the arrangements with the monks, and paid the bills. Our party had contracted with him before leaving Egypt, to conduct us through Palestine, and furnish everything necessary for our journeys.

Ramleh is a considerable village, and has several mosques crowned with minarets. It is supposed, by some, to be the ancient Arimathea, the home of Joseph, that wise counsellor who went boldly to Pilate, and begged the body of Jesus, that he might lay it in his own new tomb. A principal object of interest here is a fine old tower, a half a mile west of the village. It is about one hundred and twenty feet high, built of hewn stones, and adjoining it are ruined walls and arches of an immense edifice that might have been a church, mosque or khan, under which are vast and solidly built subterranean vaults. In the morning I ascended to the top of the tower, from which the view is wide and attractive. From the mountains to the sea, and from Carmel to the desert, the broad plain of Sharon is spread out in a diversified surface of gray villages and green fields and groves.

In a cemetery near by I noticed a number of women around a grave weeping and sighing, and was

WOMEN WEEPING AT A GRAVE.

reminded of what was said of Mary: "She goeth unto the grave to weep there!"

Two or three hours brought us near the mountains of Judea, and to the village of Latron, on the slope of a hill, and supposed to be the home of the penitent thief. A mile north of it is Amwas, a conspicuous place, and long regarded as the Emmaus where our Lord appeared to the two disciples, but it is too far from Jerusalem to be the site of that village. We had passed near some very interesting localities on our right, where Samson performed many of his marvellous exploits, and where David slew the giant Goliath. We must have been near the brook where the ruddy stripling selected his five smooth pebbles. And perhaps we were in sight of the spot where Philip, coming from Samaria, joined the Eunuch, and they continued on in a southwesterly direction to the place of baptism. A Presbyterian missionary—the author of "The Land and the Book"—who has traveled through there says, "There is a fine stream of water called Murŭbbah, deep enough, even in June, to satisfy the utmost wishes of our Baptist friends."

Entering the mountainous region, we found the country hilly, rocky, and rough, all the way to Jerusalem. The Syrian horses are sure-footed, but some of the paths are "slippery," and along precipices where a fall might be fatal, reminding us forcibly of various Scripture allusions. On our left was the village of Ajalon, and we were passing along the valley where the moon stood still at the command of Joshua, during the great battle when he routed the hosts of the five kings at Gibeon, and drove them over Beth-horon and down the valleys here. We now stopped an hour in the shade for our noon lunch.

Going up and down the mountains that are round about Jerusalem, we come to a village nestled on a hill-side with adjacent olive groves and terraced slopes. This is Kirjath-jearim, where the Ark rested twenty years, after it was brought hither from Beth-shemesh. The house of Abinadab was on this hill, whence David at the end of that period took the Ark to Jerusalem along the path we were traveling. Very likely Emmaus was near this place.

We were now, on each successive mountain-top, hoping to catch a glimpse of the City of the Great King—the city we had long desired to see. Crowning an eminence on our left, we saw a white wely or tomb. It was Mizpeh, and the tomb of Samuel.— Near this is Ebenezer, where the prophet placed the memorial stone, " Hitherto hath the Lord helped us !"

Anxious to get sight of the sacred city, I hastened on in advance, and overtook another party of Americans and English just as we got a glimpse of a hill whose slope was dotted with olive trees and whose summit was crowned with a cluster of buildings, one of which looked like a church with a spire. "The Mount of Olives!" we exclaimed, and such it was. A moment after, as we advanced, we saw domes and minarets intervening, and then the massive walls and gate of a city not more than half a mile distant. O, sacred hour! Moment never to be forgotten! A blessed memorial day! when at half-past three o'clock in the afternoon, my eyes were actually resting upon Jerusalem and Olivet! What wonderful associations do these names and places awaken! and what powerful and tearful emotions thrilled my heart as now they were really before me! Such a moment, such soul-thoughts and feelings, cannot be described. I dismounted, sat down by an old wall, and with these sacred objects before me, read from my pocket Bible portions of the Psalms and of the New Testament, referring so beautifully, tenderly, and gloriously to this city of Mount Zion and of God. Our party came up, and presently entering the Jaffa or Bethlehem gate, we began to realize the fulfillment of the beautiful passage we had so often repeated: "Our feet shall stand within thy gates, O Jerusalem!"

XVII.

The Holy City—Olivet—Calvary.

IBRAHIM had sent on in advance one of his assistants, to secure quarters for us in Jerusalem. He made arrangements for us at the Mediterranean Hotel, the best, perhaps, of the two or three in the city. It is kept by a German, I believe, named Hauser, who speaks tolerable English, and charges only a quarter of a dollar for an extra cup of tea.

On entering the Jaffa Gate, and passing through the massive wall, it was a thrilling thought that I was in the City of the Great King, and on Mount Zion! On the right was the Tower of David—the Hippicus of Josephus—an ancient building resembling a castle, and is one of the few relics of the former city. We were now in the narrow paved Street of David, filled with a motley crowd of Arabs, Turks and Franks, intermingled with camels and donkeys, among which we worked our way as best we could. Going eastward and descending the hill for a short distance, we turned to the left into Patriarch Street, a dirty lane, with small shops on each side, and in a short time were at our hotel on the left. Ascending two or three flights of stairs, and going over a portion of the roof of the building, and then descending a few stone steps, I was at length conducted to my room. Look-

CHURCH OF HOLY SEPULCHRE, POOL OF HEZEKIAH, MOSQUE OF OMAR, OLIVET.

ing out at the west window, I saw, directly beneath, the ancient Pool of Hezekiah, an immense tank of water, about two hundred and fifty feet long and one hundred and fifty wide, with the Greek convent on the north of it. This great reservoir corresponds to the account that Hezekiah "made a pool and a conduit, and brought water into the city."

I lost little time in ascending to the roof, for a view of the city and its surroundings. "Jerusalem is builded as a city that is compact together." It occupies a high broad eminence, and is surrounded on all sides, but the northwest, by deep valleys. The western part of the city is considerably higher than the eastern. The wall enclosing the city is lofty, and of an imposing appearance, its entire circuit being about two miles and a half. The four sides, though not regular, are easily made out, and nearly face the cardinal points. Mount Zion, much the largest elevation in the city, embraces its south-western portion. East of this, across a depression called the Tyropœan valley, is Moriah, the seat of Solomon's temple, now occupied by the Mosque of Omar, whose lofty and brilliant dome makes a striking appearance. Calvary is just north by a little east of Zion, and not far from my place of observation. The church of the Holy Sepulchre, a large irregular edifice, is built over it. Its principal dome is partially decayed. The Mount of Olives seems to rise up beautifully from the eastern edge of the city, but the deep Valley of Jehoshaphat intervenes. The summit of Olivet is nearly two hundred feet higher than the city, and is crowned with a mosque, and the Church of the Ascension.

The setting sun illumines its western slopes, dotted with olive trees, and disclosing occasional terraces, and three paths leading over it toward Bethany. Am I really looking upon those sacred localities? It is a wonderful view—it is a holy hour—a time when unutterable thoughts and powerful emotions thrill the soul. Within my range of vision, even near me, what strange, solemn, and all-important events have occurred!

The next morning—the Jewish Sabbath—was clear, bright and balmy, and I saw the sun rise gloriously over the Mount of Olives. A few of us had arranged for an early walk to that sacred mount. Along Patriarch Street, a little to the north, and then turning to the right near Calvary, we went down the *Via Dolorosa*, passing, just before we arrived at St. Stephen's Gate, a number of miserable lepers, sitting by the wayside begging. Going through the gate, we soon descended a steep declivity, passing the spot where it is said the martyr Stephen was stoned to death, and crossing by a bridge the bed of the brook Kedron at the bottom of the valley of Jehoshaphat, we began to ascend the slope of Olivet. An enclosure at our right, containing a number of very old and venerable looking trees, represents the Garden of Gethsemane—a sweet and holy spot, which we long to enter, but pass on, ascending the hill by the central path. Near an old dilapidated stone building, evidently once the tower of a vineyard, we paused to rest, and look back upon the city. Alone, and the sweet stillness of the morning about us, at the suggestion of Mrs. J. E. Tyler, of Louisville, whose interest with that of her husband in those sacred places was always deep and tender, Rev. William Howe, of Boston, led us in prayer, as we kneeled upon the slope where Jesus had often kneeled and spent even whole nights in prayer.

Olivet is a somewhat high hill or range of hills, running north and south, exceeding the extent of Jerusalem, of a grayish appearance, interspersed with green patches, and here and there a sprinkling of olive trees, grouped in clusters or standing in isolation, and covered with a dense, dark foliage. Limestone walls for terracing the slope, and slight ledges of rock serving the same purpose, are noticed as we pass along. On the central and highest summit are a few small buildings, including a church and a mosque.

My first view of Jerusalem from the west was partial and meager; but now, as I looked upon that wonderful city from the Mount of Olives, my anticipations were fully realized. My previous conceptions of its form and appearance were entirely met in the picture before me. There it all lay at my feet in one view. Inclining toward me, I could look upon its every building, see the whole circuit of its walls and the hills on which it stands, all seeming to rise up out of the deep surrounding valley. O what scenes had transpired in those localities beneath my gaze—events that will thrill the world forever!—the thought of which at such a time awakened most powerful emotions. What feet had been where mine were standing—what eyes had looked upon those scenes!

In every direction the view is commanding and glorious. I climbed up to the balcony of the slender minaret, and with rapt eagerness and delight surveyed the far-spreading, varying, and wondrously strange panorama. On the west all Jerusalem and its environs are seen, and in the horizon beyond there is a line of brown hills about equal in elevation to those occupied by the city. Casting the eye on northward, you see a conspicuous eminence crowned with a tower. It is Neby Samwil, the ancient Mizpeh, and Gibeon adjoins it on the right. More directly north appears Mount Scopus among groves of olive. Turning the eye southward of Zion, the Hill of Evil Council rises up from the valley of Hinnom with a rocky and terraced slope. Beyond it is the green plain of Rephaim, and still further the Convent of Elias on a ridge by the path leading to Bethlehem. Looking now to the east a wider prospect is unfolded, and the eye rests on objects of deep and thrilling interest. Just down at my right, behind a ridge or spur of the hill, is dear and beloved Bethany. Almost at my feet begins the "wilderness of Judea," gradually declining in a series of bleached and barren hills, and desolate glens, for ten or twelve miles, when it drops into the low valley of the Jordan. A long extent of this valley is visible; and the course of the river can be traced by the dark line of verdure on its banks. The valley expands toward the south into a white plain which terminates at the Dead Sea, a portion of which is distinctly seen, its waters sparkling in the morning sunlight. Beyond the Jordan valley rises the long range of Moab mountains resting like a dark wall against the sky. There, "over against Jericho," are Pisgah and Nebo; and though they cannot now be indentified, I doubtless looked upon the very summits where Moses was permitted to behold all the Land of Promise, and whence his glorious spirit went up to the Mount of God.

O Sacred Olivet! The whole mount is instinct with memories of Jesus. How often His eyes looked upon it and His feet pressed it. He trod these paths as He went over it to the sweet home of His friends. Here He came for seclusion and rest. "In the day-time He was teaching in the temple, and at night He went out and abode in the mount that is called the Mount of Olives." Here how many times the sun went down beneath His gaze, and the leaves rustled in the zephyrs that fanned His holy brow. Here, in some shady retreat or that olive garden with His few disciples seated about Him, how often He spoke to them words of heavenly wisdom and power. What sermons and parables were here uttered by the Divine Man! Here He taught, and prayed, and wept. The scene of the Agony and Betrayal was here; and just over this summit where he ascended to heaven His feet for the last time touched the earth. O what a privilege to trace His pathways here—to kneel where He knelt and suffered—to think of His tears and His triumph—and, best of all, to share His love! As we return, the sacred city lies before us in the morning light like a picture set in a frame of mountains that are round about Jerusalem, as the Lord is around about His people.

After breakfast, we went to the house of the present governor, said to occupy the site, and to be actually composed in part, of the Palace of Pilate. It is on the Via Dolorosa, directly north of the Mosque of Omar.

From the roof we had a fine view of the great mosque and its broad area, once the Temple grounds, and now like a beautiful green Park, surrounded by massive and lofty walls, with evergreen trees, the dusky olive and tapering cypress, growing here and there, while marble fountains, airy arches, richly carved pulpits and prayer-niches, and graceful miniature cupolas, give beauty and variety to the fairy scene. Moslems were leisurely walking over the grounds and the broad platform of the mosque, or praying at some shrine; but we were not permitted to enter the sacred enclosure.

Descending to the Via Dolorosa, we go up to the Church of the Holy Sephulchre. This is pointed out as the way our Saviour went from the House of Pilate to the place of crucifixion. Two old arches, now filled up, are shown in the wall where was the *Santa Scala*, or staircase, down which Jesus went from the Judgment Hall. These marble steps or stairs are said to have been removed to Rome. Nearly opposite is the Church of the Flagellation, or Crowning with Thorns, marking the place where Christ was scourged. A few rods westward, the *Ecce Homo Arch* spans the street, desginating the spot where Pilate, presenting Jesus to the people, said, "Behold the Man!" And so, as we proceed along the gloomy, narrow street, turning now to the left and then to the right, we are shown various other stations—the place where the Saviour fainted, and made an impression in the wall of a house, as he leaned against it—the spot where he met his mother—the house of St. Veronica, a woman who came out and presented her handkerchief to Jesus, that he might wipe his bleeding brow—the place where Simon took the cross—and that where our Lord said to the women who followed him weeping, " Daughters of Jerusalem, weep not for me." The Latin pilgrims regard this street and these stations with the greatest interest, seeming to believe every superstitious tradition. Not in this street as it now is, but quite near it, possibly, our blessed Lord did go from Pilate's hall to Golgotha, along a sorrowful way, bearing his cross; and the characteristics of this Via Dolorosa serve to give appropriateness to its name.

Of all holy places in Jerusalem, or on the earth, the spot where Jesus was crucified, and the tomb in which he was buried, if certain of their identity, must be regarded with the deepest interest. Notwithstanding all the doubts cast upon the traditional sites of these sacred places, I am inclined to regard them as the true ones. There is nothing about them that absolutely forbids their being such. No other sites have been discovered, answering so well to the Divine Record. These have been almost universally regarded as the real localities, from a very early date. The principal objection to them is that they are within the present city, and probably were within the city when the great events occurred. But a discovery, made a few days before I was in Jerusalem, tends to confirm the traditional sites as the true ones. An excavation had been made, a little distance southeast of the Holy Sepulchre, and after reaching a depth of more than twenty feet, a portion of what appears to be an old city wall, was found. After a personal inspection of its large beveled stones, its thickness and its direction, we could not hesitate in regarding it as a portion of the wall described by Josephus as enclosing that part of the city. If so, then Calvary, where Jesus suffered without the city and the gate, might have been exactly where tradition places it. The sepulchre was in a garden near by, or as John says, "in the place where He was crucified." The Church of the Holy Sepulchre, a very large edifice, covers both Calvary and the Tomb. It contains various chapels, and is occupied by different sects. The entrance is on the south side, from a paved court, where persons are selling beads and other souvenirs to the pilgrims. A motley crowd are within, priests and pilgrims, apparently from all the world. We observe a number of persons kneeling around and fervently kissing a marble slab elevated a little above the floor. This Stone of Unction is said to be that on which the body of Jesus, when taken down from the cross, was laid and prepared for burial. At the right of this, in order to reach the summit of Calvary, we ascend a flight of eighteen steps, and soon come to an altar where persons are reverently kneeling at the place where, it is affirmed, the cross stood. A large circular silver plate with an opening in the centre is over or around the spot; and putting my hand through it and into the hole where the cross was inserted, I could feel on its sides the native rock; and by removing a board near by a considerable portion of the rock could be seen. Entering an apartment below at the base of the rock I saw a still larger portion of it in its rough state, and noticed a perpendicular fracture, as if it had been rent at the crucifixion. All around this rocky Golgotha are numerous little chapels, altars and stations marking events and positions of persons at the time of the crucifixion. You are shown the Chapel of Adam, enclosing his tomb; the Chapel of Helena, with the cave where she found the cross, nails, and crown of thorns; and a spot called the Center of the Earth. Caring little for these traditions which attract the ignorant and superstitious, I was yet impressed with the reality of Calvary itself and its wonderful scenes. This may be the true locality; and if so, here stood the cross on which the Lord of Life hung in agony and death. What a mingled throng around this hill and from the adjacent wall watched the strange drama—sorrowful women at the cross—priests and soldiers mocking, and passers-by railing—the penitent thief asking and receiving the remembrance of Jesus —the beloved disciple catching His last words of affection—the centurion, impressed by the darkness and earthquake, and more deeply by the Dying Victim, exclaiming, "Truly this was the Son of God;" and crowds of beholders smiting their breasts as they retired from the unparalleled scene. O Calvary! there is no spot like thee—no mountain-top so near heaven as thy summit! Thou art indeed the centre of the world.

I was next anxious to "see the place where the Lord lay!" The Holy Sepulchre is about a hundred and twenty feet northwest of Calvary, and directly under the large dome of the Church. For its protection a small building of stone has been erected over it. The entrance is on the east, where the little Chapel of the Angel seems to be a sort of vestibule of the

Tomb, which is entered by a low small aperture. Stooping, as Peter did when he looked into it, I went through the door and could then stand erect. Four or five others were in the tomb, some of them kneeling and kissing the marble slab that covered the niche on the right or north side, an altar-like recess, where the body of our Lord was laid. A Greek priest was standing at the west end sprinkling holy water on those near him, and giving each visitor a flower from his large bouquet. Over the sepulchral couch hung several little pictures and bas-reliefs of the resurrection, and in the vaulted ceiling more than forty lamps of gold and silver were burning, while sweet incense perfumed the air. Notwithstanding all this bedizening array, and the constant crowding in of poor, filthy pilgrims on their knees, bowing their faces to the cold marble, and dropping their tears upon it, I experienced a feeling of awe and solemnity that words cannot describe, arising from the reflection that possibly I was in the veritable tomb of Jesus—into which Joseph and Nicodemus bore His mangled body—where it reposed over the Sabbath—where it awoke to life—where angels, the Marys, and apostles had been! It would be a far greater satisfaction to behold this "garden in its simpler guise," like that on the slope of Olivet.

"O, if the lichen now were free to twine
  O'er the dark entrance of that rock-hewn cell,
Say, should we miss the gold-encrusted shrine,
  Or incense fumes' intoxicating spell?
Would not the whispering breeze as evening fell,
  Make deeper music in the palm-trees' shade,
Than choral prayer or chanted ritual's swell.
  Can the proud shafts of Helena's colonnade
Match thy time-hallowed stems, Gethsemane's holy glade?"

XVIII.

A Walk About Zion—Bethany.

AFTER leaving the Church of the Holy Sepulchre, where the various sects were holding services amid the confusion of motley throngs, and under the blazonry of gilded altars, images, and burning candles, I went to a synagogue on the eastern slope of Mount Zion. The large irregular building, having a main audience-room and adjoining apartments, was well filled with old men, young men and boys; and the services of the day—it was the Jewish Sabbath—were proceeding. A person occupying a seat at the eastern end of the room, was addressing the assembly in an earnest and fluent manner. Near the middle of the room there was an elevated platform, enclosed by a railing, occupied by half-a-dozen Rabbis, venerable looking men. In the galleries above, and behind lattices, the faces and forms of women could be dimly seen. These, I suppose, were the younger women, as I noticed a number of elderly females sitting on the steps and seats outside of a door, not far from the speaker. Most of the worshipers had books, and occasionally made mumbling responses during the service, and sometimes nodded their assent to what was said. The preacher finished his discourse in fifteen or twenty minutes, and then rose and offered a prayer, which he uttered rapidly with his face turned to the wall. A copy of the Law was now taken from a recess and carried in a small procession around the congregation who seemed to regard it with great reverence, and some even kissed the vesture that enclosed it. The chanting was general, but not very musical. Indeed, scarcely anything there seemed like devotion. The assembly was listless and inattentive. Many of the men, with their flowing garments, tarbushes or hats, and long gray beards, had a dignified and solemn aspect; but their features were hard and stoical—heartless men they seemed, and ready, if Jesus were there, to say as did their ancestors, "Away with him; crucify him!"

Not far from here, in the Tyropœan, at the base of an ancient wall, the western boundary of the Temple area, is the Wailing-Place of the Jews, where they come every Friday afternoon, to lament over the ruins of their Temple. It is an old custom, and a piteous spectacle, to see them with mournful prayers and solemn wailings, pressing their foreheads and lips to those venerable stones, that might once have been in the foundation of their ancient Sanctuary. They take up the prayer of Isaiah, and in their Hebrew tongue pour it out in sad strains: "Be not wroth very sore, O Lord! neither remember iniquity forever; behold, see, we beseech thee, we are all thy people. Thy holy cities are a wilderness; Zion is a wilderness; Jerusalem is a desolation. Our holy and our beautiful house, where our fathers praised thee, is burned up with fire; and all our pleasant things are laid waste." Large numbers of men and women, and

WAILING PLACE OF THE JEWS.

wandering Jews from all the earth, come and drop their tears at this place of wailing. It was raining and muddy when I was there, and only a few were present.

> "Oh! weep for those that wept by Babel's stream;
> Whose shrines are desolate, whose land's a dream;
> Weep for the harp of Judah's broken shell;
> Mourn—where their God hath dwelt the godless dwell."

A little south of this spot, and in a portion of the same ancient wall, there is a remarkable ruin, discovered and described some years ago by Dr. Robinson. It is the spring of a great arch, composed of immense hewn stones, and supposed to be a portion of the grand bridge over the Tyropœan, connecting Mount Zion with the Temple. May not this wonderful bridge have been "the ascent by which Solomon went up to the house of the Lord," and which so excited the astonishment of the queen of Sheba? A personal inspection of these prodigious stones convinces you of their great antiquity and of the sublime vastness of the structure of which they are the remains. What grandeur and glory once crowned Moriah and Zion! Over this magnificent passage the people of God were wont to go to their holy Sanctuary. Solomon and his royal successors, mighty kings and princes of Israel, proceeded across it in state to pay their vows to the Lord. On this bridge, perhaps over this remaining segment of the arch, Titus stood and plead with the Jews in the Temple to submit to the conquering arms of Rome.

The Jews still cling to the eastern slope of Zion. Their houses are small and gloomy, and the narrow streets are so filthy that in passing you hold your breath and hasten your steps. Here too, near the southern wall, is the quarter assigned to the lepers. Poor, miserable, and horrid caricatures or fragments of humanity, why should they be perpetuated through succeeding generations? But a sight of them recalls many a Scripture scene and incident. You see their diseased and mutilated forms by the wayside, and hear their piteous cries for charity. At night they creep into their little huts among old mounds of rubbish that has been accumulating for centuries.

Going out of the city at Zion Gate, near the summit of that sacred mountain, we soon come to a building enclosed by a high wall. It is called the Palace of the High Priest Caiaphas, and is occupied as an Armenian church or convent. We are admitted by a priest, who shows us, under the altar, what is said to be the veritable stone that once closed our Lord's Sepulchre. The prison where He was confined is next pointed out.

A little south of this building, is the Mosque of the Tomb of David. There is no doubt that David was buried on Mount Zion, and this building is said to cover his grave. But the Moslems will not permit us to visit the royal vault. We are admitted into the Cœnaculum, however, and shown a large, lone, cheerless "upper room," in which, according to tradition, our Saviour celebrated the Passover and instituted the Supper. Here He washed the feet of His disciples. Here the apostles were assembled on the day of Pentecost, and were miraculously endowed with the gift of tongues.

A short distance to the northwest is the American Cemetery. Climbing up a corner of its high wall, I saw a row of graves in the little enclosure, where a few missionaries and travelers have mingled their dust with that of kings and patriarchs on Mount Zion.

The Christian Sabbath dawns. It is a lovely morning, and the bright sun, rising over Olivet, gilds the dome that covers the empty tomb of Jesus. A Lord's-Day in Jerusalem is a sweet memory forever! A few of us had arranged for an early walk. Passing out at the Bethlehem Gate, we went down the western slope of Zion into the Valley of Hinnom, which encompasses nearly half the city, belting it on the west and south. We crossed to the opposite slope near the Lower Pool of Gihon, a reservoir of immense capacity, being about six hundred feet long and two hundred and fifty broad, and is probably the same as mentioned in Isaiah: "Ye gathered together the waters of the lower pool." The massive city wall at its south-western angle, crowning the lofty brow of Zion, shows finely from this position. Continuing our course amidst stone fences and patches of cultivated ground interspersed with olive trees, we soon turned with the valley to the east. We passed on our right ridges of rock, along the steep declivity in which here and there tombs had been cut. Reaching a commanding position, we sat down to rest under "the shadow of a great rock," with our faces toward Zion. Behind and above us is Aceldama and the Hill of Evil Council where Judas made his shameful bargain and came to his terrible end. Before us, lofty and bold, rises

Mount Zion. The portion of it in view is now, according to fulfilled prophecy, "plowed as a field," though it was once all covered with palaces and dwellings.

The valley deepens as it descends eastward to its junction at En-Rogel with that of Jehoshaphat. Its topography is accurately marked where it is first mentioned in Joshua in the description of the boundary line between Judah and Benjamin: "The border went up by the valley of the son of Hinnom unto the south side of the Jebusite, the same is Jerusalem; and the border went up to the top of the mountain that lieth before the valley of Hinnom westward." Down in the vale before us were once celebrated the horrid rites of Moloch under Judah's idolatrous kings. "They built," says Jeremiah, "the high places of Tophet, which is in the valley of the son of Hinnom, to burn their sons and their daughters in the fire." The lower part of the vale where the brazen image stood was well adapted for the scenes of such a cruel and terrible fanaticism. It is a deep wild glen, with bare and frowning cliffs and mountain sides above. "One cannot but shudder, as sitting in the opening of some dark tomb, or beneath the gnarled boughs of some old olive, he reads its fearful history." In allusion to this abominable practice, or to the circumstance that the refuse and filth of the city were cast in here to be consumed with unceasing fires, the later Jews regarded this Gehenna as the symbol of future punishment.

After singing one of the songs of Zion, we went down to the Well of En-Rogel, which is walled around and arched over with ancient masonry and enclosed by a small building containing watering-troughs. An

Arab drew us some of the fresh cool water. It was by this well that Jonathan and Ahimaaz, David's servants, waited for instructions from Hushai during Absalom's rebellion; and here Adonijah, another son of David, assembled his friends when he aspired to be king in his father's stead.

We now turn northward, and following up the bed of the Kedron, we ascend the Valley of Jehoshaphat lying east of Jerusalem and separating it from the Mount of Olives. We soon pass a cultivated and verdant spot sprinkled with trees, and where cucumbers, onions and other vegetables are growing. This is the site of "the King's Garden," mentioned by Nehemiah. It is watered by streams from the Pool of Siloam, a most interesting fountain on the western slope of the valley. It is a rectangular reservoir fifty-three feet long, eighteen wide and nineteen deep. I descended its stone staircase to the clear water, and thought of the blind man whom our blessed Lord commanded " to go and wash in the Pool of Siloam. He went his way, therefore, and washed, and came seeing." Nehemiah says Shallum built "the wall of the pool of Siloah by the king's garden," and Isaiah speaks of "the waters of Siloah that flow softly." This Pool is connected by an under-ground passage with another some distance to the north of it, called the Fountain of the Virgin, on the side of the hill Ophel. Here several women were washing clothes, from one of whom I procured an ancient coin, probably a Roman penny. How interesting, if it were the one shown to our Saviour, when He inquired, "Whose image and superscription hath it?"

Perched on a high cliff on the eastern side of the valley, is the little village of Siloam, its houses in one place clinging to the rocks, and in another half buried in the tombs. Our blessed Lord alludes to this place in speaking of "those eighteen on whom the tower of Siloam fell and slew them."

We soon reach the south-eastern angle of the city wall, and are eagerly inspecting its ancient foundation-stones, great and beveled, laid very likely in Solomon's time, and were a part of the wall enclosing the Temple. We cannot survey these venerable relics of the past, and think of the eyes that have looked upon them, and recall the histories they awaken, without feeling that there are "sermons in stones."

In the deep valley below, between Moriah and Olivet, are the remarkable and massive tombs of Zachariah, St. James and Absalom. They are not properly excavations, but large monuments, having vaults within, and from which the surrounding rock has been hewn away. The "Pillar" of Absalom has considerable architectural beauty, marred somewhat however by the natives' throwing stones upon it in contempt of the rebel son. Adjoining this is the tomb of Jehoshaphat. Above these sepulchral monuments that have probably not materially changed since the days of our Saviour, an extensive Jewish Cemetery occupies a portion of the slope of Olivet. The graves are marked by flat stones laid over them. For many centuries the sons of Abraham have sought this spot as their last resting-place. Many of them have journeyed from the ends of the earth that they might die in the Holy City and have their dust laid here in the

ABSALOM'S TOMB (RESTORED).

valley of Jehoshaphat, where they believe the Messiah will stand and summon the dead in the resurrection. Then those who sleep here will rise at once, while those who have been elsewhere buried can only reach this favored spot by a painful under-ground journey. The Moslems have appropriated this tradition, and point to a projecting stone, in the city wall east of their great mosque and near their own cemetery, on which Mohammed is to sit and participate in the events of the final day. Back of the Jewish burying-ground and further up the slope of Olivet, are the Tombs of the Prophets. A circular, cistern-like entrance leads down to the various subterranean passages and vaults.

Again we are under the eastern wall of the city, and lingering at the Golden Gate once leading to the Temple area and perhaps to Solomon's porch. It is now solidly closed with stone, but its ornately sculptured abutments and beautiful arches remain, and cannot fail to attract special attention when we think of the feet that have pressed hither in the sacred past. Proceeding northward among a great variety of upright monuments in the Moslem Cemetery, we soon enter the city at St. Stephen's Gate.

Refreshed by our morning walk, we were prepared to enjoy a religious service in the forenoon at the English church, situated on Mount Zion, near the Castle of David and the Bethlehem Gate. It is a plain, inviting edifice of mixed Gothic, built of light hewn stone, and will seat some four hundred persons. A respectable audience was in attendance, and a good sermon was preached by Bishop Gobat, from Phil. ii. 5—11.

In the afternoon we had another delightful walk to Bethany, the home of Martha and Mary and their brother Lazarus, a place of sweet and sacred memories, and honored by the frequent visits of our blessed Lord. We went over the Mount of Olives by the northern path, the same doubtless which David took after the rebellion of Absalom. The sorrowful king "went over the brook Kedron toward the way of the wilderness, and went up the ascent of Olivet and wept as he went up, and had his head covered and he went barefoot;" and a weeping train followed with their heads also covered with earth. Jesus had often taken this same path to Bethany. We pause on the summit to enjoy again the extensive prospects it commands, and then descend its southeastern slope. Bethany, situated on that slope, is not seen at first, being hidden by an intervening ridge, where the village appears below, partly embowered in groves of olive and fig-trees. Is not this ridge or swell on the Mount, the place of our Saviour's ascension? It would seem so from its position, its distance from Jerusalem, and the circumstances of the sacred narrative.

Bethany is a small village of about twenty houses, built of stone, but having a neglected appearance. It is situated in a shallow vale on a broken plateau of rock environed with fruit trees which give it something of pleasantness and beauty. Some prominent ruins are pointed out as the house of Lazarus and his sisters, and not far from it, that of Simon the leper. We are next directed to the tomb of Lazarus, at the

BETHANY.

northern extremity of the village on the side of a declivity. It is a cave that a stone might cover. I descended into it by a number of steps, and was shown the vault where the body of Lazarus is said to have lain. Seated around the opening of the tomb, I read to our company the eleventh chapter of John. The reading of that inimitable narrative there, seemed almost to reproduce the touching, tender, and sublime scenes of the great miracle, and to impress us deeply with the blessed sympathy of Him who wept as a friend, and with His glorious Divinity as being "the Resurection and the Life."

We returned by the road leading over the southern shoulder of Olivet—the great thoroughfare from Jerusalem to Jericho—the same path along which Jesus passed on his triumphal entry to the city, when palm branches and garments were spread in his way. The road climbs the hill till it reaches a point where the southern portion of Zion appears in view, on which stood the Palace of David; and there doubtless the shout of the multitude burst forth—"Hosanna to the Son of David! Blessed be the King that cometh in the name of the Lord!" Then the road descends a little, and the city is hidden from sight; presently it mounts again, and passing a ledge of rocks—the stones that would cry out if the people held their peace—the whole city at once bursts into view—a glorious vision, nowhere so complete as at that spot. Then it was that Jesus, coming near, "beheld the city and wept over it." How vivid and impressive all this seemed as by the natural features of the place and the inspired narrative we could trace step by step the progress of the great procession! As we descend the Mount, a few fig-trees by the way remind us of the one that withered there under the Lord's curse. How delightful was this walk to Bethany, over ground that our blessed Saviour had so often trod! How sweet to visit the village where He found loving friends and a welcome home after the toils of many a weary day, and to linger amid scenes hallowed by His Divine works and gracious words, and by the gentle ministrations of those who loved to sit at His feet!

We held a religious service in the evening, and by request, I preached in the large "upper room" of our hotel. Above twenty Americans were present, and a few English and Scotch. The place, the circumstances, and the memorable localities near us, rendered the occasion one of deep and thrilling interest. The preliminary services were conducted by Rev. R. B. Booth, pastor of the Presbyterian church, Stamford, Conn.; Rev. W. C. Child, of Boston, led the singing; and Rev. R. B. Welch, of Catskill, N. Y., a minister of the Dutch Reformed Church, offered the closing prayer. With Olivet and Gethsemane immediately before me, and Calvary and the Sepulchre almost within the sound of my voice, I could preach of Jesus only—His incarnation, teaching, works, sufferings, death, resurrection and intercession. The hymns we sung were—"All hail the power of Jesus' name," "When I survey the wondrous cross," and "Jerusalem, my glorious home!" That precious Christian Sabbath in Jerusalem will long be remembered.

XIX.

Pools of Solomon—Hill Country—Hebron.

I CANNOT forget thee, O Jerusalem! There are other hallowed places, within and without thy gates, around which I would love to linger. But I leave them for a few days, for a deeply interesting excursion to Hebron and Bethlehem, the Dead Sea and the Jordan—places with which are associated sweet, sad and holy memories. It was somewhat late Monday morning, after the preliminaries of getting ready—sending off the muleteers with baggage, and selecting our horses—that we passed out at the Jaffa or Bethlehem Gate, and our numerous caravan, as two or three parties accompanied us, wound along down the upper part of the Valley of Hinnom, and crossed it at the margin of the Lower Pool of Gihon where we struck perhaps the boundary line between Judah and Benjamin. Ascending the opposite slope, we passed on our right, a fine large stone edifice, nearly completed, designed as a hospital for Jews, and built mainly through the munificence of the late Judah Touro, an American Jew.

We had now reached the Hill of Evil Council, on whose summit, at our left, are some ruins, said to be those of the country-seat of Caiaphas, where Judas arranged and received the money for the betrayal, and where Jesus was taken before Annas, after his apprehension at Gethsemane. A lone wind-shaken olive tree marks the place where the traitor hanged himself.

Down in the valley on our right, we see 'Ain Karîm, the birthplace of John the Baptist. Around us are several fields enclosed by wall-fences, and showing evidences of intelligent cultivation. Within a few years considerable land has been bought up by Jews, and others, who have come to this city to cultivate the long-neglected soil, and already the desolate hills and plains are beginning to bloom. Remarkable events are transpiring in this Holy Land, and among them the return of Jews to possess their ancient homes, is a significant sign. Looking back from the Hill, we have quite a good view, from the south, of Jerusalem and the western slope of Olivet.

Proceeding on, we are soon at the Well of the Wise Men, surrounded by loose stones, and in the center of our path. Tradition says that when the wise men departed from Herod, they wandered to this spot in uncertainty; but stopping to draw and drink at the well, they saw reflected in its clear water their guiding star. However this may be, it is interesting to think that this is the very path which the Eastern Magi must have taken, as they went from the court of Herod to the presence of the new-born King in the manger of Bethlehem; and over this path appeared the strange star which they had seen in the East, and it "went before them, till it came and stood over where the young child was. When they saw the star, they rejoiced with exceeding great joy."

A fertile plain now opens before us, gradually sloping to the right, or southwest, till about a mile distant it terminates in a deep narrow valley, Wady el-Werd, or Valley of Roses. This is the Plain of Rephaim, where David conquered the Philistines in several battles. In Joshua it is called "the Valley of the Giants." David came out from his fortress on Mount Zion, against the enemy here, by Divine direction, and with the assurance of victory. Here stood the mulberry trees, where he was to "fetch a compass behind" the Philistines, and rush forth and overpower them at the appointed signal. "And let it be, when thou hearest the sound of a going in the tops of the mulberry trees, that then thou shalt bestir thyself; for then shall the Lord go out before thee to smite the hosts of the Philistines."

At the southern extremity of the plain we come to the Convent of Elijah, a massive pile, or gray limestone edifice, inclosed by a wall. The monks have a tradition, contrary to Scripture, however, that here Elijah rested after his flight from Jezebel.

Passing over the brow of an eminence to a region of lofty hills and deep valleys, we see on our left, about a mile distant, Bethlehem, the birth-place of our beloved Saviour. O favored eyes, to look upon these sacred localities! There are the fields and hillsides where the shepherds watched their flocks by night, and heard the heavenly songs and the glad tidings. Bethlehem is finely situated on the summit of a terraced ridge, dotted with the olive, vine and fig. We long to hasten to it, but are to pass through it on our return to-morrow.

A few minutes further bring us to a deeply interesting spot—the Tomb of Rachel—a place regarded by all authorities as the one where she died and was buried. A small square building of stone, plastered white, surmounted by a dome, and standing close by the road-side, designates the sacred shrine. These "whited sepulchres" of distinguished persons are frequently seen, generally on the side or top of a hill. We dismounted and entered the building, where we saw something like an inclosed sarcophagus written over with visitors' names. It is a comparatively modern structure, but the authenticity of the site being unquestioned, we lingered a little while with deep interest, and read from the Bible the touching account of Rachel's death. Many years after that sorrowful event—for here Benjamin was born—when Jacob was nigh unto death in Egypt, he thus tenderly refers to it in the presence of his and Rachel's son, Joseph: "As for me, when I came from Padan, Rachel died by me in the land of Canaan, in the way, when yet there was but a little way to come unto Ephrath; and I buried her there in the way of Ephrath; the same is Bethlehem."

Descending into a valley, we soon reached the Pools of Solomon—three immense open tanks or reservoirs, stretching away at our left, partly hid at first by a large rectangular old khan or castle. These remarkable Pools, excavated in part from the rocky bed of the valley, and in part built up of stone masonry, are so arranged on different grades, that the second might be emptied into the third, and the first into the second, evidently for the purpose of collecting much water.

They are rectangular-shaped, varying in size from four hundred to six hundred feet in length, about two hundred and twenty in width, and from thirty to fifty in depth, all containing clear water. After lunch under the shadow of the old castle and near a well-like opening leading down to rushing and roaring streams through vaulted chambers of stone work, I walked about the Pools, and in the middle one took a refreshing bath. They are supplied by a large fountain some forty rods to the northwest, but flowing under ground, the water is not seen till it reaches the well.

If Solomon built these stupendous works, and such I believe is the general verdict, then this well may have been the "fountain sealed," to which in his Song he compares the sister spouse, and the "garden enclosed" may have occupied the intervening space down to the first pool. Here were his country-seats and pleasure-grounds, as described by himself: "I made me great works; I builded me houses; I planted me vineyards; I made me gardens and orchards, and I planted trees in them of all kinds of fruits; I made me pools of water, to water therewith the wood that bringeth forth trees." The site was admirably chosen, only six or seven miles from Jerusalem, in a region finely diversified with glens and hills and fountains, and the soil capable of the highest and most blooming fruitfulness. The hill-slopes around these relics of the old and solemn past, now for the most part rocky and bare, have the appearance of once being terraced and cultivated to their very summits.

As I look over the prospect and recall the past, what splendid pictures, what regal forms, what varied scenes and striking contrasts rise and glow and pass and fade! The imagination is burdened with the gorgeous vision, as the whole scene reappears as it was when Solomon was in all his glory. His boundless wealth, and his matchless wisdom and skill crowned the hills, and adorned these vales with enchanting beauty and luxuriant loveliness. Here were the blended glories of nature and art—all kinds of fruit-trees robed in verdure and bloom, and ripened treasures of gold and crimson—vines creeping up to the summits of the terraced hills, and bending with the white and purple clusters—shade-trees and flowers adorning the winding walks, along which streams murmured and fountains played—bird-songs in the tree-tops, and music from instruments and human voices in the groves and the villas and mansions crowning the summits or dotting the slopes—and then comes the king himself in gorgeous splendor, with a magnificent retinue—and mirth and melody, feasting and dancing, beauty and revelry are in those brilliant abodes of wealth and pleasure. Ah, Solomon! thou art making the grand experiment of all this world can do or give to satisfy man's longing, boundless nature. O thou wisest of men—and most foolish too—what is thy solution of the great problem, that has so engaged the attention of all ages? "Vanity of vanities; all is vanity and vexation of spirit."

Years pass—and the old king is led a silly captive into foolishness and idolatry. He goes down to the grave. The voices of mirth are hushed; the sound of revelry has died away. The villas and halls in which so many feasted and rejoiced, have decayed, fallen, and mingled with the dust. The vineyards have died on the hillsides. The groves, orchards and gardens have disappeared. The olive, the orange, the pomegranate and the fig—fruits and flowers—walks and fountains—all have faded away, and only the bare and rocky slopes, with these stupendous pools—relics on which the storms of more than twenty-five centuries have beat—remain to suggest, by desolate contrast, the ancient beauty and grandeur over whose sad blight and death, the "fountain sealed" still murmurs its lone and solemn requiem.

Early in the afternoon we resumed our journey. For some three hours there is nothing of special interest to observe, except a continual succession of hills and valleys, mostly bare and rocky. Limestone ridges, gray and dingy, crop out from their sides and crown their summits. Narrow glens run in tortuous courses through the wilderness to the Dead Sea, lying directly east of us, but out of sight. Dwarf oak, arbutus, and other shrubbery, very scantily robe the hills. There are no forests. Gay wild flowers, beautiful and brilliant, of almost every form and hue, mingle a sweet cheerfulness with the general desolation. The soil of the valleys is evidently rich, and the remains of terraces on the hills indicate a former cultivation. The solitude of this neglected and forsaken region, once thickly populated, is broken by the drumming of partridges, almost the only inhabitants. A few wandering Arabs pass us, and perhaps donkeys loaded with dry sticks gathered on the hills, and sometimes women carrying bundles of this fuel on their heads.

We think of the patriarchs and others who traveled this path long ages ago. We have no account of our Saviour's journeying here, during his ministry, but it was probably along this very road that he was borne while an infant, in his mother's arms, in the flight into Egypt. Abraham, Isaac and Jacob, David, Solomon and Saul, often looked upon these mountains and valleys.

Only a little to the left of us are the deserted ruins of Tekoa, "whence Joab called the wise woman to plead with David on behalf of Absalom." There, too was the home of the prophet Amos, who kept his sheep and gathered wild fruit among these mountains and glens, till the Lord summoned him to a higher office, and made him a preacher of judgment and mercy to sinning Israel. And not far off is the Cave of Adullam, in which David often took refuge. He was familiar with all these hills and vales, for here he kept his father's sheep—here he retreated when pursued by Saul—here, amid the strongholds of nature, he not only fled from his enemies for safety, but also wrote some of those beautiful and sublime Psalms, in which he sings of Jehovah as his Refuge, Rock and Strong Tower. This "hill country of Judea," through which we are passing, is holy ground. Every footfall is upon soil trodden by ancient worthies, and every view around was seen by their eyes. Their cities and homes have crumbled to ruin, but the natural scenery remains. The everlasting hills, the valleys, the rocks, the fountains, are all here. Hence, the sacred and undying interest that clusters about them. Never poet or minstrel sang such sweet and glorious strains as those which flowed from the inspired heart and lips of the Shepherd King among these mountains.

> "The harp the monarch minstrel swept,
>   The king of men, the loved of Heaven,
> Which Music hallowed while she wept
>   O'er tones her heart of hearts hath given—
>   Redoubled be her tears, its chords are riven!
>
> It softened men of iron mould,
>   It gave them virtues not their own;
> No ear so dull, no soul so cold,
>   That felt not, fired not to the tone,
>   Till David's lyre grew mightier than his throne!
>
> It told the triumphs of our King,
>   It wafted glory to our God,
> It made our gladdened valleys ring,
>   The cedars bow, the mountains nod;
>   Its sound aspired to heaven and there abode!"

We pass close by the border of the Valley of Berachah on our left, remarkable as the scene of the great battle and victory of Jehosaphat against the children of Moab, Ammon and Mount Seir. The faith and energy of Judah were inspired in this contest by the sublime assurance: "The battle is not yours, but God's." An old stone tower is soon observed on our right, and a little beyond we come to a fountain, surrounded by massive foundations and excavated tombs. Several women are washing clothes in the stone troughs. The present name of the tower is Beit Zur, suggesting at once the Beth-zur of Joshua, mentioned in connection with Halhul, which we find a little further along. On the left, as we proceed, is an old ruin, consisting of large foundations of hewn stone, as though a great castle or other building had been commenced there, but never finished. It is called the House of Abraham.

We soon find ourselves in the famous Valley of Eschol, suggestive of vineyards and clusters of grapes. And here they abound to this day. Nowhere did I see such luxuriant vines, covering the hill-slopes and filling the valley. Vineyard after vineyard met our eyes as we passed along the stony path, and their arrangements immediately recalled one of our Lord's parables: "There was a certain householder who planted a vineyard, and hedged it round about, and digged a wine-press in it, and built a tower." The Eschol vineyards are thus enclosed with walls and hedges, and have their towers for watchmen. Here came the spies, sent up by Moses to observe the land. Here, by this brook, "they cut down a branch with one cluster of grapes, and they bare it between two upon a staff." Caleb and Joshua were among them. They looked upon these hills—walked in this path—drank of this flowing stream—gathered grapes here, and pomegranates and figs—and these fruits are found here still. Here they saw the children of Anak, sons of giants, and their walled cities; but the hearts of those faithful two failed not; and they alone, of all their associates, were permitted to cross the Jordan to the promised possession. And this very place was afterwards captured by Joshua and given to Caleb. So much for being hopeful, trusting and brave, and looking on the bright side.

Descending a little further the narrow valley of Eschol, our eyes are soon resting on the city of Hebron—a city that has had a continuous existence for almost four thousand years, having been built "seven years before Zoan in Eygpt." It seems difficult to believe one's own eyes in the presence of localities so ancient and sacred, while thought runs back, far back through the ages, and recalls the men, the histories, the scenes associated with these places. But here is the reality, positive, evident, unmistakable. This is Hebron—this picturesque city, stretching away on the slope east of the valley, and divided by gardens into two sections. Here lived the father of the faithful, and his son Isaac, and his grandson Jacob; and they were all buried in that Cave of Machpelah. There, too, their wives were buried—Sarah, Rebekah, and Leah; and I am looking upon the building that encloses their dust!

But now we have arrived at our camping ground— a gentle grassy slope opposite the city, and overlooking it. There our tents are being pitched, and two or three other parties are pitching theirs near by, making quite an array of white tents.

As the sun still glimmers over the vale, and lights up the adjacent hills, we take a walk down into the city. We pass the large, ancient Pool of David, over which he hanged the murderers of Ishbosheth. There are no walls enclosing the city, as at Jerusalem, but there are gates at the entrance of the principal streets. We enter one, and pass along the narrow alley between houses, till we come to the Haram or Mosque covering the Cave of Machpelah. This large and very ancient edifice is built of hewn stone of great size, and beveled like those in the substructions of the

Temple walls. It is believed that these stones were laid in the original edifice by the immediate descendants of the patriarchs buried in the tombs within. The Moslems have had possession here for a long period. They have a high regard for Abraham, and will for no consideration allow any "Christian dog" to enter the building. As we came up to it, and to the verge of an alley of steps leading still further, a number of these Moslems stepped in rather insolently before us, to prevent our proceeding another inch. It is outrageous that these sacred places should be in their exclusive possession. It will not be so always, nor many years, I fancy. They sometimes allow Jews to look through a little hole in the wall. I got one of our Mohammedan guides to go in and bring me a piece of the cave or tomb.

I read here the account in Genesis of Abraham's purchase of that field from Ephron the Hittite, and the death and burial of Sarah. Then the patriarch and others following were gathered to their rest here, till the embalmed body of Jacob was brought up from Egypt and laid beside his father. Perhaps the mummied form of the last is preserved here still, and had permission to enter been given, I might have looked upon the veritable body of Jacob, and seen the dust of Abraham! At Thebes I saw mummies of persons who lived probably as early as did these; and I brought away a human hand that may have aided in building the Pyramids, or in planting and gathering some of the corn that Joseph stored in the years of plenty.

We returned to our tents just before sunset, and

found them ready for us, and dinner prepared. Our table is sometimes set within a tent, but more often outside. Three of us occupy a tent, each person having an iron bedstead raised about a foot from the ground, and provided with suitable bedding. This was our first night in the tents, in which we were to domicil for the next three weeks. Here began our tent-life, in the place where Abram pitched his tent in "the plain of Mamre, which is in Hebron." Nor did we forget the altar of prayer.

It is our custom after dinner to repair to our tents, and at our little table, with a candle thereon, write up our journal of the day's experience and sight-seeing, read over the history of the places we had visited, and press the flowers we had gathered. This done on that first evening in the tent, I went out and looked from the dim outline of the city and adjacent hills, up to the bright and glorious stars, beaming serenely on that Holy Land, just as they did when Abram saw them, sitting in his tent-door; when Isaac went out at eventide to meditate; when the shepherds saw them from the Bethlehem hills; and when Jesus himself beheld them from the Sea of Galilee, and from the retreats of Olivet. While all else seemed strange about me, those beautiful stars looked familiar and home-like, and carried me in thought to dear and loved ones far away. O, what varied scenes, in ages past, those heavenly orbs have witnessed here! and beyond them, eyes, pure and holy, are ever looking down upon this strange and wonderful earth.

XX.

Home of the Patriarchs—Bethlehem—Mar Saba.

Morning dawns over ancient Hebron. The earliest sunlight, glittering from the mountains of Moab and the hills of En-gedi, comes lovingly to the doors of our tents. The night was unusually cool, and some of our party emerged shiveringly from their frail tabernacles, by no means enraptured with the first comforts of tent life. But those who had a supply of heavy shawls to add to their bed-quilts, found them quite useful. Breakfast was soon prepared, and we were summoned to the table, surrounded with camp-stools and chairs, and furnished with mutton-chops, chickens, eggs, bread, potatoes, boiled rice, and *dibs*, or grape molasses, sometimes called honey in the Scriptures, and tea and coffee. We frequently had *mish-mish*, or dried apricots stewed, which were a fine relish. A considerable company of the natives gathered around us, Moslems and Jews, the latter having several qualities of Hebron wine for sale. In the meantime, our tents were struck, and the baggage piled on the mules, and they started off. After a brief ramble or climbing a hill, our horses were ready—they had been tied through the night near the tents—and we filed away.

With deep and earnest interest, we look over the

city and its hills, to fix the picture in our memory, while sacred historic characters and associations come thronging to the mind. This is old Hebron, originally Kirjath Arba, city of Arba, father of Anak, and progenitor of giants. Here dwelt the patriarchs. These valleys were their camping-grounds. Their flocks and herds grazed on these hills. On these slopes and summits, on these rocks and rills, the eyes of the venerable Chaldean shepherd often looked from his tent door, under the oak of Mamre. Here Jehovah condescended to converse with him — commended his fidelity, and cheered him with glorious promises. Here to his peaceful home came the news of his nephew Lot's misfortune and captivity, in the plundering of Sodom, and hence he set out with his servants on his successful pursuit of the enemy. Here, a few years later, he was visited by angels, whom he entertained, and from whom he received the promise of a son, and knowledge of Sodom's coming doom. On one of those high hills under our gaze, perhaps, he plead with the Lord for its wicked inhabitants, and from the same height the next morning he surveyed the smoking ruins of the destroyed cities. Abraham, Isaac and Jacob spent most of their lives in this vicinity, experiencing, as is common now, various events of joy and sorrow. Here Joseph dreamed, and incurred the hatred of his brethren. From hence his father sent him to Shechem, to see those brethren. He found them in Dotham, and they sold him into Egypt. From Hebron, Jacob's ten sons went into Egypt to buy corn in the time of famine; and after Joseph was known, and had sent for his father, it was from Hebron that the patriarchal family departed for Egypt, by the way of Beersheba. One of the six cities of refuge, it also became, after the death of Saul, the royal residence of David. Here he reigned over seven years, and most of his sons were born here. The Jews have a high regard for Hebron. They cling especially around the Cave of Machpelah, the burial-place of their fathers, dropping there their tears and chanting their prayers, as they do at the ruins of their ancient Temple in Jerusalem. The present population of Hebron is seven or eight thousand, the Mohammedans largely preponderating—the rest are Jews; no Christians reside here. The houses, built of stone, have a substantial look, are generally two stories high, with little domes rising from the flat roofs.

Taking a northwesterly direction, through olive groves and vineyards, we soon reached a very interesting locality and object—the Oak of Abraham—the traditional site of his tent, and place where he entertained the angels. This splendid old tree stands alone in a beautiful spot. Under it is the smooth greensward, and near it a well of sweet, crystal water. It is a favorite place for Jewish pic-nics and social gatherings. This venerable oak measures twenty-three feet around the trunk, and its foliage covers a space ninety feet in diameter. Evidently of great age, it is still sound and flourishing. While it cannot date back to the days of Abraham—some, however, claim it as the veritable tree under which he pitched his tent—it may be a representative of his oak, springing from its roots or acorns, and may spread its branches over the same soil.

What a sweet, cheerful picture, to recall the patriarch as his tent was here, as he communed with God, and received celestial visitants! Adjoining was Sarah's tent—and here peace and simplicity reigned in those olden days of pastoral life. Here they lived, and yonder they sleep—ages elapse—but heaven and earth shall meet here again in the great and joyous resurrection. I gathered a few twigs from the old oak, and we sang under its boughs a portion of the hymn:

> "Children of the heavenly King,
> As ye journey sweetly sing—
> Ye are traveling home to God
> In the way the fathers trod."

Then retracing our steps through the Valley of Eschol, I stopped at a vineyard where some men were trimming the vines, and got a few slips, which I subsequently put in a little box of earth from the Garden of Gethsemane, to take home.*

We returned to the Pools of Solomon by the way we came, with little to interest us, save the thought, perhaps, that we were in the same path that Abraham took in his mournful journey to offer up Isaac on Mount Moriah. At the Pools we turned to the right, and wound over the shoulder of a large hill, following the old acqueduct leading to Bethlehem, and even to Jerusalem, crossing the valley of Hinnom near the lower Pool of Gihon, where its remains may still be

---

* One of them lived, and is doing well in its new, far-off nursery, having grown thirty feet in the second summer.

traced. It is of rude masonry, slightly rising above the surface, and occasionally, where a stone had been removed, we could see the water still flowing in this artificial channel.

On our right, and below us, was the village of Urtas and the vale of Etam—a beautiful green spot, some of it highly cultivated and filled with fruit trees, in bright and variegated bloom, making a sweet contrast with the desolate hillsides. Over the gray surface, amidst rocks and ruined terraces, we journeyed nearly an hour, and—

> "Lo, Bethlehem's hill-site before me is seen,
> With the mountains around the valleys between;
> Where rested the shepherds of Judah, and where
> The song of the angels rose sweet on the air."

Yes, that is Bethlehem; and the bold ridge or elongated hill, stretching from west to east, on which it is picturesquely situated, is in full view. The village houses stand along the western part, and the eastern brow and chief summit is crowned with an immense convent or pile of buildings, looking like some old castle of feudal times. The hill-slopes below are quite steep, and the curved and stair-like terraces are well kept, and covered with rows of thrifty olives, and intervening figs and vines. The eye glances down hence upon the fields once occupied by Boaz, where Ruth gleaned after the reapers, where David, her great grandson, kept his father's sheep, and where the shepherds were watching their flocks when they were startled by the strange and glorious displays attending our Saviour's birth.

BETHLEHEM

CHURCH OF THE NATIVITY. 243

After coming in sight of Bethlehem, we pass over a moderate valley amidst olive groves and vineyards, with occasional pomegranate and almond-trees, and ascend the hill at the west end of the village; and proceeding through its one street, along which are various little shops and all sorts of people, we at length come to the Church of the Nativity, the large building already alluded to. It was erected in the year 327 by the Empress Helena, mother of Constantine, and is one of the oldest monuments of Christian architecture in the world. It is supposed to cover the place where our blessed Lord was born. We first enter a large audience room, dingy and dilapidated, through which extend double rows of Corinthian columns of marble, evidently very ancient, and taken, as some think, from the porch of the Temple at Jerusalem. Faded mosaics meet the eye on the walls, and above are cross-beams or hewn timbers of the cedars of Lebanon. Entrances from this room—in which are traffickers in various mementoes—lead to the three chapels, Latin, Greek and Armenian; and from each of these there are winding stairways down to the Grotto of the Nativity, the great attraction.

There are various caves, chapels, altars, and tombs under this church, adorned with pictures and other tawdry trappings of Romish and Greek churches. Here is the tomb of Paula and Eustachia, that of Jerome also, and the study where he spent some thirty years, and made a translation of the Scriptures in Latin, the famous Vulgate version. Here is the altar of the Innocents, said to mark the spot where two thousand children, slain by Herod's order, were buried.

After going through a number of long, narrow and dark passages, we are conducted to the Chapel of the Nativity. It is a low room or vault, thirty-eight feet long and eleven wide, and seems to have been hewn in the rock. A little recess at the east end is the *sanctum* of the whole building. There, in the center of a marble slab fixed in the pavement, is a silver star circled by the words—*Hic de Virgine Maria Jesus Christus natus est.* "Here Jesus Christ was born of the Virgin Mary." Sixteen silver lamps are suspended around this star, and continually kept burning. In the corner of this Grotto is shown the place of the manger. Over it is a good painting of the Virgin and Child, with the shepherds, set in a silver frame, and behind a screen of silver wire, and illumined by five silver lamps. The station of the Magi is near, and the Chapel of Joseph is a long dark vault leading out of the Grotto.

Whether Jesus was born and laid in a manger in *this* cave, no one is able to say with certainty. Tradition makes this the spot, and it *may* be even so. No doubt there are natural caves here; and such caves were then, and are still used in the East as stables. At any rate, this is Bethlehem, and here, or in some spot near me, beneath my eye, my blessed Saviour was born. Here, a helpless infant, He was cradled in a manger—so humble and lowly was the advent of the Son of God. This wondrous fact was rendered deeply impressive as I wandered through Bethlehem, and knew that this great event *here* transpired—the new star was in this sky, shone over these hills, and directed the Wise Men to the humble abode where they found and worshiped the young child—as I looked off upon and went among the hills and valleys where the shepherds heard the angel voice and the song of heavenly hosts—and as I saw in that very place shepherds now with their flocks, reminding me of that momentous event and hour, when,

> "— In that stable lay, new-born,
> The peaceful Prince of earth and heaven,
> In the solemn midnight,
> Centuries ago."

We left Bethlehem, with regret that we could not linger longer upon its hill, and even spend the night there, amidst associations of heaven and earth so wonderful. We descended the steep hill eastward, looking back for a fine view of the town, gathering flowers as we went, observing here, for the first time, that little white-spangled flower, called the Star of Bethlehem, and singing, too, amid those hills and vales, the sweet hymn, "When marshaled on the nightly plain." We recall the historic scenes and characters of Bethlehem—the sad story of Naomi; the romantic fortunes of Ruth; the remarkable adventures of David. Here that son of Jesse was born, drank at his favorite spring, learned to sling stones, and was anointed king by Samuel. But, O Bethlehem Judah, "City of David," thy one great event absorbs the mind—the birth of David's greater Son, even Him who is Lord of lords and King of kings. How favored are these eyes that look upon thee, and these feet that tread thy soil!

On we went amidst bold gray hills, and deep winding valleys, and about sundown pitched our tents near the Convent of Mar Saba, an immense building on the steep declivity of the yawning gorge of the Kedron—one of the wildest, most romantic, and desolately rocky places in Palestine. I was desirous of spending the night in this remarkable edifice, and two others of our party being like-minded, we were politely received by the Greek priests in charge, who offered us refreshments, and showed us to our lodgings in a large and comfortably furnished chamber.

Early in the morning we went through the various apartments of that singular and romantically situated edifice, built up of stone on the perpendicular side of a deep and frightful chasm. It clings to the rugged precipice in such an irregular outline and manner, that the artificial and natural rocks are curiously blended. A Greek priest showed us the chapel containing the tomb of St. Sabas, who died in the year 532—a palm-tree planted by that saint in one of the yards—a charnel-house containing heaps of bones of martyred worthies—and the cave, the original nucleus of the establishment, where Sabas spent many years of his life. This was a lion's den at first; but when the saint intimated to the beast a desire to occupy it for a religious purpose, he quietly resigned his claim to it—so the story goes. This strange old building passed through various fortunes in the fierce wars between the Crescent and the Cross. It is said to contain rich treasures, which the wild Bedawîn of the region would like the opportunity of seizing, but it is strongly guarded. No woman is ever allowed to enter its doors. The famous traveler Madame Pfeiffer spent a night alone in a tower-loft outside.

XXI.

The Dead Sea and the Jordan.

Leaving Mar Saba at seven o'clock in the morning, we journeyed eastward through the rough and romantic wilderness of Judea. High, bold and gray limestone hills, with deep and dark ravines, were all around us. Now and then, through the opening gorges, we caught glimpses of the Dead Sea. It is usual to go there under the protection of a guard, as the region is infested by wild Arab robbers. Indeed, the Sheik of the place will be likely to rob you, unless he is engaged as an escort to protect you. We had his son, with a few assistants, as our guard. The young Sheik is a fine specimen of a wild Bedawy. He rode an Arabian mare, perfectly trained to every movement, and fleet as the wind. He was dressed in the gay costume of his class, with a variously colored silk turban wound around and streaming from his tarbush. He had a long gun slung across his back, a sword at his side, and a knife and pistols in his girdle. He would ride towards us with the velocity of lightning, brandishing his drawn sword as if to take off our heads, and then turn at a right angle within a few feet of us. He would throw his gun into the air and catch it, and even pick it up from the ground, while at a full gallop. My repeating pistol, manufactured by the New-Haven

Arms Company, greatly interested and astonished him, and he was anxious to get possession of it.

We were four hours going to the Dead Sea. On some lofty hills, about half-way there, we had fine views of that wild and desolate region. Stretching off on our right to the southeast, rugged, dreary and bare, is the "wilderness of En-gedi." Before us, lying low in its bleak-bordered bed, is the Sea of Death, now with dark shadows flitting over it, and then sparkling with sunlight gleaming through the clouds. Down to its eastern shore come the dark, wall-like mountains of Moab, stretching far to the North, and bordering the vale of the Jordan. About two miles on our left is a white wely on a hill-top. It is the Neby Mûsa of the Mohammedans. The real tomb of Moses is among those mountains yonder, east of the Jordan, "in a valley in the land of Moab, over against Beth-peor; but no man knoweth his sepulchre."

About an hour before reaching the Dead Sea, we descend the steep hills to the barren plain. Here our guard professed to be somewhat alarmed, or wished us to be, and declared that they saw Arab robbers lurking about our path. But we saw none, and I presume it was only a *ruse* on their part, to magnify their importance and increase their claim to *bucksheesh*. Over the light-brown, parched and crusty plain, with scarcely any vestige of vegetation, we are approaching the northwestern shore of the Dead Sea. We reach the water's edge, and dismount amidst pebbles of nearly all colors, many being black and pitchy or bituminous, and dead branches of trees, which have come down the Jordan, and been thrown upon the

DEAD SEA FROM THE NORTHWEST.

beach. What a strange place to stand upon—to look abroad and around from—and to silently meditate! Every spot that the eye rests upon, near and far off, has some Scripture account or scene connected with it; and what thrilling accounts and tremendous scenes! Lift the curtain of history, and what a succession of events come and go—changeful, beautiful, fearful, wonderful, terrible! What eyes have looked upon the clear waters of this lake, with its bold, bleak shores! Patriarchs and kings have beheld it. Our blessed Lord, too, must have seen it from the Mount of Olives and the heights above Jericho.

Who does not admire lake scenery—often so beautiful, charming and romantic? The foreign tourist will not soon forget his visits to the emerald-bordered lakes of Killarney in Ireland—the sublime frames in which those Scottish pictured gems, Lomond and Katrine, are set—and the rich beauty and romantic grandeur of the Swiss waters nestled among her glorious mountains. Around all these lakes there are verdure and fruitfulness, groves or vineyards, as well as rocky palisades. Flowers fringe their margins, and harvests wave behind, while fishes sport in their depths, and shells often glitter along the shore.

But this lake of Death is a strange and unique exception. There is nothing of life or of beauty here. The gradually sloping plain on the north is barren and bleached, crackling like egg-shells under one's feet. The rocky bluffs on the west and south, and the Moab-cliffs on the east are dark and desolate. Not a living thing inhabits its waters—not a flower, not a green willow or shrub, except where a fresh stream flows in, smiles on its borders. Nothing of the loveliness or the music of nature is here. Its waters, heavy, and intensely bitter and pungent, are rarely ruffled by the breeze. All is silence, and gloom, and death. Forty miles long and ten broad, the Dead Sea lies in a sort of grave. Its surface is lower than that of any other body of water in the world, being thirteen hundred feet below that of the Mediterranean Sea. During most of the year an intensely hot sun is shining upon it, causing a vast amount of evaporation, sufficient perhaps to exhaust the influx of the Jordan, and of several small streams. This often fills the air with hazy vapors, adding to the somber desolation that rests over it. Without any knowledge of its early history one would naturally feel that a blight and curse are here. And how well it still testifies to the great and solemn event that long ago changed its whole aspect!

What features did this lake present near four thousand years ago, before "Lot pitched his tent toward Sodom?" From the heights of Bethel he looked down upon this beautiful and tempting region, "and beheld all the plain of Jordan, that it was well watered everywhere, before the Lord destroyed Sodom and Gomorrah, even as the garden of the Lord, like the land of Egypt, as thou comest unto Zoar." The water of the lake was probably once fresh, and it must have been much smaller than it is now, allowing a broad margin for the fertile fields, especially on the southern side, where it is supposed the Cities of the Plain stood. Here, according to Gentile and Jewish records, was the earliest seat of Phœnecian civilization. The

Assyrian kings coveted the rich spoils of these cities; and here, in the "vale of Siddim," the first battle in Palestine was fought. Lot was taken and his goods, but he and they were recovered by Abram. The peculiar nature of this region is indicated in the Scripture account of the battle of the five kings, where mention is made of the slime-pits of bitumen in the vale of Siddim. These became elements in the destruction of those guilty cities, when the measure of their exceeding wickedness was full. One day the patriarch, from one of the hills toward Hebron, looked down upon the Eden-like beauty of this plain, and the splendor of its cities teeming with the busy and tumultuous life of a gay population; but, on the next morning, what an appalling sight was before him, as from the same spot, "he looked toward Sodom and Gomorrah, and toward all the land of the plain, and beheld, and lo, the smoke of the country went up as the smoke of a furnace!" Strange contrast! Beauty has turned to ashes, and life to death. And so it has remained through thousands of years. So I see it, a picture of sterility and gloom, suggesting impressive and solemn lessons of God's word and providence.

I lingered there an hour or two, gathered a few characteristic pebbles, bathed in the buoyant water in which it was impossible to sink, tasted its saline bitterness, filled a bottle with it to bring home, and then turned away toward the northeast, on a visit to the river Jordan, where our blessed Saviour was baptized. But I seem to see it now—that Sea of Death, the little dark island near the shore where we stopped, the sluggish waves slightly moved under a strong breeze, the desolate heights of En-gedi on the west, the bold promontory jutting out into the sea from the gloomy mountains of Moab on the east, the conical salt hills far to the south, where Lot's wife lingering perished, and the low plain on the north, where the fresh waters of the Jordan flow in and are absorbed.

Over a mostly level plain, with a very rare sprinkling of stunted vegetation, we were about an hour and a half in reaching the traditional place of the baptism of Jesus. On our right, we could trace the winding course of the river, from the strip of verdure and small trees among which it flows, though we could not see the river itself. On our left, the plain was broad, terminating in the abrupt, light-gray hills of Judea, overlooking the site of ancient Jericho. It was not till we came almost to the brink of the Jordan, that we got a glimpse of its swiftly-flowing and slightly turbid waters. O favored eyes! O hallowed moment! Can the emotions awakened by such a sight be described? And this is the Jordan—the sacred river, flowing as of old—in whose stream and on whose banks such scenes of wonderful interest have transpired! And here it rolls still, graceful in its sweep, musical in its flow, and every murmur of its waters seems to repeat and confirm the events of Bible history. O sweet and quiet spot for sacred meditation! Here let me sit down by this tree on the bank, and watch the rushing stream, and recall the past!

After reading passages of Scripture relating to the place, I wandered up and down the bank, gathering a few mementoes to take home. Just above, there was

THE JORDAN AT THE SUPPOSED PLACE OF CHRIST'S BAPTISM.

a bend in the river to the right, and a considerable growth of trees and shrubbery on the banks not far below, as well as above, prevented a view of the river to any great extent. The width of the Jordan here, I judged to be twenty yards or more, and its depth was probably ten feet. The banks were somewhat precipitous, and increasingly so at a little distance either way; but the water's edge could be easily approached for a number of rods at our stopping-place. This is the traditional place of our Saviour's baptism, the passage of the Israelites, and the farther miraculous dividing of the river by Elijah and Elisha. Here, or near this spot, all these wonderful events must have transpired. This is confirmed by Scripture allusions to localities in the vicinity.

Just beyond the plain, on the eastern bank, are the dark mountain ranges of Moab and Ammon. Up under their shadow, when the long journey of forty years in the wilderness was nearly finished, the great caravan or procession of the Israelites had come. Then it was that Balak, King of Moab, sent for Balaam, who loved the wages of unrighteousness, to come and curse Israel. On yonder mountain-heights, Pisgah and Peor, did the wicked King rear altars, and take thither the false Prophet. There he uttered his remarkable parables. But God's people were not to be cursed, but blessed.

From the mountains of Abarim, before Nebo, the Israelites came and pitched in the plains of Moab, by Jordan, near Jericho. At this encampment, just over the river from my position, what deeply interesting and solemn scenes transpired! What laws and counsels were given to Israel! What hallowed words and sublime strains fell from the inspired lips of Moses! A faithful, patient, earnest and successful leader he had been. The people had sinned and fallen by the way. Beside himself, only two remained of the men who left Egypt; and he, having once erred, must now finish his course without passing the Jordan. But he shall have a glorious view of the long-sought and cherished land of promise. "And Moses went up from the plains of Moab unto the mountain of Nebo, to the top of Pisgah, that is over against Jericho, and the Lord showed him all the land." Blessed vision! type of the heavenly land he was so soon to enter; for there the Divine Hand took the great Moses to his rest and burial.

> "Sweet was the journey to the sky,
>   The wondrous Prophet tried;
> 'Climb up the mount,' says God, 'and die;'
>   The Prophet climbed—and died.
>
> " Softly his fainting head he lay
>   Upon his Maker's breast;
> His Maker kissed his soul away,
>   And laid his flesh to rest."

Joshua succeeds Moses, and preparations are made for entering the Promised Land. Long had it filled their dreams and inspired their hopes, and now they can look over upon its borders. Its mountain-tops are beautiful in the sunlight, and its green valleys are enchanting. But the swift-flowing and now full Jordan intervenes. How shall they pass the bridgeless flood? A Divine promise is their encouragement. Down to the river's edge they come and camp. The following day the priests, with the Ark on their shoulders, advanced till their feet touched the water along the shelving bank. The immense procession of people stretched far behind them, with Reuben, Gad and Manasseh, fully armed, in the van. No sooner had the priests' feet touched the water than it receded before them, leaving the bed of the river dry. The waters, coming down from the Sea of Galilee, "stood and rose up," while those below flowed off into the Dead Sea. Thus was a broad path opened through the river by the hand of God. In the midst of the dry bed the priests bearing the Ark remained till all the people passed over, and the twelve stones had been taken out of the river, to serve as a memorial of the miracle in after times. Now the feet of Israel's mighty host were pressing the soil of Canaan, and the hearts of their enemies melted at their approach.

Nearly six hundred years later, two remarkable men were standing at or near this place, on the west bank of the Jordan. They are Elijah and Elisha; and fifty sons of the Prophets, back on an eminence, are watching them with intense interest. Elijah takes off his outer robe or mantle, wraps it together, and smites the waters. They at once divide hither and thither, and the two pass over on dry ground. While they are talking together on that plain beyond, suddenly "there appeared a chariot of fire and horses of fire, and parted them both asunder; and Elijah went up by a whirlwind into heaven." Wonderful translation! glorious vision! Elisha saw it and cried, "My father! my father! the chariot of Israel and the horsemen thereof." He caught the mantle of the ascending

Prophet, returned to the Jordan, and swept its waters with it, calling upon the Lord God of Elijah. Another miracle divided the river, and the lone Prophet re-crossed it. The young men who had watched him perceived, as he returned to them, that the spirit of Elijah rested upon Elisha, and they bowed before him to the ground.

Nearly a thousand years after the passage of the Israelites, an event transpired here, perhaps at this very spot, of most thrilling interest. O Jordan! thou wast honored by the Lord of Life and Glory, who bowed his holy form in thy river, and made it forever sacred. Along those hills and vales of the wilderness of Judea, in this region of the Jordan, and beyond the river, came the bold and earnest Forerunner, preaching repentance, and the kingdom of heaven at hand, in the spirit and power of Elijah. And this, too, was the place where Elijah last appeared. How alike they were—these two great Prophets of the Jordan wilderness—alike in dress, in character, in their sublime utterance of truth, the one under the Old Dispensation, the other the herald of the New. Here came John the Baptist, preaching in "raiment of camel's hair," with a "leathern girdle round his loins" —clad like the present sons of that desert—eating the "locusts and wild honey" of the wilderness. "He came baptizing," says the Rev. Mr. Stanley, of the Church of England, "that is, signifying to those who came to him, as he plunged them under the rapid torrent, the forgiveness and forsaking of their former sins. Ablutions in the East, have always been more or less a part of religious worship—easily performed and always welcome. Every synagogue, if possible, was by the side of a stream or spring; every mosque still requires a fountain or basin for lustrations in its court. But no common spring or tank would meet the necessities of the multitudes who, from Jerusalem and all Judea, and all the region round about Jordan, came to him, confessing their sins. The Jordan, by the very peculiarity of its position, which renders its functions so unlike those of other Eastern streams, now seemed to have met with its fit purpose. It was the one river of Palestine—sacred in its recollections —abundant in its waters; and yet, at the same time, the river, not of cities, but of the wilderness—the scene of the preaching of those who dwelt not in kings' palaces, nor wore soft clothing. On the banks of the rushing stream the multitudes gathered; the priests and scribes from Jerusalem; the publicans from Jericho and the Lake of Gennesareth; the soldiers on their way from Damascus to Petra; the peasants from Galilee, with ONE from Nazareth. The tall reeds or canes in the jungles waved, shaken by the wind; the pebbles of the bare clay-hills lay around, to which the Baptist pointed as being capable of being transformed into children of Abraham; and at their feet rushed the refreshing stream of the never-failing river."

Such was the scene, when the Mightier, of whom John spake, came to the Jordan to be baptized of him. Recognizing the Son of God, he shrank in such a holy presence, and said, "I have need to be baptized of thee." But Jesus assured him—"Thus it becometh us to fulfil all righteousness." And they went down the bank, and the Blessed Saviour was baptized in the Jordan. "There," observes Stanley, "began that sacred rite which has since spread throughout the world, through the vast baptisteries of the Southern and Oriental Churches, gradually dwindling to the fonts of the North and West; the plunges beneath the water diminishing to the few drops which are now, in most churches, the sole representative of the full stream of the Descending River."

How sacred, how solemn is such a place! How thrilling, how divine its associations! Jesus was here —here he was baptized—here the heavens opened at the scene. Here was heard the approving voice of the Father, and here the Spirit Dove came down upon the Lamb of God. The devout tourist would scarcely leave such a spot before bathing in the hallowed river. So I felt, as thrice I bowed my head in the Jordan and heard the murmur of its waters above me.

Had my visit to the Jordan been a few weeks later, at the Greek Easter, I might have witnessed that singular and exciting scene, the bathing of the pilgrims, which is an annual occurrence. From all the East, and from most of the countries of Europe, pilgrims gather at Jerusalem, and to the number of several thousands go down to Jericho and encamp, and early the next morning repair to the Jordan, to bathe in the sacred river where our Lord was baptized. It is a motley crowd, under the escort of a Turkish guard. They plunge into the stream, most of them in white dresses prepared for the occasion, and then kept as the shrouds in which they are to be buried. The pilgrimage, often long and painful, they deem highly meritorious; but it is not necessary to repeat it, and children are frequently brought to receive the one immersion or bath, which will save them the expense and peril of a pilgrimage in after life.

Reluctantly we left the Jordan, and not till we had sung the "Shining Shore," and "On Jordan's rugged banks I stand," thinking of dear ones who had passed over into the heavenly Canaan, beyond the river, since we left home, and that blessed hope and faith that look for a Divine hand to divide the stream, or give support in its swellings, when our feet come to touch its waters.

XXII.

Jericho to Jerusalem.

THE sun was nearing the high hills of Judea, when we made our way westward from the Jordan in the track of the Israelites under Joshua, to their encampment at Gilgal. In a little more than two hours, traversing mostly a level plain, with a small growth of shrubs and grass here and there on the arid sandy soil, we reached our tents, on a little eminence just beyond which flowed the brook Cherith, now called Kelt. Perhaps our tents covered a portion of the Israelites' camp at Gilgal. And as I went down to the brook and drank of its pure sweet water, it might have been at the place where Elijah drank and was fed by the ravens, nearly three thousand years ago. Over the brook is a miserable-looking village, of low filthy huts, like those on the Nile, and guarded by hedges of thorn-bushes. Some of the swarthy inhabitants gather around our tents, appearing more dirty, ragged and degraded than is common. One fellow is most fantastically arrayed. That wretched village is probably the site of Roman Jericho, and a part of ancient Jericho, stretching farther to the northwest. A solitary stone building, in a ruinous condition, is all that remains of the city, and that is called the house of Zaccheus.

Jericho had a beautiful situation. It must have presented a splendid and imposing appearance, as the Israelites surveyed it from their camp at Gilgal. It lay between there and the gray, barren, bold mountains of Judea, rising abruptly in the west. It was embowered in a magnificent grove of palm-trees, stretching far to the north and south. The walls and towers of the city, "high and fenced up to heaven," rose proudly above the grove—the walls over which the spies had been let down from the house of Rahab, and were concealed in the "mountain" back of the city, while their pursuers vainly sought them at the Jordan. Mighty as were those walls, they were soon to fall by the signal power of God, in the presence of the encompassing Israelites.

Here, at Gilgal, after the fall of Jericho, the camp and tabernacle remained till the latter was removed to Shiloh. Here Joshua marshaled his armies, and led them up northward to the battle of Ai, near Bethel. Here Achan's crime was detected, and he was punished with death in the adjacent Valley of Achor. Here came Samuel from year to year, and held his court as a judge in Israel. Here the kingdom was renewed to Saul, and here he took the fatal steps which led to the loss of that kingdom. "And Samuel hewed Agag in pieces before the Lord in Gilgal." Here came David on his return from exile, and was met by thousands of people.

After the rebuilding of Jericho, it was the seat of a school of the prophets, and often visited by Elijah and Elisha. One of the most important springs, flowing from the hills, watering the plain and supplying the city, had become worthless and blighting, and was healed by Elisha. Up the wild mountain pass, a day's journey to Bethel, the prophet was going when he was mocked by the wicked children, whom the two she-bears from a neighboring forest destroyed. Elisha appears to have been at Gilgal when he was visited by Naaman, whom he sent to the Jordan to be cured of his leprosy. In later times, when the Roman sway extended over Palestine, Jericho, with its palm-groves and balsam gardens, was given by Antony to Cleopatra. Of her, Herod the Great bought them, and made this one of his royal cities, which he adorned with many stately buildings, and here that monster of iniquity died.

Many wonderful scenes had transpired at Jericho. Distinguished prophets and mighty princes had been there, but at length, in the person of our blessed Lord it had a visitor greater than them all; and some of His gracious words and astonishing works are forever associated with the place. After His baptism, He was led up of the Spirit into the wilderness. Then followed the long fasting and the temptation. It was doubtless to the wilderness of Judea, back of Jericho, up to which the Saviour was led, passing near or through the city. The boldest of those lofty, white limestone hills is called *Quarantania*, from the forty days' fasting of our Lord. It rises abruptly from the verdant plain, its rugged side dotted with the dark openings of numerous caves and grottoes, once tenanted by hermits, and its summit is crowned by a small chapel. Tradition also makes this the high mountain where Satan showed Jesus all the kingdoms of the world.

The sun was not much above the mountains of Moab, when we left our camping ground near the brook Cherith, where our slumbers had been somewhat disturbed by barking dogs, braying donkeys, and tramping horses. We rode through the filthy hut-village of Riha, with its barracks of thorn-brush, crossing the brook and other streams, bordered by fine patches of luxuriant wheat and other growing crops. These cultivated spots had a green and beautiful appearance, in the midst of the general barrenness and desolation. They showed what capabilities are in the soil, and how, with proper irrigation from those abundant fountains, and a suitable tillage, the whole plain of Jericho could be made fruitful as a blooming garden, or as the vale of Jordan when it first met the eyes of Lot. Such, doubtless, it will become, when it passes into other and more enterprising hands.

We observed thorn and other trees, and a peculiar kind near the brook Cherith, bearing a fair round yellow fruit, tempting to the eye, but bitter, nauseous, and said to be poisonous. It is called by some the Apples of Sodom. The ancient grove of palms, so majestic and beautiful, has entirely disappeared. About twenty years ago, travelers speak of seeing a solitary palm-tree, but that lone representative of the past long since disappeared. We noticed a few old hewn stones and pottery mounds, indicating, probably, the site of ancient Jericho. On our left, near the base of Quarantania, we saw the stone remains of old sugar mills, in operation, perhaps, two thousand years ago.

But now we come to 'Ain es-Sultan, the Fountain of Elisha—the identical spring, it would seem, into which that prophet cast the salt, and it was miraculously healed. At the foot of the hills, it bubbles up profusely into a rude reservoir, and then flows away in a clear stream of sufficient size and force to carry a mill at once. And so its pure sweet waters have bubbled and flowed since the day when Elisha stood at its margin, and wondrously healed the fountain. How interesting to stand there, to sit down by the fountain-side, and drink of the spring where, no doubt, the prophet quenched his thirst, and where, perhaps, our blessed Lord himself had come and drank.

Standing on the high bank from under which the fountain gushes out, and looking over the whole range of the plain, what thrilling associations and emotions are awakened! What a wonderful cluster of Scripture localities are in view! What a long, changing, eventful history is there! Through the varied scenes of the drama, what forms and figures move! Patriarchs and prophets, kings and conquerors, and our Divine Lord himself have been there. At my feet is all that remains of the great, powerful, and walled city of Jericho. The mountains back of me, and those beyond the Jordan, remain as of old, but all else how changed! I can look down where the Cities of the Plain stood, where Lot heard the angel voice, "Escape to the mountain." I can see the heights where Moses viewed "the landscape o'er," and ascended to glory, and where Elijah followed in a chariot of fire. I can look far up the valley, and trace the windings of the Jordan downward to where it was thrice miraculously divided, where the stern, earnest Forerunner preached and baptized, and where our blessed Redeemer bowed his sacred form in the Descending River. Across this plain He went up to the wilderness to fast and to be tempted. Over it He subsequently walked with his disciples. Coming from the eastern side of the Jordan, conversing with the sons of Zebedee in regard to their singular request, they reach the palm-shaded borders of Jericho, and there sat blind Bartimeus, whom He healed; and there was the sycamore from whence He called the tax-gatherer Zaccheus. Nothing in all thy history, O City of Palms, is so beautiful as these scenes of mercy and salvation! What a memorable visit of Jesus to Jericho! Gracious, heavenly, and joyful words fell from His lips here—words that have comforted and gladdened many a heart since they were heard by the poor beggar and the rich collector. Solemn, thrilling, earnest lessons and eloquent voices, come to the heart from all these places and associations. The perished cities speak of the doom of sinners. Nebo speaks of the saint's prospects and of heaven. The Jordan, of following Jesus, and the believer's safe passage over the river to his home. The battles of Joshua, of the victories of faith after we have enlisted for Christ. The fountain at my feet murmurs of the Fountain opened for sin. Its being divinely healed is an emblem of a soul renewed and purified, henceforth to flow on in a tide of everlasting salvation. Before leaving we sang "The voice of free grace," and "There is a land of pure delight."

After our Lord's entertainment at the house of Zaccheus in Jericho, and His uttering of the solemn parable of the pounds, "He went before, ascending up to Jerusalem." He took the usual path, the only thoroughfare between the two cities. It remains the same to-day—a road "ascending up"—an almost continual climbing of high hills. In this path it was my privilege to go, tracing the footsteps of our blessed Saviour.

After leaving the Fountain of Elisha, we turned southward for a little time, along the fertile margin of the plain of Jericho, under the high Judean hills. Crossing again the Cherith, we turned to the right near the base of Quarantania, and entering the wild, deep gorge of Wady el-Kelt, we began to climb up our narrow path among the mountains. Far down on our right, at the bottom of the precipitous ravine, the Cherith flows like a silver ribbon. On our left, and all about us, are lofty, bold, gray and white limestone slopes and summits, giving to the region an aspect lonely, desolate, and sublime. The wild pass we are ascending is the "going up to Adummim," mentioned by Joshua in his description of the boundary, as lying on "the south side of the river," or brook. Our course is westward, over flinty rocks, on the edge of this glen or abyss, whose almost perpendicular walls are nearly five hundred feet high. Caves and grottoes are in their sides, once the abodes of hermits and anchorites, and the ruins of a few chapels crown the rugged heights beyond. We now pause and look back, from our high and comanding elevation, to take one last near view of the plain of Jericho, the Jordan valley, the Dead Sea, and the adjacent mountains. The view is wide and varied, grand and gloomy, embracing numerous Scripture sites, with which are associated some of the most interesting and thrilling events of sacred history.

We journey on, and I think of that last journey of Jesus over this same path, going up from the house of Zaccheus, his new friend in Jericho, to the house of Lazarus, his older friend in Bethany. It was just one week before His crucifixion, that He passed along here, over these same flat rocks that are beneath my feet. O, what a week was that! How crowded with blessed and tender instructions, with strange, solemn, and wonderful events!

We come to the summit or rather shoulder of a hill, and begin to descend. The region, broken up into high elevations and deep ravines, is wild, gloomy and desolate. A little way from our path, on the right, are the stone ruins of some ancient building. Our guides tell us it is the remains of the inn to which the good Samaritan took the poor traveler who, in coming down from Jerusalem to Jericho, fell among thieves, who stripped and wounded him, and left him half dead. This spot has always been noted as the lurking-place of robbers. And no traveler now passes through there, without perceiving how admirably adapted the region is for deeds of violence and blood, especially if he gets a sight of the wild, fierce, demoniac-looking Bedawin, crossing the path, skulking in the ravines, or hanging around the rocks. I saw in that vicinity several such in their tattered garments, with their lances, long guns, pistols and clubs, watching an opportunity to pounce upon the solitary or unprotected traveler. Ibrahim was continually cautioning us to keep together. Some years ago, at this most dangerous part of the road, an English gentleman was way-laid, stripped, wounded and left for dead. Very likely he might have been thinking of our Saviour's account when he fell under the Bedawy's club. As we were passing, I intimated to Mustapha, one of our sturdy Arab assistants, to designate the place where the scene in the Gospel narrative transpired. In a short time he pointed to the ground, and then with both hands swung his huge stick within a few inches of my head, as a partial illustration of the scene. In a valley a little further along, we sat down to our lunch amidst some old ruins near a little fountain, perhaps the same that Joshua calls "the waters of En-shemesh."

Climbing along this bleak, hilly region, amidst slight showers of rain, an hour's ride brings us near to Bethany. Emerging from the "wilderness of Judea," we begin to ascend the southeastern slope of Olivet. Bethany comes into view. Here, as we reach the border of the town, is the place where Martha came to meet Jesus, and in her regretful anguish greeted him: "Lord, if thou hadst been here, my brother had not died." Then Mary came here and addressed Him in the same words. He was beyond the Jordan when they sent to their Lord the message —"He whom thou lovest is sick." Down this long dreary path, through the valley, and over these dark, bleak hills, they had gazed with anxious expectation, and watched for His approach. O long and sad hours and days! but, after three suns had set upon their brother's grave, the form of Jesus was seen coming up the ascent. And here they met Him, and heard His glorious words of Resurrection and Life and Immortality. Here came the sympathizing Jews and mingled theirs with Mary's tears. Here the Redeemer " groaned in spirit and was troubled, and said, Where have ye laid him?" And here *Jesus wept.* O Bethany! how sweet and hallowed are thy associations with Jesus! How much of His human side, His precious love, His dear friendship and tender sympathy thou didst witness! The night before His betrayal, He came to visit and feast with His friends in thee. His last look upon earth was upon thee; for the risen Lord led his disciples " out as far as to Bethany"—to that shady ridge between thee and Olivet's summit—" and He lifted up His hands and blessed them, and was parted from them, and was carried up to heaven."

> " Jesus wept! those tears are over,
>   But His heart is still the same;
> Kinsman, Friend, and elder Brother
>   Is His everlasting name.
>   Saviour, who can love like thee,
>   Gracious One of Bethany.
>
> " Jesus wept! and still in glory,
>   He can mark each mourner's tear;
> Living to retrace the story
>   Of the hearts He solaced here.
>   Lord, when I am called to die,
>   Let me think of Bethany."

XXIII.

City of the Great King—Gethsemane.

ONCE more in Jerusalem, to spend a few days, including another precious Sabbath, and to visit over and over again localities of most sacred and tender interest. Around no city in the world do such hallowed associations cluster. No other spot has been so honored of God. None has such a wonderful history. No city has been loved like this. The mountains in and round about it are unparalleled in the scenes they have witnessed. No hills or summits have such associations as Moriah and Zion, Calvary and Olivet. Every foot of soil is sacred; every rock has its story; every fountain its memories; and every path its footprints of God. I think of the glories of the past—the Temple and the throngs who came to worship in it—and I do not wonder that God's people should sing: "His foundation is in the holy mountains. The Lord loveth the gates of Zion more than all the dwellings of Jacob. Glorious things are spoken of thee, O city of God."

> "And throned on her hills sits Jerusalem yet,
> But with dust on her forehead and chains on her feet
> For the crown of her pride to the mocker hath gone,
> And the holy Shechinah is dark where it shone."

Compared with its former greatness and glory, Jerusalem is scarcely more than a ruin now. It is, however, a walled city, nearly square, and contains, probably, not over 15,000 inhabitants, comprising in the order of numbers, Jews, Moslems, Greeks, Latins, Armenians, and others. The hills and valleys remain much as they were in ancient times. Some relics of the old walls and towers are left. Pools and fountains still exist or flow as in former days. A few trees— olive, fig, palm, cypress, and pomegranate—remain as representatives of those that once crowned the hills or adorned the gardens. As I walk on the walls, or make the circuit of the city without them, imagination is ever busy in restoring the original grandeur of this City of the Great King, reviewing its changeful history and astonishing events, and seeing again the vast throngs that once crowded its thoroughfares, and the wonderful persons that walked its streets. How deeply interesting to "walk about Zion"—how beautiful the scenery by the way—if we could see the city as it was in its glory, the hills and valleys in their verdure and bloom; if we could "tell the towers, and mark the bulwarks, and consider the palaces," that were long ago destroyed! The visitor is reminded of the prophet's lamentations: "How doth the city sit solitary that was full of people? How is she become as a widow! She that was great among the nations, and princess among the provinces, how is she become tributary!" O chosen city, how art thou fallen! and what glorious, what sad memories are thine!

> "Jerusalem, Jerusalem,
> *Thy* cross thou bearest now!
> An iron yoke is on thy neck,
> And blood is on thy brow;

> Thy golden crown, the crown of truth,
> Thou didst reject as dross,
> And now thy cross is on thee laid—
> The Crescent is thy cross."

I have in a previous chapter described an excursion around Zion, or the southern part of the city, from the Bethlehem Gate along the valleys of Hinnom and Jehoshaphat to St. Stephen's Gate. I will now attempt to describe the northern part of the circuit.

We went out at the Bethlehem or Jaffa Gate, and first visited the Upper Pool of Gihon, a few hundred yards west of the northwest corner of the city. Here the Valley of Hinnom commences. This pool is an immense open tank, of rectangular form, excavated in the rock. It is partly full of water. The prophet Isaiah was commanded of God to go forth and meet Ahaz "at the end of the conduit of the Upper Pool, in the highway of the Fuller's Field." Here, also, Rabshekah stood and delivered the haughty message of his royal master, the King of Assyria, to the Ministers of Hezekiah. We also read that Hezekiah stopped the upper outflow of the waters of Gihon, and brought it down to the west side of the city of David.

Turning to the right, we go round the northwest corner of the city, and make a gentle descent to the east. Scattered olive trees, rocks, and old tombs are about us. We are now not far from the Damascus Gate, near the middle of the northern wall. We go to the Tombs of the Kings, sometimes called the Tomb of Helena, about half a mile north of this gate. They are extensive excavations in the native rock, embracing an open court, chambers, passage-ways, and various side vaults, all smoothly hewn, and exhibiting much skill and taste; but as they contain no inscriptions, it is uncertain when or for whom they were made. Crawling into the low and narrow entrance, we explored these dismal cells with candles.

Returning by the Grotto of Jeremiah, a huge cave in a rocky hill-side, we come back to the wall, a little east of the Damascus Gate, and climbing over a mound of soft earth and rubbish, we discern a low cavernous entrance under the wall. Provided with a guide and lights, we go down, as we are obliged to, in a horizontal position, and are soon lost to daylight. We now find ourselves in an immense rocky cavern, extending far under the hill Bezetha, or northeastern part of Jerusalem. We explored this nether city to the distance of about a quarter of a mile. Sometimes the rock-roof was high above us, and at other places we had to stoop to avoid a contact with it. We walked over loose stones, and passed huge pieces of rock, all white limestone. This was evidently an immense quarry, for the marks of the quarrying instruments are plainly seen, and blocks that have been split from the rocks remain. There can scarcely be a doubt that the stones for the Temple-walls were taken from this quarry. Here they were dressed and prepared, as is evident from the many piles of chippings. And this agrees with the account of the erection of the Temple. "And the house, when it was in building, was built of stone, made ready before it was brought thither; so that there was neither hammer nor axe, nor any tool of iron, heard in the house while it was building." Here, in Solomon's time, we must believe, those immense beveled stones, now seen in the base of the city wall at its southeast corner, were quarried and hewn. Occasionally we passed huge, rugged columns of rock, left by the workmen to support the roof. After an hour's ramble in these vast, dark, and dreary halls, that so long ago echoed the sounds of the "tools of iron," it was pleasant to emerge again to daylight. This cavern was unknown to foreigners till a few years since, when it was discovered by Dr. Barclay, an American missionary, who observed his dog crawling into it.

Proceeding eastward down the hill, we enter the Valley of Jehoshaphat, amidst a cluster of olive trees, and turning south cross the bed of the Kedron. Just over the bridge, on the left, is the Tomb of the Virgin Mary. It is a church also, and I was surprised to find it so ample and so brilliantly adorned. It is mostly under ground, and the main room, gleaming with lighted silver lamps and splendid altars, is reached by a descent of sixty steps. About half way down on the right, are shown in a niche or little chapel, the tombs of Joachim and Anna, parents of the Virgin. Joseph's tomb is on the left, and Mary's is in the church below.

A pilgrim's tent was pitched near this building, and on some rude seats under a large tree adjoining it, several persons were sitting or lounging, whenever I passed.

A few rods to the southeast brings us to the northwest corner of the enclosure of Gethsemane, on the lower slope of Olivet. A stone wall, roughly stuccoed, and about seven feet high, surrounds the Garden. The space enclosed contains perhaps a third of an acre. We pass along the north wall, turn the corner, and find, near the south end of the east wall, a low door or gate, the only entrance. This is locked, but a few raps thereon bring a monk, who lives in a little apartment in the Garden, and he politely gives us admission.

We are now in the Garden, and the scenes of our Saviour's agony and betrayal throng upon the mind with indescribable solemnity and power. Jesus praying, Jesus suffering, the cup of anguish, and the traitor's kiss—how vividly they reäppear! We can scarcely think of anything else. We care not for the tradition that points out the precise spot or grotto where Jesus prayed, the rocky bank where the three Apostles slept, and the place of the betrayal. We know they were all near, and we give ourselves up to the great and awful realities they witnessed.

There is a walk around the Garden, close to the wall, to which, at every few steps, rude pictures are attached, representing the various scenes in our Lord's passion. In the center of the enclosure there are also walks, and flower-beds bright with roses and other blossoms. But the most striking feature is that of eight very old, large and venerable olive trees. Their trunks are partially decayed, and are supported by stones piled about them. No other trees on the mountain are like them, so ancient and solemnly grand. It almost seemed that I was looking upon the very trees under whose boughs our blessed Lord and His disciples sat—where He taught them the glorious mysteries of His kingdom—and where afterwards He knelt and prayed in agony, and His holy soul was overwhelmed with sorrow. Though not dating so far back, yet the olive is often very long-lived, and even these may be the immediate successors, or have actually sprung from the roots of those that were here in the time of Christ. With their gnarled trunks and and scanty foliage, these venerable trees are sacred and affecting memorials—"the most nearly approaching to the everlasting hills themselves, in the force with which they carry us back to the events of the Gospel history." In a secluded spot under the shade of one of those glorious old trees, I read aloud the names of my Christian flock, from a list of them I had with me, and commended all to God in prayer, and to the abounding grace of Him whose soul for us was here exceeding sorrowful, even unto death. Far apart though we were, yet prayer and faith and love, and fellowship with our suffering Redeemer, brought us near together, and into sweet union with Him and with each other.

After we had been nearly two hours in the Garden, our little party got together in a retired place, near the western wall, where we might review more minutely the solemn memories of this hallowed spot. We sat down, affected with its powerful and tender associations—our tearful interest all the while profoundly increasing, as I read aloud, one after another, the several accounts in the Gospels of our dear Saviour's agony here, and concluded by reading the fifty-third chapter of Isaiah. Our tears flowed most freely. So overpowering were my emotions, that I could hardly read audibly. I never had such a near view of Christ before—of His majestic holiness and Divine glory—of His infinite pity, tenderness and love—of the unspeakable intensity of His sufferings and sorrows—of the importance and greatness of His atoning work—of the terrible guiltiness and ill desert of sin in the sight of God—of my own unutterable unworthiness and sinfulness, and the sweet, glorious preciousness of Jesus as a Saviour. I never before felt such a personal nearness to Him, or had such a vivid sense of His enduring all that unsearchable agony for *me*. If I had not then been conscious of a sweet hope in that suffering Saviour, a loving reliance upon Him, and a personal interest in His blood and righteousness, I should have been most miserably wretched. So doubtless we all felt, as we kneeled down there where our blessed Lord had knelt and prayed, and poured out in tears and cries our souls to Him, recalling the bitter anguish of

"——that dark and doleful night,
When powers of earth and hell arose
Against the Son of God's delight,
And friends betrayed Him to His foes."

From the Garden, the whole eastern wall of the city, with the slope of the hill below, can be seen, and perhaps our Saviour caught a glimpse of Judas and his band, issuing from a gate, or round a corner of the wall, just at that moment when He seems to speak abruptly to His disciples—"Rise, let us be going; behold, he is at hand that doth betray me."

I often visited this sacred enclosure. The first morning after my arrival in Jerusalem, and the last morning of my stay there, I lingered at this spot. And who could visit such a place, and not be affected to tears? Who could feel indifferent to the lone Sufferer there—the steadfast Saviour, under the infinite pressure of a world's guilt—the blessed Lamb of God, betrayed, taken, and borne away as a criminal! O Gethsemane! How strangely wonderful are the scenes thou hast witnessed! How thy every tree, and stone, and turf speaks of Jesus! The breeze in the boughs whispers of His prayers. The dew-drops on thy rose-leaves remind us of His tears. Each crimson flower tells us of His bloody sweat. Sad and precious Gethsemane! thou art to-day a witness for Christ. Thou, on that everlasting hill, dost seem to repeat His instructions heard by thee. Thou art ever repeating the story of His love, His tears, His conflicts, His victories!

> "O Garden of Olivet! thou dear honored spot,
> The fame of thy wonders shall ne'er be forgot;
> The theme most transporting to seraphs above;
> The triumph of sorrow—the triumph of love!"

Kindly permitted to take a few flowers, rose-leaves, an olive branch, and a little box of earth from the Garden, we recrossed the Kedron, and climbed the steep and high ascent to St. Stephen's Gate. Near the gate, on our right, is a well or fountain, and men are raising water for their horses and other animals. A flock of sheep there, too, with their keepers or owners, apparently counting them as they each pass under a rod, reminds us of certain passages of Scripture, and suggests the locality of Bethesda. "Now there is at Jerusalem, by the Sheep market, a Pool, which is called in the Hebrew tongue Bethesda." We enter the wall and turn a few steps to the left, and reach the traditional site of this far-famed Pool, whose angel-troubled waters were so efficacious. It is now a large excavation, in a neglected and ruinous state. But it is easy to recall the five porches, filled with the various impotent folk—a sad and sorrowful spectacle—as they waited for a cure. We think of the poor cripple, suffering eight and thirty years, sitting by the brink of the Pool, and yet unable to avail himself of its virtues. We see Jesus come and speak to him kindly, tenderly, and heal him by a wonderful word.

XXIV.

Benjamin—Gibeon—Gibeah—Bethel.

I MIGHT still linger with interest at Jerusalem, and dwell on other chapters of its long and wonderful history, its strange and astonishing scenes. I might speak of climbing the massive Tower of David, one of the few relics of the former city, and of the glorious view from its top—of looking down again from the House of Pilate, at the northern foot of Moriah, upon the broad and beautiful grounds of the Temple, where were the home and altar of Melchisedek; where Abraham offered his son Isaac; where was the threshing-floor of Ornan, and the angel with the drawn sword hovered above; where Solomon built the glorious Sanctuary; where our blessed Lord was often found teaching the people; where multitudes of infatuated Jews perished in the burning Temple; where now the great octagonal mosque, with its splendid dome, stands in the center of that charming area, by far the most beautiful building in the Holy City. And while thinking of all this, from a minaret on my right is heard a shrill voice breaking over the stillness; it is the muezzin's call to prayer. I might speak of repeated walks in and around the city, and on the top of its high, massive wall, and of never-wearying visits to Calvary, Gethsemane, Olivet and Bethany. But

I must tear myself away from these sacred attractions. Having procured various little memorials of Jerusalem and the Mount of Olives, arrangements were at length made for our departure. We had passed two Sabbaths in the Holy City, on each of which we had a delightful religious service, with preaching, in an "upper room" on Mount Zion. The sermon on the second Lord's day was from the Rev. Mr. Booth.

It was a beautiful day, March 27th, at noon, when our agreeable party of thirteen Americans took leave of these intensely interesting localities. I have already mentioned several of our company who had visited Eygpt together; the others were Messrs. P. Snyder, of Albany, A. R. Wiggs, of Alabama, and the "two Marys," Miss Foot, of Brooklyn, and Miss Billings, of Elmira; and we were now joined by the Rev. J. L. Jenkins, of Lowell, the Rev. W. B. Clarke, of New Haven, and Mr. Porter, a Theological student, of Boston. We went out by the Jaffa Gate, where we first entered the city, and turned to the north into the Damascus road. Over an uneven surface, abounding in rock-ledges and tombs, with olive trees and occasional patches of cultivated ground, we passed the upper end of the Kedron valley, and reached, at the distance of about a mile, the heights of Mt. Scopus, and paused to take a last look of the city. The view was charming and delightful, and can never be forgotten. Jerusalem, under the light of a vernal sun, lay like a beautiful picture in a frame of hills. Long and earnestly, silently and tearfully, we gazed, feeling that we should never again behold that sacred and wonderful city. How clearly we see each object, ren-

dered familiar by frequent visit and observation!—
The encircling walls of massive stone—the domes of
the Church of the Holy Sepulchre—the Castle of
David—the Mosque of Omar, and various minarets
shooting their slender spires upward—Zion, Moriah,
Bezetha and Aksa, hills within the walls—and without, the slopes and heights of surrounding elevations,
rising from the deep valleys of Hinnom and Jehoshaphat, most prominent and most tenderly attractive
being those of Olivet, while the dark, wall-like mountains of Moab, beyond the vale of the Jordan, were
just visible, and enhanced the beauty and interest of
the picture. As our moistened eyes took in this last
view of the Holy City, and as its unparalleled events,
especially those connected with the closing scenes of
our blessed Saviour's mission, came thronging upon
our minds, our emotions, my own, at least, are not to
be described. I opened my pocket Bible, and read
aloud the forty-eighth Psalm, and from our position we
could readily appreciate the glowing description—
"Beautiful for situation, the joy of the whole earth, is
Mount Zion, *on the sides of the north*, the city of the
Great King." We could appreciate the strong attachment of the captive Israelites to the city of their
solemnities, and felt like adopting their powerfully
affectionate and plaintive strains: "If I forget thee,
O Jerusalem, let my right hand forget her cunning;
if I do not remember thee, let my tongue cleave to the
roof of my mouth; if I prefer not Jerusalem above my
chief joy." "Thy servants take pleasure in her stones,
and favor the dust thereof." We joined our voices in
singing these lines:

JERUSALEM FROM THE NORTHEAST.

"The hill of Zion yields
    A thousand sacred sweets,
Before we reach the heavenly fields
    Or walk the golden streets.

"Then let our songs abound,
    And every tear be dry;
We're marching through Immanuel's ground
    To fairer worlds on high.

"O then my spirit faints
    To reach the land I love,
The bright inheritance of saints,
    Jerusalem above."

We then set our faces to the north, and going down the slope, we saw Jerusalem no more. Farewell, O Sacred City! Thy wonderful history extends through long centuries, is crystalized on the immortal pages of Revelation, and embraces the most exciting, touching, tender and glorious scenes. What a precious privilege to have looked upon thy walls, to have entered thy gates, to have walked among thy hallowed localities—all of which are now as familiar as childhood scenes, and to be recounted with perpetual pleasure—bright and charming pictures that memory will hold dear and cherish forever!

We soon found ourselves entering a rich cluster of Scripture sites, with which are connected events of thrilling interest. We are among the heights and passes of Benjamin, on the main road to Galilee, along which our Divine Lord and His disciples often went, and previously traversed by kings, prophets and patriarchs. The general appearance is that of hilly and rocky desolation. A few stunted trees scarcely attract a notice. Isolated patches of cultivated ground seem a vain attempt at husbandry, but are often really rich and productive. Old terraces, belting the hills to their summits, indicate a former thrift which might be again renewed. Here and there, under the hand of cultivation, are spots of luxuriant verdure, abounding in groves of olive, fig, pomegranate and vines, showing the capacity of the soil where all looks forbidding. On the slopes and summits there are frequent villages, in a ruined or dilapidated state, that are scarcely distinguishable from the gray rocks around them.

A hill close on our right, covered with old ruins, among which are several rock-hewn reservoirs, is supposed to be the site of Nob, where the priests were slain by the cruel order of Saul; and in the vale declining to the east, David probably lay concealed, and had his interview with Jonathan. Farther to the east on a broad ridge, we see Anathoth, interesting as the birthplace of Jeremiah. West of us rises Mizpeh, a conspicuous commanding elevation, often mentioned in Scripture, the scene of thrilling events, and the gathering of vast assemblies preparatory to battle or the choice of a king. There Saul was chosen, and the shout first heard in Israel, "God save the king!" To this height came the chivalrous Crusader, Richard of England; but before looking upon Jerusalem, he buried his face in his hands, and exclaimed—"Ah! Lord God! I pray that I may never see thy holy city, if I may not rescue it from thine enemies!" At the northern foot of Mizpeh, a hill crowned with a village rises up from a beautiful plain, whose verdure is enlivened with clustering vineyards and olive groves. This village is Gibeon, one of the royal cities of Scripture history. Here that singular piece of strategy was planned, that curious expedition, which beguiled the Israelites into a league with the Gibeonites. The latter became hewers of wood and drawers of water to the former, and up that hill they carried the wood, and from that fountain below bore the water to the altar and the sanctuary. On this little plain, the five kings of the Amorites encamped against the Gibeonites. The latter sent for Joshua, and over that broad, stony ridge at our right, the Israelites suddenly rushed, and came down across our path upon them with the first beams of the morning sun. They were slain with a great slaughter at Gibeon, and driven westward over the pass Beth-horon, where many more perished by the falling stones and hail. It was during this great battle that Joshua commanded the sun to stand still upon Gibeon, and the moon in the valley of Ajalon. "And the sun stood still and the moon obeyed, until the people had avenged themselves on their enemies. And there was no day like that, for the Lord fought for Israel." It was deeply interesting to look upon the scene of this stupendous miracle, and from the place where it transpired, look up to the same sun now in the sky, and, by faith, to the same God in the heavens above. He still fights for His people; and suns, days and ages wait for the triumph of His kingdom.

Gibeon is a place of battles and scenes of blood. Doubtless, at this pool or reservoir, still seen seen on the eastern slope of the hill, Abner and Joab met at the head of the armies of Israel and Judah. Before them the twelve men of Judah fought with the twelve of Benjamin, resulting in the slaughter of the twenty-four. Then followed the battle terminating in the defeat of Abner and the death of Asahel. Here, too, "at the stone which is in Gibeon," Amasa was treacherously slain by Joab on saluting him, "Art thou in health, my brother?" It was in Gibeon that Solomon offered a thousand burnt-offerings, and here the Lord appeared to him in a dream, and was pleased that he asked for wisdom as the best gift.

Passing down a rocky declivity, over a valley, and up a steep, bare hill, we find on its summit a confused heap of ruins, which mark the site of Gibeah—sometimes called Gibeah of Saul—the city that gave Israel its first king. There is a horrid story of a Levite, in the Book of Judges, connected with this place—an event that resulted in nearly annihilating the tribe of Benjamin. On this hill, the Gibeonites hanged the seven descendants of Saul, in revenge for the massacre of their brethren. And here occurred that touching scene of maternal tenderness, when Rizpah, the mother of two of the victims, "took sackcloth and spread it for her upon the rock, from the beginning of harvest until water dropped upon them out of heaven, and suffered neither the birds of the air to rest on them by day, nor the beasts of the field by night." From April till the early rain of autumn, that lone, sad mother watched by the wasting skeletons of her sons, day and night, through the long Syrian summer. A sorrowful spectacle, and yet how suggestive of the strength of her affection, and the depth of her grief!

Descending the hill, in half an hour we come to Ramah of Benjamin, a small, poor village, with fragments of columns and beveled stones built into the modern houses. This site is identified, from the Bible account of its lying between Gibeon and Beeroth. To the latter place another half hour brings us. It is now called Bireh, and is a large Mohammedan village. Tradition makes this the place where Joseph and Mary, having been to Jerusalem with Jesus when he was twelve years old, turned back, not finding Him in their company.

We have passed Geba and Michmash—lying off to the right—places mentioned in Isaiah's prophetic description of Sennacherib's march towards the Holy City:

"He is come to Aiath, he is passed to Migron;
At Michmash he hath laid up his carriages
They are gone over the passage;
They have taken up their lodging at Geba
Ramah is afraid; Gibeah of Saul is fled.
Lift up thy voice, O daughter of Gallim;
Cause it to be heard unto Laish, O poor Anathoth!
Madmenah is removed;
The inhabitants of Gebim gather themselves to flee.
As yet shall he remain at Nob that day;
He shall shake his hand against the mount of the daughter of Zion,
The hill of Jerusalem."

With the eye upon places mentioned in this highly poetic description, it is easy to trace the successive steps of the proud Assyrian, rushing on with his mighty army amid the terrified inhabitants, till at the last station he gets a glimpse of the Holy City he would despoil. So accurate is the topography of the

Bible, that in wandering through the lands it describes, their history is reënacted before the eye of the mind.

Turning now to the right from the main path, we ascend the low southwestern slope of a stony hill, and enter a village not very attractive in its present condition, or beautiful in its appearance, but a location of deep and thrilling interest; for this is the site of ancient Bethel, associated with sacred, sublime and glorious scenes. As we come to this hill, and look upon these rocks, and tread these paths, and gaze upon those higher hills beyond and around, and know and feel that this is indeed Bethel, how do sweet and sacred associations cluster and throng about us! What wonderful scenes have been witnessed here! The forms of venerable patriarchs are before us—altars, sanctuaries, vows and pledges, the worship of God, the presence of angels—all are here, and Heaven itself has been near this spot. Dreams of glory and promises of prosperity cluster here. O Bethel! sweet name; hallowed place—how would I like to lie down, even with stones for a pillow, as the pilgrim Jacob rested here, worn and weary, with heaven's canopy for a tent, and the watchful stars above him, and dream gloriously as he dreamed, and see such angelic and Divine visions as he saw—heaven and earth united, and a stairway up to the Excellent Glory. As we entered the village, we saw the tents of a party of friends already pitched near a fountain at the southern base of the hill; and it would have been a pleasure to have pitched ours there too, as the sun was nearing the horizon, but they had gone forward to another camping-ground.

Bethel is about twelve miles north of Jerusalem. The present village, called Beitin, consists of some twenty inferior houses, mingled with fragments of ancient ruins. The whole ridge or hill is exceedingly rocky, and Jacob could find a pillow of stones at any place. It is between two fertile valleys, running north and south. Near the western base of the hill is a massive old stone reservoir. It is a green spot watered by two little fountains, where, no doubt, the cattle of Abraham often drank, and where the maidens of Sarah came and filled their pitchers, just as do the Arab maidens from the village now. Here Abraham first pitched his tent, as he journeyed south on his way to Egypt; and to this spot he returned, "unto the place of the altar which he had made at the first." It is easy to fix the eye upon the precise locality of the patriarch's tent on that high hill or "mountain," "having Bethel on the west and Ai on the east." No position in the neighborhood affords so fine a view; and from that height Abraham and Lot could easily survey a vast region to the right and left. Lot looked down thence upon the rich plain of Jordan, then beautiful in its crystal springs and luxuriant fruitfulness, and chose his inheritance among the Cities of the Plain. They parted on that hill, and Lot descended the ravine along the thoroughfare leading to Jericho. Then Abraham was divinely directed to look from that hill over the land, with the assurance that it should be his, and the number of his descendants should be as the dust of the earth. Wild and dreary hills then met the lone patriarch's view, but at length they were crowned with cities that flourished and were remembered with honor long after the blooming "garden," with its proud seats of a splendid but corrupt civilization, was reduced to an utter desolation, washed by the Sea of Death. It is certainly most deeply interesting to visit and behold sites so unmistakably identified, where Abraham stood near four thousand years ago. There are the same hills, valleys, plains, and broad view that met his eye. The accuracy with which the Bible describes these minute geographical features, wonderfully confirms its truth.

About a hundred and fifty years elapse, and Jacob, flying from his enraged brother Esau, comes a solitary wanderer to this spot, and "tarried all night, because the sun was set; and he took of the stones of the place, and put them for his pillows, and lay down to sleep," and dreamed that glorious dream of the ladder and the angels, and received promises of blessing and prosperity. He awoke, and saw but the bleak hills and arching heavens, but deeply impressed with the divine vision, the place was hallowed, and he exclaimed, "This is none other than the house of God, and this is the gate of heaven." So the name of the place was changed from Luz to Beth-el, "House of God." Here, after thirty years, Jacob came again with his household, and reared an altar, and was honored with a visible manifestation of the Divine presence. While they lingered here, "Deborah, Rebekah's nurse, died, and she was buried beneath Bethel, under an oak; and the name of it was called Allon-bachuth," the oak of weeping.

Bethel has a long and varied history. From the pillar that Jacob set up came at length the Sanctuary of Bethel, and the Holy Place of the northern kingdom. Jeroboam sought to rival the Temple at Jerusalem, by building a splendid one here after the Egyptian style, in which feasts and assemblies were held, and idolatrous offerings made to the Golden Calf. The desecration of the place finally gave it the name of Bethaven, "House of Idols." Prophets denounced divine judgments upon it, and the desolation that followed, and has reigned for ages, fulfilled the prediction: "Bethel shall come to nought." How strange that men could become idolators at such a place as Bethel, so hallowed by the presence of angels and promised blessings of the living God!

A little east of Bethel is Ai, one of the most ancient sites in Palestine, and the next place conquered by Joshua after the fall of Jericho. The first attempt to capture it was a failure; but it resulted in the conviction and execution of the covetous Achan. In the second attack, an ambuscade was placed at night in the valley to the west, while the main body took their position beyond the glen, on the north. In the morning they crossed the valley as if to assault the city, but pretending a panic, suddenly retreated. The stratagem was successful. While the male population rushed out aftèr the fugitives, Joshua gave the signal from one of those hills at the north, and the "liers-in-wait" at once took possession of the defenceless city, and laid it in ashes. I read the Scripture account of these battle-scenes as we passed along by the hills and valleys where they transpired so long ago.

From several of these heights may be seen, a few miles to the northeast, the light chalky peak of Rûmmon, and the dark conical hill of Tayibeh, which it would be interesting to visit, if we had time to make the necessary detour. The first is the "rock of Rimmon," whither the six hundred Benjamites fled from the terrible battles of Gibeah in which the crime of their tribe was so severely avenged. There they abode four months, till at length the Israelites "repented for Benjamin their brother," and sent some to the "rock Rimmon to call peaceably unto them." The other height is crowned with a village that probably represents the site of Ophrah, to which in the reign of Saul one of the "three companies" of "spoilers" went from the camp of the Philistines at Michmash. It is supposed also, from its position on the border of the Jordan valley and from its similarity of name, to be the "city called Ephraim," which was "near to the wilderness," and to which our Lord retired with His disciples after the raising of Lazarus.

XXV.

Ephraim—Shiloh—Plain of Moreh—Jacob's Well.

DESCENDING from Bethel, our northward course was among a succession of rocky hills and vales, with occasional patches of wheat, scattered olives, vines and figs. In an hour or so, we came to a scene of beauty and luxuriance springing up amidst the general desolation. It seemed hardly possible that there could be such fertility in a region naturally so unpromising. It reminds us that we have entered the territory of Ephraim, who was blessed with "the precious fruits brought forth by the sun—and the precious things of the lasting hills." The village of Yebrûd is on the left, crowning an isolated eminence, whose sides are belted by tiers of handsome terraces. The skillful hand of intelligent cultivation is evident. The fig orchards are remarkable for their extent and thrifty appearance. And yet the region is exceedingly rough and rocky, as we wind along steep declivities, and cross ravines where many a wintery torrent has rushed and roared. The scenery is picturesque, often wild and enchanting, with old ruins sometimes frowning from the tops of the stony hills.

We soon enter a romantic valley, called Wady-el-Jib. Here, as the first shadows of evening begin to fall, our camping-ground, dotted with white tents, is a pleasant sight. The remains of a large cistern are near, and not far off a stream trickles from the side of a cliff. The appropriate name of this spring is Ain el-Haramîyeh, "the Fountain of Robbers;" and it is said that scarcely a year passes but some bloody tragedy here transpires. It is a strange, wild, lonely spot, yet the adjacent fields are well cultivated. In surveying this narrow, deep glen, in the dark evening, and looking up its terraced sides to the bright stars above, it had the appearance of a vast, oval amphitheater, and reminded me of a night view of the Coliseum at Rome. We slept undisturbed, except, perhaps, by the tramping of a horse or braying of a donkey belonging to our escort. In the bright, fresh morning, we proceeded up the valley, gradually widening, and the hills becoming less steep. In our enjoyment of the fine weather and romantic scenery, we could appreciate the lively description found in the Hand-Book: "The ride through this district in spring is most charming. The terraced hills are so quaint; the winding valleys so picturesque; the wild flowers, anemones, poppies, convolvolus and hollyhocks, so brilliant and so plentiful; the somber foliage of the olive, and deep green of the fig, and bright green of the young corn on the terraces, all give such exquisite hues to the landscape. Add to this the gray ruins perched on rocky hill-tops; and the peasants in their gay dresses—red, and green, and white; and the strings of mules, and donkeys, and camels, defiling along the narrow paths, their bells awaking the echoes; and the Arab with his tufted spear or brass-bound musket; and the shepherd leading his goats along the mountain side, or grouped with them round a fountain; and the traveler from the far west—the oddest figure among them all—with his red face, and white hat, and jaded hack, and nondescript trappings."

We journey on amid such scenes—rocks, hills, valleys, one or two little villages, looking like loose gray stone heaps on the distant oval summits or slopes— and in an hour or so, turning off the main path to the right, we come to a very interesting locality. It is Seilûn, the ancient Shiloh. Naked, rounded hills, with ruins here and there, and a few cultivated fields, mark the place. We passed the remains of an old church, whose walls are supported by buttresses, and within are some broken Corinthian columns. A little farther down the hill is another old building, that may have been a mosque. In front of it is a fine oak tree. Here I read several passages of Scripture relating to Shiloh. Its location is well described in the Book of Judges, as being "on the north side of Bethel, on the east of the highway that goeth up from Bethel to Shechem, and on the south of Lebonah." This is so accurate in every particular, that there cannot be a doubt that we are here on the very site of Shiloh. Here, probably on the top of this little hill, the Tabernacle of the Lord was first permanently set up in the land, being brought hither from the camp at Gilgal. Here the whole congregation of Israel assembled again to receive each his allotted portion of the promised and now accepted possession. Here Elkanah came every year from Ramah to offer sacrifice; here Hannah prayed; here the child Samuel was brought and lent to the Lord by the grateful mother; and here that child served the Lord and heard his voice. Here the aged Eli, who restrained not his sons, fell down dead on receiving intelligence of their death in battle, and the capture of the Ark by the Philistines. Eli was probably buried in one of those rock-hewn sepulchres in the valley a little to the east. The Shiloh maidens were accustomed to dance by themselves at an annual festival held in honor of the Ark. At the foot of the hill are the ruins of an old well, and it was probably there that the scene transpired. The remnant of the Benjamites, who were forbidden to take wives of Israel, lay concealed in the adjacent vineyards on the hillside, and rushing suddenly among the dancing virgins, seized and carried off two hundred of them. How lifelike these distant events appear, when we look upon the localities where they occurred. We can almost see the disguised wife of Jeroboam stealing hither to consult the prophet Ahijah about her sick child. She received no comfort, but rather heard terrible judgments denounced upon the wicked house to which she belonged. Shiloh not only lost its glory in the capture of the Ark, but it would seem, from a passage in Jeremiah, that its ruin was accomplished not long afterwards. "But go ye now unto my place which was in Shiloh, where I set my name at the first, and see what I did to it for the wickedness of my people Israel."

It was an interesting thought, as I was on this journey from Judea to Galilee, that I was passing along the same path, among the same hills and valleys, where our blessed Saviour had journeyed with his disciples. His eyes had rested upon some of the same objects that now greet mine—these rocks, these hillsides, these fountains. Probably He had looked back from Mount Scopus upon the Holy City. He saw Gibeon, and Mizpeh, and Anathoth; He passed through Gibeah, Ramah and Beeroth; He looked upon Bethel and Shiloh. Passing through these localities, then ancient and hallowed by Scripture history and Divine manifestations, on His way to Jacob's Well, what were the thoughts of His mind, to whom all events and all history were equally transparent, and what communications did He make to His disciples by the way!

After gathering a few flowers and other memorials amidst the ruins of Shiloh, we crossed several wheatfields, and descended on the north into a little glen, which we followed westward till we joined the main road. We were now in a beautiful green plain, about a mile in length, enclosed by dark, lofty hills. A narrow ravine through the western ridge affords an outlet for a winter-stream to the plain of Sharon. On a hillside at the left, is the village of Lubban, the modern representative of the city of Lebonah, that in the days of Israel's judges lay between Shiloh and Shechem. Over the beaten path on this level and fertile plain, some of our Arab horses gallop with a fleetness and grace for which they are justly celebrated. We cross a valley at the end of the plain, having passed an old khan or castle on our right, while now and then a village is seen on the stony hills stretching away on either hand. A mountain-like elevation is now before us, which we climb by a long, winding path, among rocks and ridges, gray, bleak and desolate. It is a wearisome ascent, but the vista that opens to the view on reaching the summit is fair, far and beautiful. We stop as if entranced, and silently admire the varied loveliness and splendor of the landscape.

Up to the crest of this ridge our divine Saviour came, on the bright morning of that day when He journeyed with His disciples and rested at noon by Jacob's Well, which, were it an object of sufficient prominence, might be seen from this point. In reflecting that His feet have pressed this soil, and His eyes have looked upon these hills and plains, one wishes that he might have been here to journey with the Lord, to hear His words, and to receive His blessing. And then the thought springs up—Well, the blessed Saviour is still with His disciples, graciously, lovingly present, wherever they are. Did He not say, " Lo, I am with you always ?" and this dear promise, with the fact that He was once bodily here, brings a refreshing and heavenly sweetness to the heart.

" O here with His flock the sad Wanderer came;
These hills He toiled over in grief are the same:
The founts where He drank by the wayside still flow,
And the same airs are blowing which breathed on His brow."

What continually strikes the traveler, and makes Palestine so different from our land and other lands, is the utter absence of forests, the scarcity of trees, and the denuded, discrowned appearance of the hills and mountains, together with the perpetual stoniness, especially of the regions of Judah and Benjamin. But we are now entering a different country. The mountain territory of Ephraim is distinguished for its little fertile plains, several of which we have already passed. We constantly see evidences about us, in the abundance of vines, figs, olives and corn, that Ephraim was blessed with "the chief things of the ancient mountains." It was not in vain the dying patriarch deliberately rested his right hand on the head of Joseph's younger son, and said, " In thee shall Israel bless, saying, God make thee as Ephraim."

The view before us from this high ridge, as we look down northward upon the plain of Moreh, gives us fresh impressions of the exuberant richness of this central portion of Palestine. The plain stretches away for a dozen miles, perhaps, while its breadth, in its widest parts, does not exceed two. Neither fence nor village is seen on its lawn-like surface. A few olive groves fringe its borders, bounded on the east by a low, irregular line of dark hills, and on the west by much higher elevations, whose grand summits are also more bold and barren. The most prominent of these is Mount Gerizim. On its top we see a white wely marking the place where once stood the Samaritan Temple. Mount Ebal, partly hidden, is just beyond; while in the valley between the two is Nablûs, the site of ancient Shechem or Sychar. We descend the hill and enter upon this beautiful plain, now called el-Mukhna. Its great fertility is evident, and thriving corn-fields seem to cover its entire surface. Villages appear on both sides, perched high up on the slopes or summits, built there, not for convenience, but for security. The natives have a wild and fierce appearance, and the men are all armed with long guns, pistols, daggers, and knob-headed clubs. We frequently meet these fellows straggling along in tattered garments, part of them driving donkeys loaded with grain or straw. They all go armed while at work in the fields, watching their flocks among the hills, or on their journeys, lest they shold meet some representative of a hostile tribe or family, and the revenge of an old blood-feud should be gratified in the murder of a new victim.

A few years ago it was unsafe for a time, on account of hostile tribes, for travelers to pass through this region. But no hostile intentions were ever manifested towards us, though the neighborhood has a bad reputation. We are accustomed to address these fierce-looking men, as well as others, when we meet them, with the usual salutations in Arabic, and they almost universally return them with a pleasant recognition and a graceful bow, at the same time bringing their right hand to their forehead, breast and lips.

As we proceed up the plain, we journey under the shadow of Gerizim, the Mountain of Blessing, which rises loftily on our left. Passing along to the point of a low spur projecting from the base of Gerizim to the northeast, we soon reach that very ancient and most interesting spot, *Jacob's Well*. A pile of shapeless ruins, including several fragments of granite columns, lie around it. A vaulted chamber formerly covered the entrance, in the floor of which was the opening to the well. Within a few years a portion of the vault has fallen in, and completely covered up the mouth, so I had not the pleasure of looking down into the depths of the well. We could drop into it, however, a small pebble, through the crevices of the loose stones. The Samaritan woman said to our Saviour, "The well is deep." Travelers have described it as being seventy-five feet deep, excavated in the solid rock, nine feet in diameter, perfectly round, and the sides being smoothly hewn. The few old columns and building-stones lying about are probably the ruins of a church that is said to have been built over this well by Helena, to commemorate a spot so hallowed by the presence of Jesus. Jerome, in the fourth century, speaks of a church being here. There is no doubt about the authenticity of the site. It must be, from its position, and the objects mentioned about it, the identical well where our Divine Lord, weary with his journey up the plain, sat down at midday to rest—just as travelers still stop here in the noon or evening of the spring-day—just as we stopped and sat down on that well a little past noon on the 28th of March. How intensely interesting a place! How vivid the review of its sacred historic scenes! A little to the west of it are the twin mountains Gerizim and Ebal. Between them, in a narrow picturesque valley, is the site of Shechem. A little north of the well is Joseph's Tomb, a small white building, partly embowered in trees. The adjacent plain stretches away in beautiful verdure, covered with the young and growing wheat.

To this place, divinely called and directed, Abraham came from Ur of the Chaldees, and from Haran, and entering this rich plain from the north, pitched here his tent for the first time in the Land of Canaan.

he came to the place of Sichem unto the plain of Moreh." Here he "builded an altar unto the Lord, who appeared unto him," and promised to give this land to him and his posterity. The first altar in the Holy Land must have been within a few rods of the place where we are sitting at the well. Abraham journeyed south to Bethel and Hebron, but his grandson Jacob, many years afterwards, on his return from Padan-aram, having crossed the Jordan with his two bands, "came to Shalem, a city of Shechem, and pitched his tent before"—that is, east of—"the city;" and so it must have been near this spot. "And he bought a parcel of a field, where he had spread his tent, at the hand of the children of Hamor, Shechem's father." On that "parcel" he made his well, and the bones of his son Joseph were brought up from Egypt and buried here, perhaps at the spot now indicated by the little wall-inclosed building known as his tomb. Jacob removed to Hebron, but still retained possession of his field here; and it was to this spot he sent Joseph to look after his brethren, when "a certain man found him wandering in the field," and directed him to Dothan, whither they had gone.

Interesting as this spot is, in its connection with the patriarchs, it had to me a deeper and holier charm in its association with our blessed Lord, who held here a memorable conversation with the woman of Samaria. As we sat on the well, I read aloud that inimitable narrative in the fourth chapter of John's Gospel, and read it with new interest, looking upon objects it mentions. The Divine Man "must needs go" past this spot, when "He left Judea and departed into Galilee." Wearied with the journey, and oppressed by the heat, He sat down at noon by this well. Up that passage in the valley, between Gerizim and Ebal, His disciples went away into the city to buy food. Down the same passage or gorge came the woman to draw water, according to the unvarying custom of the East, which still, in the lively concourse of veiled figures round the wayside wells, reproduces the image of Rebekah and Rachel. She came to this well, instead of procuring water in or near the city, because it might have been of better quality here, or very likely she attached some special sacredness to the water of *Jacob's* Well. "Jesus said unto her, Give me to drink;" and considering the universal hospitality and courtesy of the Orientals, her refusal and reply were indicative of the bigotry and enmity of the Samaritans against the Jews. Then followed the wondrous dialogue which so interested and astonished the woman, as Jesus directed her attention from the well to the Water of Life. "Our fathers worshiped in *this mountain*," said she, pointing, no doubt, to the Samaritan sanctuary full in view on the summit of Gerizim. Our Lord then unfolded the freedom and fullness of the Gospel, dispelling the idea of special virtue or sanctity in particular localities, and announcing the essential spirituality of true worship. His divine words led her to think and speak of the Messiah, and then came the glorious announcement, "I that speak unto thee am He." Her heart had been touched, and her faith received this blessed revelation. She forgot her errand —for she left her water-pot—in the joy of finding her

Saviour, and hastened up the vale to the city to publish the glad tidings.

The disciples had returned, and were conversing with the Lord, while the beautiful plain was spread out before them, verdant with the young wheat, suggesting the beautiful figure: "Say not ye, There are yet four months, and then cometh harvest? Behold, I say unto you, lift up your heads and look on the fields, for they are white already to harvest"—pointing, perhaps, in the other direction up the valley, where the people of Sychar, whom the woman had called, were now flocking down towards Him. It was a harvest of souls that was ready, and the reapers not only received wages, but gathered fruit unto life eternal. O blessed story of Jacob's Well! Though the daughters of Samaria come no more to draw from its depths, yet the Living Water still flows. The footprints of patriarchs are here, and those of Him who is greater than Jacob, and the echo of His heavenly voice lingers here, in the gracious words that fell from His lips.

XXVI.

Nablus—Shechem—Mount Gerizim.

THE Tomb of Joseph is a short distance north of Jacob's Well. The interior of the little building is covered with pilgrims' names in various languages, the Hebrew being quite prominent. Jews and Samaritans, Christians and Moslems, all concur in the belief that this is the veritable spot where the patriarch was buried. This is a portion of that "parcel of ground which Jacob bought of Hamor and gave to his son Joseph." If this ground were excavated, perhaps the sarcophagus might be found in which his embalmed remains were placed, as they were brought out of Egypt to their burial here, according to the Divine record. The tomb has an agreeable situation, and stands a little nearer the base of Ebal than of Gerizim. Turning westward, we are soon in the valley of Nablûs, and the city itself is before us, most picturesquely nestled between the two mountains. Its white domes and slender minarets are gleaming in the sunlight, while gardens and groves surround it. No city in Palestine has a situation and surroundings more romantic and delightful. Corn fields and orchards, abounding in fruit-trees of various kinds, enliven and diversify the view. Fountains and streams murmur at our feet, and most musical bird-songs greet us from the tree-tops. The greater part of the town lies on the south side of the valley, clinging to the base of Gerizim. The fine fertile vale opens like a gateway from the plain of Moreh, and the two mountains rising steeply from its smooth bed, shut it in with their dark rocky sides on the north and south. Nablûs occupies the highest part of the vale, and is the site of ancient Shechem, one of the oldest cities of the world. As we approached the town between these two bold mountains, I thought of that vast assembly and most impressive scene, when the whole congregation of Israel was gathered here to listen to the reading of the Law by Joshua. The valley is narrowest—the mountains come nearest to each other—towards the eastern end. There, no doubt, the immense concourse was gathered. "All Israel, and their elders, and officers, and their judges, stood on this side the ark, and on that side, before the priests and the Levites, which bear the ark of the covenant of the Lord—half of them over against Mount Gerizim, and half of them over against Mount Ebal." What an immense procession was that of the tribes, with the women and children and strangers, that came up here according to the command of Moses. They doubtless swept up the plain, and gathered around the Ark here in this narrow pass. On Gerizim the blessings and on Ebal the cursings were pronounced in the presence of this vast assembly, and their thunders of response were like the sound of many waters. The scene must have been incomparably august and impressive. And now I was passing along the very spot where that immense multitude stood thirty-three centuries ago, and the echoes of the blessings and cursings, with the mighty AMEN from the answering throng, seem to linger amid the cliffs of those sublime mountains, still bearing their ancient names, and still silently, boldly witnessing to the truth of the inspired record.

We enter the city of Nablûs, and ride through its long street, partly flooded, nearly its whole length, with a fine stream of water. The houses and shops, full of staring people, are thickly ranged on either side, and sometimes built on arches spanning the narrow path. Our camping-ground is an olive grove, just outside of the city, on one of the lower slopes of Gerizim. The city is larger than I supposed, and contains a population of about eight thousand, including some five hundred Christians, one hundred and fifty Samaritans, and a still smaller number of Jews.

During the rule of the Judges, Abimelech seized Shechem, and was proclaimed king by "the oak of the pillar." This was the occasion of Jotham's ascending Mount Gerizim, and lifting up his voice, addressed the Shechemites in that beautiful and cutting parable of the trees going forth to anoint a king over them; and as one after another refused, they called the *bramble* to reign over them. Here Rehoboam, son of Solomon, was declared king over all Israel. But soon after, in consequence of his folly, the ten tribes revolted, making Jeroboam the son of Nebat king, and establishing the seat of the new monarchy in Shechem, which subsequently yielded the honor to Samaria. It became, however, the metropolis of the Samaritans as a sect, and remains so still. The Emperor Vespasian rebuilt Shechem, and called it Neäpolis, from which the present Arabic Nablûs is derived. Justin Martyr, whose interesting account of the early Christians has been preserved, was a native of this place, where he was born in the latter part of the first century. Nablûs appears to be a thriving city; its business is considerable, and its chief productions are soap, cotton and oil. The last is celebrated for its excellence. The olive groves, so abundant in the Holy Land, are very numerous here. Every village and hamlet is embowered in these pleasant and evergreen trees. The olive matures slowly, lives long, and is the most productive of all trees or crops. It constitutes a great part of the wealth and comfort of the people. The berries are pickled and eaten as a relish. All dishes are cooked in oil. It supplies the lamps in every dwelling. All the soap in the country is made from it. Isaiah speaks of "the shaking of an olive tree." The berries ripen in November, are shaken from the trees by men, and picked up by women and children, who carry them away on their heads. They are placed in the circular cavity of a rock, and a large stone rolled over them. The crushed mass is gathered into mats, and put into the rude press. The liquor flows off, is heated slightly, and the oil is skimmed from the top, and poured into skins or earthern jars.

I was not willing to forego a visit to the site of the Samaritan Temple, and the gratification of a view from the summit of Gerizim. About four o'clock in the afternoon, a few of us began the ascent. It was a long and fatiguing, as well as agreeable walk. The steep path follows a beautiful glen south of the town, and is for some distance bordered by dwellings embowered in a variety of foliage, palm-trees, and bold cliffs. Birds sing in the boughs, and streams murmur at our feet. We pass women and children, having an unusually cheerful and agreeable appearance. Soon we get above trees and fountains, and find a long and very steep ascent to climb. At the top a broad and broken plateau stretches out before us. Loose stones are abundant, but the soil is here and there cultivated in little patches. We proceed along eastward about half a mile over this dreary surface to the base of a rocky knoll, which is the summit of the mountain. Here is a little spot of level ground where the Samaritans encamp at their Feast of the Passover. Near by is a circular pit, in which the Paschal lambs are roasted. We reach the summit by an ascent of about two hundred yards, and find there the remains of an immense structure of huge stones, old and massive walls, towers, and various apartments. The main edifice appears to have been nearly square, each side measuring about two hundred and fifty feet. At the northern side is a conspicuous Moslem wely. These ruins indicate the site of the Samaritan Temple, though a more modern edifice, perhaps a Roman fortress, may have been built over its foundation-stones. To the Samaritans this is a sacred place, and they locate around it several events in Jewish history, which elsewhere transpired. For instance, under the western wall there are a number of flat stones, and we are told by some that *under* these are placed the "twelve stones" brought out of the bed of the Jordan, while others affirm that these are the veritable stones themselves. A smooth surface of natural rock lies a little south of these ruins, its western edge terminating in an irregular excavation or rocky pit, in which I observed water. Here is the Samaritan shrine, or "Holy of holies," towards which they turn in prayer, and on approaching which they take off their shoes. They have a tradition that on this rock Abraham sacrificed the ram, instead of his son. Our guide tried hard to make us understand just where Isaac was laid on the altar, and where the ram was caught in the thicket. Here, they say, Jacob had his heavenly vision, and named the place Bethel; and that here the Ark was placed, and the Tabernacle set up. It was important for the Samaritans, being imitators and rivals as well as haters of the Jews, to locate these events in their own territory; and what place so befitting as Mount Gerizim?

This rocky knoll rises like a crest from the broad summit of the mountain, and almost overhangs the beautiful plain on the east. The view here is diversified, charming, glorious. I shall never forget the vision presented, as I stood amidst those old ruins in the mellow rays of the declining sun on a vernal day. The rich and velvety plain of Moreh, or Mukhna, is at my feet. A green arm of it breaks into the dark hills on the east, directly across from the vale of Nablûs. A village north of that arm, in a cluster of olive trees on an acclivity, is called Salim, and it may occupy the site of that ancient "Shalem, a city of Shechem," near which Jacob pitched his tent when he returned from Padan-aram. Yonder, at the northeast, the patriarch crossed the Jordan with his two bands, coming through the deep cleft in the dark mountain-wall beyond, made by the Jabbok in its flow toward the Jordan. Through the same vale, no doubt, Abram came from the land of the Chaldees, and pitched his tent near the place of Jacob's Well, which I see beneath me. The eastern view is bounded by the long, somber mountain-chain of Gilead and Moab. On the north, the eye traces rugged ridges and rounded peaks succeeding each other till the far climax is reached in the shadowy form and snowy crown of Hermon. On the west, through breaks and gorges among the hills, I get glimpses of the plain of Sharon, and of the glassy, cloud-like surface of the Mediterranean Sea, stretching away beyond. All around me are the mountains of Ephraim—the stronghold and rich possession of the house of Joseph. The fertile plains and winding vales below are verdant with the growing corn, and are clothed with the fatness of the olive and the vine. " Joseph is a fruitful bough, even a fruitful bough by a well, whose branches run over the wall." There are many examples of the practical foresight and sagacity of Jacob, and these traits are strikingly illustrated in his securing this rich possession in the heart of Canaan, and reserving it for his favorite son. "The blessings of thy father have prevailed above the blessings of thy progenitors, unto the utmost bound of the everlasting hills; they shall be on the head of Joseph, and on the crown of the head of him that was separate from his brethren."

The next morning was bright and clear, and the sun rose in golden beauty upon our tents, while we were greeted with bird-songs of peculiar sweetness.

After breakfast we were conducted, through the most filthy of lanes and tunnel-like alleys, to the Samaritan synagogue in the south part of Nablûs. It is a small old building, and we were required to remove our boots and shoes, and enter it in our stocking-feet. There we were shown a famous copy of the Pentateuch. The parchment was unrolled from its tin case, and we inspected the venerable manuscript, said to have been written by Abishua, the son of Phinehas, the son of Eleazar, the son of Aaron, and so must be about three thousand three hundred years old. It is a huge roll, dingy and patched, and sufficiently curious to attract attention.

The Samaritans still observe their ancient rites, and in solemn processions go three times a year to the top of Gerizim, reading the Law as they ascend. These occasions are the Feast of the Passover, the Day of Pentecost, and the Feast of Tabernacles. On Friday evening they pray in their houses, and on Saturday—their Sabbath—in their synagogue, accompanying the public services with various prostrations, and loud and hurried recitations. It is a singular fact that their number—hardly a hundred and fifty, all told—has remained about the same for several centuries. They still hate the Jews as cordially as they did when the woman declared to our Lord that the two nations had no dealings with each other. This rule is sometimes departed from when they can strike a good bargain in business or trade.

We left our camping-ground amid the songs of birds in the olive groves, in strange contrast with the moaning importunity of begging lepers, reaching forth their stumps of hands, and upturning their terribly disfigured faces. Perhaps they are the descendants of Gehazi, the dishonest servant of Elisha, on whom the curse of this fearful disease was pronounced forever. The road from Nablûs to Samaria is, like all the other roads in the Holy Land, a foot or bridle-path, winding among hills and valleys. There are no fences to protect the fields, which are cultivated close to the path, so that some of the seed scattered by the sower would naturally fall "by the wayside." The "stony places" are abundant, and the plant that has "no deepness of earth" is soon "scorched" by the hot Syrian sun. As we descend from the city, leaving Gerizim and Ebal behind, but still follow the valley that divides them, we find, for some distance, an exceedingly rich, well-cultivated and picturesque region, abounding in orchards of olive, fig, apricot, apple, and pomegranate, intermingled with gardens and vineyards, and murmuring waters, rushing on in their natural or artificial channels, now turning a mill-wheel, and then forming a cascade amidst old Roman ruins. Flowers of different forms and hues border and fringe our path. Fields of wheat and barley, and one of oats—the only one I recollect to have seen—are observed as we proceed. Long lines of donkeys, and camels tied one behind the other, and heavily laden with sacks of wheat and flour, pass us with their Arab attendants. We find shepherds with their flocks at some fountain near the wayside, or going "before them" among the hills, and calling their own sheep by name. In rough places, I have seen the shepherd with a lamb under his arm, and another in his bosom, its little head protruding from the opening in the loose garment above the girdle—recalling at once the beautiful prophecy of the Good Shepherd: "He shall gather the lambs with his arm, and carry them in his bosom." It is easy to see how quickly the eye of the "shepherd divideth his sheep from the goats," as the former are white and the latter black. Savage-looking Bedawîn, crossing our path, or ranging the fields, are frequently seen, wretchedly clad, and armed with long clubs having knotty heads, and often with old rusty guns on their shoulders, and daggers in their girdles. The valley grows broader as we proceed, and turning to the right, we climb among the hills, while a considerable plain lies off to our left. Village after village meets the eye on the round tops of the hills, or clinging to their slopes amid the rocks.

XXVII.

Samaria—Dothan—Passes of Manasseh.

Having arrived at the top of a ridge commanding a wide view, our eyes fasten with deep interest on the "hill Samaria," which King Omri bought of Shemer, and where he erected his palace, before Homer began to sing his wonderful songs in the villages of Greece. This bell-shaped hill rises about six hundred feet above the broad green valleys that separate it from the encircling mountains beyond. It has a fine plateau on the summit, hardly reached by the modern village clinging to the eastern slope. The situation is splendid, and the landscape enchanting. No wonder it attracted the eye of King Omri, as the seat of his capital and palace. It is a beautiful gem among the hills of Ephraim, set in as rich a framework as the country affords.

Descending the long slope into the valley among olive trees, we then climb the hill Samaria by a short, steep acclivity amidst rubbish and ruins. In the walls of the village houses and in the walls of the terraces on the hillside are seen various relics of ancient structures that must have been ample and gorgeous. Near the summit on the east is the ruined Church of Saint John, now used for a mosque. It is a conspicuous object, and once must have been a splendid edifice. Its roof is gone, but its walls of hewn-stone and Gothic window-spaces remain. It was built in honor of John the Baptist, as there is an old tradition that here he was buried, a deep excavation in the rock under the church being still shown as his tomb. Subsequently this spot was also regarded as the place of his imprisonment and execution. Passing along the southern brow of the hill shaded with olive groves, we observe by the way a large number of round stone columns standing erect in the soil—I should think there must be a hundred of them—while others lie prostrate amid masses of ruins. I noticed also in a terrace-wall a single Corinthian capital, a relic of those that once crowned these columns. They must have formed a part of some magnificent temple, or grand colonnade. They are about two feet in diameter at the base and rise above the ground perhaps a dozen feet, and extend for quite a distance around to the western brow of the hill. Perhaps they were the ornaments of a magnificent street, and indicate the splendor of the city in which they stood. But they are now the grim skeletons of a glory departed, and the hill that once glittered with palaces and temples is almost as bare as it was when Israel's king bought it. Looking from amidst " these solitary columns shooting up from clustering vines and green corn, on the piles of hewn stones in the little terraced fields, and on the great heaps among the olive trees below, we cannot but recall the striking, the fearful prediction of Micah," that has been so remarkably verified: "I will make Samaria as an heap of the field; and I will pour down the stones thereof into the valley, and I will discover the foundation thereof."

The present inhabitants, about four hundred in all, have a bad name, and are sometimes insolent and troublesome to travelers. A number of them, including a group of children, followed us around the hill, but did little more than to wall up in one instance our path. As we descended the northern slope we observed in a nook or depression of a green open field, a striking group of standing columns similar to those already described. They are probably the remains of some structure built by Herod the Great, who erected magnificent edifices in Samaria, and gave it the name of *Sebaste*, in honor of Augustus, it being the name of the Emperor rendered into Greek. The Arabs call it Sebustieh.

Samaria had an eventful and chequered history. It was the capital of Israel about forty years, and was often the seat of idolatry and crime. Ahab, adopting the religion of his Sidonian wife, built here a temple for Baal, which was destroyed with a great slaughter of idolators by the impetuous Jehu. From those mountains of Gilead at the east came the bold and wonderful prophet Elijah to rebuke the wicked king, and herald the long drouth. Probably in the vale at the northern foot of the hill were encamped the great besieging army of Benhadad from Damascus, so signally defeated by a handful of Israelites. Ahab was fatally pierced by an arrow from "the bow drawn at a venture," in the battle which he and Jehoshaphat fought against the Syrians for the recovery of Ramoth-Gilead. His blood-stained chariot returned from the valley of the Jordan with his dead body to Samaria. Here he was buried; "and one washed the chariot in the pool of Samaria"—perhaps the same reservoir that still exists near the old church. Here Elisha had his home for a time, and several striking events in his history occurred. Up the northern slope of this hill he must have led the Syrian army struck blind at Dothan. Here came, through the influence of a captive Hebrew maid, the Syrian captain Naaman to be cured of his leprosy, and applying to Elisha probably at Gilgal, was directed to wash in the Jordan. Here was the scene of the interesting story of the four leprous men sitting at the entering in of the gate, during a Syrian seige when the famine was so severe that women killed and eat their infant sons. Here came Philip, after the death of Stephen, and preached the Gospel with wonderful success, where the sorcerer Simon had long thrived by his impostures. Under the monarchs of the northern kingdom, and under Herod the Great, the city was distinguished for its glaring idolatries and monstrous crimes, as well as for its beauty and grandeur. Its present condition repeats the prophecy: "Samaria shall become desolate, for she hath rebelled against her God."

In leaving Samaria we found the northern slope of the hill and the valley below entirely devoid of trees and presenting a dreary appearance. We are passing now from the territory of Ephraim to that of Manasseh. From the valley we wind up a rocky acclivity, and pass over terraced hills and among orange groves and little villages here and there on the slopes or summits. Now, as we rise to a mountain-like ridge, a glorious panorama is spread out before us. A little green plain, rich and fertile, seems a beautiful picture in a rough rock-frame, while vine-clad hills and verdant valleys relieve and diversify the scene. One of the largest villages we pass is Jeba, a flourishing place, quite picturesquely situated on a slope looking down into a green vale, and surrounded by the thriving olive and fig and fragrant thyme. Here is an intersecting road direct from Nablûs. Emerging from our course through a narrow valley half an hour beyond, we come to the circular plain of Sanûr. It is three or four miles in diameter, has a low, marshy, lake-like appearance, a portion of it being covered with water. Having no outlet through the surrounding hills a large body of water collects here in winter, but it dries up in summer, and the plain is then cultivated. The natives call it the "Drowning Meadow." At the southwest corner of this plain is the village of Sanûr, enclosed by a fortress, and inhabited by a rude, turbulent, and quarrelsome people, whose acquaintance some travelers have found to be decidedly disagreeable. About a mile beyond this plain we obtain a fine and splendid view from the crest of a rocky ridge. Before and below us is the village of Kŭbatieh, nestled among flourishing groves of olive, while to the west of it there is a beautiful net-work of plains and vales. Northward we can look through these passes of Manasseh into the great plain of Esdraelon, whose broad green surface stretches away to the hills of Nazareth.

We are now about six miles from Samaria and twelve from Shechem. Here, under the shade of an old olive, we spread our carpet and sit down for lunch. And here let us read and think of the interesting and thrilling events that have transpired in that beautiful and fertile spot a little west of us. There is a charming green plain with adjacent rounded hills—a most delightful place, admirably adapted for pasture-grounds and the feeding of flocks. That verdant hill near the southern side o the plain still bears the familiar name of *Dothan*—or Tell Dothain—doubtless the same spot that bore that name three thousand six hundred years ago. Jacob was then living in Hebron, and from thence came his favorite son Joseph to inquire after the welfare of his shepherd brethren. Not finding them near Shechem, he was directed hither where they had removed with their flocks. As he came to the top of the hill we have just ascended, and which overlooks Dothan, "they saw him afar off," recognizing his brilliant robe, and in their envy, "conspired against him to slay him." Perhaps a diligent search would be rewarded by finding the identical pit into which Joseph was cast. These pits, or dry cisterns, are common in Palestine. I have seen them in various places; there are some on the Mount of Olives. The opening, three or four feet in diameter, is level with the ground, and they may be twelve feet deep, and about the same at their largest diameter, being circular in form. The sides are smoothly plastered or cemented, and a person falling into one of them, as sometimes happens, could not get out without help. These pits are often referred to in the Bible. They are the store-houses of the farmers. All kinds of grain, after being threshed and winowed, are housed in them. They are perfectly dry and tight; and the opening being hermetically sealed and covered with earth, grain and other stores are there safe from rats, mice and ants, and also concealed from robbers. In Jeremiah there is an account of ten men saving themselves from Ishmael's slaughters by saying, "Slay us not, for we have treasures in the field, of wheat, and of barley, and of oil, and of honey." Their treasures were hid in these dry cisterns or pits. Poor Joseph's cries were disregarded, and his cruel brothers sold him to Midianite merchants passing with their loaded camels from regions beyond the Jordan down to Egypt, just as they do at this day over the same thoroughfare. Indeed, I saw in that vicinity some of these trading Ishmaelite caravans moving down in the same direction.

Another wonderful event transpired at Dothan. More than eight hundred years after Joseph came here, that hill around which his brethren watered their flocks, was crowned with a city, and for a time it was the resort of the prophet Elisha. The king of Syria was at war with the Israelites and sent his armies to attack them at Samaria. Elisha, anticipating his movements, often thwarted his purposes. Enraged against the prophet, he sent a legion to Dothan to take him. The army came down through these mountain passes, and with their horses and chariots, "a great host," surrounded the city. This was done in the silence of the night, and Elisha's servant in the early morning was overwhelmed at the sight. "Alas, my master! how shall we do?" The calm and trusting prophet replied: "Fear not; for they that be with us are more than they that be with them." And as he prayed that the young man's eyes might be opened—

> The earthly film before his face
> Was drawn aside, and in its place
> Came a soft medium, crystal clear,
> In which celestial things appear.
> Bright glories, crowning Dothan's hill,
> His raptured spirit strangely thrill;
> All round the dazzling height he sees,
> Amid the rocks and through the trees,
> A white-robed host in armor bright—
> Chariots of fire and steeds of light.

In this vision of those ministers of flaming fire that God sends to aid His people, the servant saw the words of his master verified. There are always more for them than against them. The prophet prays again, and the Syrian host are smitten with blindness, and he leads them at will to Samaria. How interesting to look upon the hill once crowned and blazing with that glorious heavenly army! Precious are the lessons of Dothan, and a blessed thought is suggested to the traveler far from home: "He shall give His angels charge over thee, to keep thee in all thy ways."

Soon after resuming our journey we past through the large village of Kŭbatîeh, finely located in a fruitful and romantic region abounding in olive-trees of uncommon size and thrift. A few miles, winding along the plain, over a rocky plateau, and through a verdant glen with terraced sides, bring us to the northern frontier of the central hills of Palestine—a region rich in Scripture associations. Among these hills Gideon was reared, the great captain of Manasseh, whose territory lay along this frontier from the distant hills of Bashan and Gilead beyond the Jordan valley on the east, to Carmel and the sea on the west. Here, as the hills break down into Esdraelon, we cross the boundary between the provinces of Samaria and Galilee; and these are the passes that were so often defended against the invaders from the north, by the " horns" of Joseph, the " ten thousands of Ephraim, and the thousands of Manasseh."

Our tents are pitched just west of Jenîn, on the border of the green plain of Esdraelon, and beside a clear, flowing brook—a part of the river Kishon near its sources. Jenîn, whose Scripture name is En-gannin, a city of Issachar, is pleasantly situated on a slope that overlooks the great and fertile plain. Rich gardens, hedged with tall cactus or prickly pear, skirt the base of the hills, which rise somewhat steeply back of the town, while a few palm-trees below give an oriental aspect to the place. It contains a population perhaps exceeding two thousand, all Moslems, and of a quarreling disposition. En-gannim signifies the " Fountain of Gardens," and the fountain which made its ancient gardens so flourishing still flows to enrich and beautify its present gardens. It is a pleasant spot to spend the night. I walked out by the stream in the evening, thinking of the wonderful events that had transpired at Dothan, and looking at the sweet stars so beautifully bright in the clear skies of the Holy Land. The croaking of frogs by the brook, the first I had heard, recalled familiar sounds of the spring-time and the streams in childhood days.

XXVIII.

Plain of Esdraelon—Jezreel—Shunem—Nain.

BEAUTIFUL, clear, balmy and delicious was the Spring morning when we left our camping ground at Jenîn. Our course was northerly, leaving at this point the mountains and passes of Manasseh, and the crystal brook, one of the sources of the Kishon, that had murmured by our tents through the night. We were now in the margin of the great plain of Esdraelon, so memorable as the ancient battle-field of nations. To the traveler who has wandered over the "hill country" and "wilderness" of Judea, the mountains of Benjamin, Ephraim and Manasseh, including the hills of Samaria, the contrast presented by the aspect of Issachar and Zebulon, especially Issachar, as seen in this broad, smooth and fertile plain, is as striking as it is pleasing. I was surprised at the perpetual hilliness and stoniness of southern and central Palestine, and delighted to find a region here in Galilee so entirely different. The form of this grand plain approaches a triangle, the eastern side running along on the margin of the Jordan valley, the northern by the mountains of Galilee to Carmel, and the southwestern by the northern base of the Samaritan hills. A line from these hills to those of Galilee on the north, which are the roots of Lebanon, passes through the central and widest part of the plain, a distance of about eighteen miles; and this is what is called in Scripture the Valley of Megiddo. Its only river is the Kishon, so fatal to the army of Sisera, flowing to the northwest and emptying into the Mediterranean near Mount Carmel, where there is an opening to the plain of Acre. From Esdraelon on the east, three valleys break down to the Jordan; the first between the hills at Jenîn and Mount Gilboa, the second between Gilboa and Little Hermon, and the third between Little Hermon and Mount Tabor. The central one is properly the ancient valley of Jezreel—the richest and most celebrated—the scene of great events in Bible history. This in time gave its name to the whole plain; Esdraelon being only the Greek rendering of Jezreel.

The appearance of this vast plain of Esdraelon as I beheld it and journeyed through it in the blooming springtime, was that of a beautiful prairie, not entirely level, but in portions undulating—an unbroken expanse of verdure. The rank grass and weeds, and the luxuriant cornfields, or young wheat, on the few spots cultivated, give ample evidence of the fertility of the soil. Still, as you scarcely see an inhabited village on its whole broad surface, so much of which is mere waste land, there is an aspect of desolation amidst living beauty. Lawless Bedawîn, from beyond the Jordan, sweep over it on their fleet Arabian horses and escape with their plunder in defiance of an inefficient government. From earliest history, it has never been secure. The iron chariots of the old Canaanites rolled over it in triumph; the Midianites, and the Amalekites, the Philistines, and the

Syrians, in turn, devastated it with their hostile caravans and armies. In the division of the land this plain fell to Issachar, a tribe that found it difficult to maintain their exposed possession, and so became somewhat assimilated to their heathen neighbors and even their tributaries. Only once did they shake off the Canaanite yoke, when hard pressed by Sisera, "the princes of Issachar were with Deborah." "Issachar is a strong ass, crouching down between two burdens; and he saw that rest was good, and the land that it was pleasant; and bowed his shoulder to bear, and became a servant unto tribute."

Wonderful events have transpired on this plain and the mountains that border it, and it is deeply interesting to look upon these ancient and Scripture-hallowed localities. On the left are visible the sites of Taanach and Megiddo—the scene of two great battles, one a grand victory for Israel in the complete rout of the hosts of Jabin and Sisera, the other a sad defeat, in which the good King Josiah was slain by the Egyptian archers of Pharaoh-Necho. But a more prominent object is Mount Gilboa, on our right, associated with Saul, and Jonathan, and Gideon—with sad memories of death, and touching, tender lamentations over those slain upon their high places. Its naked ridge rises up a few hundred feet, and its summit is crowned with a village. Its jagged brow is bleak and bare, reminding us of the pathetic strain of David: "Ye mountains of Gilboa, let there be no rains upon you, neither dew, nor field of offerings; for there the shield of the mighty was vilely cast away—the shield of Saul as though he had not been annointed with oil." Our path is close by its western base, and leads us over into the valley of Jezreel.

We soon reach and ascend a little round elevation in the midst of the valley. A cluster of wretched houses and an old tower crown the hill. Here, on this commanding and beautiful spot stood the ancient and splendid city of Jezreel. The country around is luxuriantly rich—the velvet lawn of verdure stretching away to Carmel on the west and to the Jordan on the east; to Little Hermon on the north, and to Gilboa on the southeast. So fine and central a situation might well be coveted by Ahab and his queen as the seat of their court. Round the village, called Zerin, are heaps of rubbish, a number of artificial caves or cisterns, used as store-houses for grain, and several sarcophagi of hewn stone, serving the purpose of watering-troughs. Yet this is royal Jezreel where Ahab built his palace, and the scene of some of the bloodiest tragedies on record. We look down the eastern slope of the hill and recall the sad story of Naboth and his vineyard which doubtless was there. The crafty and cruel Jezebel had procured his death; and as Ahab went to take possession of the vineyard he was met by Elijah with words of terrible denunciation and doom. Up that valley from the Jordan we see how Jehu's troops might be observed advancing—his own furious driving being watched from the tower that stood perhaps where this old tower now stands. In that vineyard he met the two sovereigns, and sent a deadly arrow to the heart of Joram, while Ahaziah fled over the plain toward the "garden-house," or En-gannim, but was overtaken and wounded, and died at Megiddo. As

Jehu reached the open space by the gate, the disguised Jezebel was thrown from a window of her palace-chamber and trampled under the hoofs of his horses. Around the dead queen the voracious dogs gathered and feasted, as to this day they prowl about these old mounds for whatever may be thrown out to them. The heads of the seventy sons of Ahab were brought here in baskets, and lay in "two heaps at the entering in of the gate until the morning." These events of Bible history are most strikingly ilustrated and confirmed by the natural features around us.

Looking down the green valley at the east we see a rounded hill, the site of ancient Bethshean. It was one of the Canaanite strongholds. To its wall the dead bodies of Saul and his sons were fastened. They had been slain on the heights of Gilboa, just south of it, now in full view from Jezreel. Beyond Bethshean is the bed of the Jordan, and over that, loom up the dark mountains of Gilead and Bashan.

At the northern base of Gilboa there is a large fountain—a noted spot in sacred history—the scene of one of the most memorable victories, and of one of the most memorable defeats, in the annals of Israel. At this fountain or the brook flowing from it, the three hundred men of Gibeon lapped, and here is where they conquered the Midianites and their allies, as they broke their pitchers, blew their trumpets, and shouted on the midnight air the wild war-cry, "The sword of the Lord and of Gideon!" Here, too, was fought the battle in which Saul was overcome by the Philistines.

Two or three miles to the northwest of Jezreel we

see a mound in the plain, the seat of a fortification in the times of the Crusades, and remarkable in recent times as the central point of the battle between the Turks and the French led by the brave Kleber under Napoleon, called the Battle of Mount Tabor, in which three thousand French soldiers "resisted successfully ten times their number, during the period of six hours in an open plain."

We descend the hill on which Jezreel was situated, and pass in the valley an encampment of wild Bedawîn—their tents "black as the tents of Kedar," and not differing materially from those of their ancestors, the Midianites, in the days of Gideon, near three thousand years ago, when they filled this valley like grasshoppers in multitude. They came for the purpose of plunder, as do their descendants. Passing through rich cornfields and ascending the slope on the northern side of the valley at the southwestern base of Little Hermon, we come to the village of Sulem, suggesting the name Shunem, which was here. Rank and lofty hedges of prickly pear border like a wall this thrifty place. Here the Philistines encamped before the battle of Gilboa. But as the scene of the touching story of the Shunamite woman which I read here, this spot awakens a deep and lively interest. Here dwelt "that great woman," the hospitality of whose house the man of God shared. She with her husband built and furnished for Elisha a little chamber on the wall, where the wayfaring prophet found a cordial welcome and a home. Houses are still seen with such a chamber on a corner of the flat roof. Into one of those fine cornfields on the plain south of the village went the dear child to his father among the reapers; and there under the hot sun in time of harvest—just as would happen now unless particular care were taken to shield the head—he sank under a sun-stroke, and was carried home to his mother, and sat on her knees till noon, and then he died. Poor woman! She laid him on the prophet's bed, and hastened to him at Carmel, at least twelve miles distant; and I could see over the level plain the whole way that she traveled to the mountain. "Is it well with the child?" That must have been a trying question, but her faith failed not.

As we passed through the village I observed a woman by the wayside winnowing wheat, and she pleasantly gave me a handful of it—so I brought home some wheat which very likely grew on the identical field where the Shunamite's boy went out to the reapers. I wondered what interest the present mothers of Shunem take in this tender story, and whether, when any of their children die, they think of the prophet's chamber, and the sad mother's journey to Carmel, and long for some Elisha to come with power to revive their dear dead ones! Whenever I made inquiry of the people living in Scripture localities, they seemed to have a knowledge of the events that had there transpired, but manifested very little interest in them.

A little way beyond Shunem, passing around the western base of Little Hermon, we had our first view of Mount Tabor, five or six miles distant over the level plain, from which it rises in beautiful form and outline, a perfect gem of a mountain, exciting our admiration and delight. It looks not much like any picture I ever saw of it, but rather like the segment of a great sphere, dotted with trees to its summit. It has a charming grace of proportion and position that surpass our expectations. From the slope of Little Hermon I enjoyed a wide and enchanting prospect. As we journeyed towards Tabor, I noticed a little village about two miles to the right of us. Inquiring of Ibrahim what place it was, and learning that it was *Nain*, I was unwilling to pass by, as we were doing, a place of such sacred and tender interest, without an actual visit. I mentioned this to one of our company near me, and proposed to strike off for Nain. He seconded the proposal; and just then seeing a path leading in that direction, I shouted, Ho! for Nain! and galloped away; but no one followed. Perilous though it might be; I ventured on alone, and visited that memorable place—the same Nain where our blessed Saviour wrought one of His great and glorious miracles. Its houses are few and poor, but its situation nestled on the slope of Little Hermon, commands a wide view over the plain and the mountains of Galilee. Heaps of rubbish and old building-stones lie around the village. Caves and tombs in the hillside a little southeast of the town no doubt mark its ancient cemetery. To that spot, winding around the northern part of the city, the funeral procession, with the dead young man on an open bier, was moving with a weeping train, when it was met by another large procession, coming down the slope from the northeast, with Jesus at its head! Blessed and tender words were those to the sorrowing mother—

"Weep not." Never was another funeral procession thus stopped and dismissed! Sweet Nain! It was a precious privilege to visit it and look upon the existing though silent witnesses of the glorious miracle. Seeing an old man and woman washing clothes at a fountain as I was leaving the village, I inquired for a nearer way to Jebel et-Tûr, or Mount Tabor. They kindly directed me to the right path, and I soon overtook the party.

Endor, like Nain, clings to one of the lower slopes of Little Hermon. We saw it on our right, a small village, and remarkable as the home of the witch whom Saul consulted the night before his death. He looked from his camp at the base of Gilboa across the valley to the host of the Philistines at Shunem. "He was afraid, and his heart greatly trembled." In his desperation he commits this last great error. The sun had gone down over Mount Carmel, and in the darkness of the night the king, with his two attendants, steals across the valley of Jezreel, leaves the camp of the Philistines on his left, winds over Little Hermon just east of Nain, and descends the declivity to Endor. Perhaps in one of those wild cavern-like excavations, a suitable home for a witch, the interview transpired, with the astonishing appearance of Samuel, predicting the defeat of Israel and the death of Saul and his sons on the morrow. With a heavy heart the doomed king must have retraced his steps amid shadows prophetic of a gloomier night.

Another hour over the rich, verdant plain brings us to the base of that beautiful and memorable mountain, Tabor. Our tents are pitched in the border of a little village called Deburieh, probably the site of Daberath mentioned in Joshua and elsewhere, but suggesting the name Deborah; for here was the scene of her wonderful exploits. As she gave the signal on the summit of Tabor, Barak with the troops rushed down the slope, perhaps at this spot, and met the mighty foe out on that beautiful plain of Megiddo, where "the stars in their courses fought against Sisera," and where "the river Kishon swept them away, that ancient river the river Kishon."

> "Here sleep the still rocks and the caverns which rang
> To the song which the beautiful prophetess sang,
> When the princes of Issachar stood by her side,
> And the shout of a host in its triumph replied."

XXIX.

Mount Tabor and the Sea of Galilee.

AROUND the mountains and plains, the hills and valleys of Palestine, what sacred associations cluster! How favored are the eyes that look upon those rocky slopes and summits, those green vales and wild glens, the crystal fountain, stream, or lake—the same as of old—and how privileged the feet that tread where mighty warriors, royal monarchs, inspired prophets and apostles, and, above all, the world's Redeemer, left their foot-prints! So I felt as we began the ascent of Mount Tabor about three o'clock in the afternoon. Our path wound around the western base of the mountain where by a narrow vale it is separated from the hills about Nazareth. We passed over to the northern side in our gradual ascent, and found it considerably covered with moderate-sized trees, mostly oak, crowned with a fresh, green, luxuriant foliage. We saw no other hill or mountain in Palestine adorned with such a forest. It was a pleasant and home-like sight. It required three-quarters of an hour to reach the summit—not quite two thousand feet above the sea-level—and in some places the path was so steep and rocky that our horses found it difficult to pick their way along. On the summit is an oblong area or nearly level surface about half a mile in length east and west and a quarter of a mile in width, surrounded by masses of old masonry or wall-like structures built on ledges of the natural rock. The best preserved of these relics is a Saracenic arch called the "Tower of the Winds." Tangled thickets of thorn, dwarf oak, and rank thistles, half cover the ruins, rendering some places difficult of exploration. Here and there are found deep cisterns or pits hewn in the rock. The center of the area is an open space of garden-like beauty— a grassy lawn beaming with gay and lovely flowers. Among the ruins near this there is a human habitation occupied by one or two monks or hermits. Priests of the Latin and Greek churches come here at certain festival seasons to perform mass or other services.

But the eye is eager to be drinking in the glorious views which this mountain-top affords. It is a vernal afternoon, clear and still; the sun is nearing the horizon over the hills of Nazareth, and the whole scene with its associations—the far-spread panorama of diversified objects of strange and sacred interest— seems to throw an extatic spell over the mind as I stand on that old gray-grown arch, the highest point, and look around in every direction with silent wonder and inexpressible delight. First of all, I am looking over the plain toward the northeast to a vast crater-like opening or basin, some fifteen miles distant, where I know reposes the most memorable, sacred and lovely lake in the world. Yes, there it is—the SEA OF GALILEE!—and I see it now, a glimpse of its clear waters at its northwestern shore, near the sites of Capernaum, Chorasin and Bethsaida. O blessed vision—rapturous moment! The long-cherished desire is being fulfilled. I behold a portion of that sea to which I have so often gone in thought and imagination and lingered round its shores and glanced over its smooth or storm-tossed surface, as I have traced there the footsteps of Jesus, listened to His wondrous words and witnessed His stupendous miracles.

> "Blue sea of the hills!—in my spirit I hear
> Thy waters, Gennesaret, chime on my ear;
> Where the Lowly and Great with the people sat down,
> And thy spray on the dust of His sandals was thrown.
>
> "Beyond are Bethulia's mountains of green,
> And the desolate hills of the wild Gadarene;
> And I pause on the goat-crags of Tabor to see
> The gleam of thy waters, O dark Galilee!"

The view on every hand is magnificent. The course of the Jordan for a long distance can be traced, and still further east a boundless perspective of hills and valleys stretches over ancient Gilead and Bashan. Directly south, reaching even to the hills of Samaria, lies the vast and beautiful plain of Esdraelon—the renowned valley of Megiddo—an unbroken expanse of verdure, a velvet lawn of loveliness, soft, tranquil, dream-like and unencumbered, yet in ages past the theater of great and thrilling events. Bordering it on the left is Little Hermon, with the small gray villages of Endor and Nain, and beyond it rises the summit of Gilboa on which the sunlight lingers with radiant glory in strange contrast with the gloomy day when the King of Israel perished there and Jonathan fell, slain in their "high places." Still further south are seen the mountains of Ephraim along which and over the valleys the mind glances to Ebal and Gerizim, Bethel and Mizpeh, Zion and Olivet. Then the eye sweeps across the broad plain to "the excellency of Carmel" on the west, and follows its bold ridge northward till its farthest slope dips into the Mediterranean Sea which lies like a dark line in the purple horizon. Intervening are the hills of Galilee, enclosing the ever-memorable and charming village of Nazareth. Fields of blooming shrubbery and rich plains break off at the north from which rise the Horns of Hattin, a double-peaked elevation known as the Mount of Beatitudes. Still farther are the ranges of Lebanon, on one of whose nearest heights is Safed, "a city set upon a hill," and in the dim distance beyond rises the cone of Mount Hermon, snow-crowned and majestic, like a dome of glory. Thus "Tabor is among the mountains and Carmel by the sea;" and one here sees how naturally the poet-king groups the glorious scenery of the Holy Land: "The north and the south, Thou hast created them; Tabor and Hermon shall rejoice in Thy name."

The name of this beautiful mountain, frequent in the Old Testament, is not once mentioned in the New. But our blessed Lord must have been familiar with it from childhood. Thousands of times His holy eye rested upon it, as it is but six miles east of Nazareth, and in full view from the western bank of the Sea of Galilee. Indeed, we have been accustomed to associate one of the most wonderful events in our Saviour's life with this mountain-top—His sublime, glorious, heavenly transfiguration. And surely no

15

place could be more befitting; and notwithstanding the objections urged on account of the fortress on the summit, I thought, as I wandered around the brow of that summit, and saw how many retired and shady nooks were there—how many secluded spots of charming loveliness admirably adapted to such a celestial scene—it surely *might* have transpired here. This may be "the high mountain apart," where Jesus led His three chosen apostles and was transfigured before them. Astonishing, glorious sight! the like of which earth had never seen before. Here, in that still night, under the sweet and solemn stars, as Jesus prayed with His beloved three, a marvelous change came over Him. His sad, sweet, holy human face brightened into the glory of the Godhead, out-shining the sun. At the same time His apparel, simple and travel-worn, changed to an unearthly whiteness and glowing splendor, excelling the robes of angels. And there were seen poised in the air about Him, in celestial raiment Moses and Elijah, and they talked of Calvary and the Cross and the dying Lamb of God. Enraptured and overpowered with the glorious majesty of the heavenly revelation, Peter says, hardly knowing what he uttered, "Lord, it is good for us to be here," and proposed to build tents for his transfigured Saviour and the celestial visitants. Then, to crown the dazzling glory of the scene, a beaming cloud as if descending from the throne of God overshadowed them, and a wondrous voice broke from it on the stillness of the night air—"This is my beloved Son, hear Him." The apostles sank overwhelmed to the earth. At length a gracious hand touched them—they arose, looked up, and saw Jesus only. Whether this sublime event transpired here upon Tabor, or on one of those peaks toward Hermon yonder, we shall not certainly know in this world; but the scene is a beautiful and blessed glimpse of Heaven and of our glorified Redeemer there; and it is a precious privilege to have under one's eye the place where it did transpire, and perhaps to stand on the very spot that witnessed it all.

Looking from the summit of Tabor over broad Esdraelon's plain—so long the Armageddon of old—now so green and beautiful, so flowery and fruitful, I think of that strangely contrasting view of it, some twenty-eight hundred years ago, when the wicked Ahab had his palace and throne at Jezreel; when Elijah prayed to God from yonder Carmel; when the heavens became as brass, the early and latter rain were withheld for three and a half years, and this goodly plain was all a parched, bare and arid waste—a hot and gloomy desolation—and men and beasts wandered hither and thither for aught to allay their raging thirst and hunger. The prophet and king met on this plain. The trial of God and Baal was arranged. On that southeastern cliff of Carmel the test was made. Baal was discomfited by power and fire from heaven. His priests were slain by the Kishon yonder. Elijah prays again on that mountain slope. The little cloud gathers from the sea beyond, and the showers descend. The prophet runs before the chariot of the king to Jezreel; and so closes one of the most wonderful days in history, filling the ages with its lessons, and inspiring even our prayers and encouraging our trust in Israel's God.

Along these battle-fields of Megiddo our blessed Lord came, the Prophet of a New Dispensation, the Herald of life and peace. Yonder He taught the multitudes, fed the famishing thousands, and stilled the stormy sea. There, at Nain, He stanched the tears of sorrow and mourning, and raised the dead to life. Here He was gloriously transfigured; and on that far-off hill He bowed in death on the cross, and from the mount over the vale He ascended to heaven. O, earth's battle-fields shall yet glow with the sweet and blessed victories of the Prince of salvation. Where strife and death and mourning have reigned, peace and life and love and songs of joy shall abound. Beautiful Tabor! Gladly would I have lingered long amidst visions so attractive, so grand and sublime—amidst surrounding objects in themselves so sacred and enchanting, and suggestive of reflections that throng the mind and almost etherealize the soul.

In good season the next morning we were leaving our camping-ground, and passing around the western and northern base of Mount Tabor, on our way to the Sea of Galilee. It is the last day of March, and never could a morning be more beautiful or charming. The sun shines in a cloudless sky, and drinks the pearly dew-drops from leaf and blossom. The birds are singing in the trees. Tulips and other brilliant flowers are smiling upon us from the ground. The woody slope of Tabor, in its fresh full foliage, is grateful to the eye. And as we move on in the delightful valley, the form of the hills and the small oak-trees and other shrubbery that cover them, so different from the general aspect of Palestine, yet so like certain landscapes at home, recalling the scenes of childhood, that for a moment I seemed to be in New England on a June morning. But before emerging from these shady ravines to the plain beyond, we have evidence of our position among the wild sons of Ishmael. We observe the dark figures of these strolling Arabs—now a solitary Bedawy lurking by the way, and then knots of three or four of them crossing our path—all having a fierce and savage loook, and armed with guns, daggers and clubs—watching for the unprotected or unarmed traveler. Many a robbery and doubtless worse crime have been committed in this retired spot and amid these leafy and flowery beauties of nature. Our dragoman overheard a group of them conversing about us. "They are a large party," said one of them; "we must let them pass undisturbed." I thought of the lines—

> "Where every prospect pleases,
> And only man is vile."

Alas, that this should be, so near the home of our Saviour at Nazareth and Capernaum, and the Mount of Beatitudes where He announced the Golden Rule.

In crossing the open plain, rich in cornfields, we passed a huge old stone khan, with loopholed towers at the corners, the only building we saw. A few natives are in the fields where once crowds followed in the steps of Jesus. Along this plain He must have passed when, rejected at Nazareth, he took up His abode at Capernaum. The Mount of Beatitudes is near us on the left, and perhaps we are on the spot where the "disciples were an hungered, and began to pluck the ears of corn, and to eat." Two or three of us, anxious for an early sight of the Sea of Galilee, speed on in advance, and as we come to the edge of the high bank, the beautiful and glorious vision is before us. With tearful gratitude we look down upon the sweet, tranquil and sacred lake, and then uncover our heads and shout in joyful exultation. The bank here is somewhat higher than I had supposed, otherwise everything looked much as my fancy had often painted it. The extent, the shape, the hills surrounding—now high and rocky and then depressed to little vales and plains—all things about the lovely sea had a familiar look, I had so studied its topography, and pictured it so often in my mind, and lingered with such intense interest about its hallowed shores. And now I am actually gazing upon it! How near I seem to come to the days of Jesus and the wondrous scenes associated with His ministry here!

As we stand on the high and sloping bank about a third of the distance from the southern to the northern extremity of the lake, its surface lies about a thousand feet below us. Its length is perhaps thirteen miles, and its width about half that distance in its broadest and central part. The city of Tiberias is before us close to the water's edge. South of it there is a promontory that excludes a view of the southwestern shore. Turning to the north the eye glances over another promontory behind which is the little rich plain of Gennesaret, and then follows the curve of the shore, bending away to the northeast, where the bank is not very high, and where was the central field of our Lord's labors. At the farthest point of the Sea the Jordan flows in through a ravine. Tracing the eastern coast down, at first there is a very gradual slope to the water and a green, lawn-like spot, that you feel must be the place where Jesus fed the five thousand as they sat in companies on the grass. Farther down, the bank rises and becomes bolder and rocky, till you are sure you discover the "steep place" where the herd of swine ran violently down into the sea. You distinguish also in those rocky palisides, with the help of a glass, some excavations or tombs, where no doubt dwelt the wild Gadarene whom Jesus healed. Looking back of us we see the arched form of Tabor and the hills of Nazareth, and north of these the ridges of Lebanon and the city of Safed; and away beyond the extremity of the lake in the dim distance is the snow-crowned brow of Hermon—a conspicuous and beautiful object—which, just as it now appears, must often have met the eyes of our blessed Lord. The hills of Gilead and Bashan lie in the eastern horizon, a portion of that long mountain wall that bounds the Jordan valley on the east.

We descend the declivity part way and stop, as it is now midday, and spread our lunch under a large fig-tree. Here we seem to have reached another climate. The bracing atmosphere of the hills is exchanged for the wilting heat of the valley under a smiting sun. The whole descent of the bank must be a mile and a half, though it appeared far less. We pass various trees, prominent among which is the tropical thorn, with a sprinkling of oleanders, and near

Tiberias we find several specimens of the graceful palm. The city has a dilapidated and shrunk appearance. Its walls are broken down here and there, having never been repaired since the great earthquake in 1837. Its present inhabitants, about two thousand in number and half of them Jews, have a pale and sickly appearance. According to Josephus the city was founded by Herod, the murderer of John the Baptist, and named after the Roman Emperor Tiberius. It is but once mentioned in the New Testament. It became the capital of Galilee, and after the destruction of Jerusalem, was the chief residence and metropolis of the Jews in Palestine for a long time. Many a learned rabbi—among them the great Maimonides—was buried in the tombs in the hillside back of the city. As I was returning from the Hot Springs, which are about a mile south of Tiberias, I met a funeral procession. The corpse was wrapped in cloths and borne on a rude bier and the wailing mourners followed. Those mineral springs, by the way, are remarkable. They are quite near the lake, and a little cluster of buildings covers them. The water issues almost boiling hot from the base of volcanic hills. A large circular tank, capable of accommadating several bathers at once, is frequently resorted to by those afflicted with rheumatism and similiar complaints. It was the *hottest* bath I ever took. This is supposed to be the site of Hammath, a town of Naphtali, mentioned by Joshua.

XXX.
Plain of Gennesareth—Capernaum—Sea of Galilee.

Our tents were pitched just north of Tiberias, near the shore of the lake. After a little rest, several of us made a most deeply interesting excursion along the hallowed margin of this lovely sea, and almost to its northern extremity, amidst localities associated at every step with the ministries of our glorious Redeemer. There is a good bridle-path near the water's edge; for the banks, though high and mountainous with here and there depressions and grassy slopes amid the rocky cliffs, do not pitch abruptly into the lake, but leave a beach of more or less width all round it. This rendered it convenient for its ancient purpose of fisheries and for landing at any part of it. Smooth pebbles of different colors and sometimes shells line the shore. The water is exceedingly transparent, deep and sweet. We saw an abundance of fishes, some of large size, and a solitary fisherman, angling from a rock, reminding us of some of the scenes and miracles in our Saviour's history.

Three or four miles brought us to a very interesting spot near the center of the western shore and widest part of the lake. It is also at the southern border of the rich and beautiful plain of Gennesareth, to form which the high bank for a few miles gives way. Here we reach a little village containing about twenty houses and a ruined tower. It is Mejdel, or Magdala, the home of Mary Magdalene. It is now the only village on the plain once so thickly peopled. It clings to the bank that rises high above it, and thence looks out upon the lovely lake and over the blooming plain, while it touches the margins of both. A large thorn-tree stands near it, and a clear stream sweeps by it into the sea amidst a thicket of willows. It flows down from a deep ravine, looking up which we get a glimpse of the Mount of Beatitudes. Two other ravines open on the plain through its western barrier of green swelling hills slightly broken by rocky crests. This plain of Gennesareth is a sacred spot. At its northern margin Dr. Robinson locates Capernaum, the home of Jesus. But Dr. Thomson places it at Tell Hûm, a little farther up the lake, where it probably was. This plain is crescent-shaped, three or four miles in length, and about half as wide. We noted, in passing, its luxuriant richness, its fine fields of wheat, and barley, its rank grass, mustard, weeds, and thistles. Josephus described it as an earthly paradise, where perpetual spring reigned, and the choicest fruits abounded. Its fertility is still wonderful. Oleanders and thorn-trees fringe the shore, and amid the thickets back of these, we observe here and there clusters of small palm. Quails, turtle-doves, and other birds of gay plumage and musical notes, are abundant. Fine streams come flowing through it into the sea. Along this shore our Saviour and His disciples were often found. Here He uttered parables. Here He wrought miracles. Here perhaps the sons of Zebedee were found mending their nets where one of these clear brooks empties itself into the lake. Probably in the mouth of the stream lay the little ships on which Jesus addressed the crowds standing about Him on the land. How often He and His disciples came to this shore or departed from it, crossing the lake. Not far from here He walked upon the water, and they heard his voice, "It is I, be not afraid." O how much there is here to remind one of His presence and words! Many of the things He alluded to in the parables are here still. The sower, the wayside, the thorns, the stony places, the tropical heat, the good ground are all here to repeat His solemn truths. The clear, beautiful lake exists as of old in its rugged frame of hills. Tempests sweep down upon it now through the ravines, and suddenly transform its tranquil surface into raging billows, as when He said, "Peace, be be still."

We find a few old ruins at the northern extremity of the plain. They may be the remains of ancient Chinnereth, frequently mentioned in the Old Testament, as is the "sea of Chinnereth," from which the plain and sea of Gennesareth derived their name. The bank now becomes abrupt and rocky, and our path, bending somewhat eastward as it follows the line of the shore, passes over the edge of a cliff through which the road is cut in the rock. In fifteen or twenty minutes we come to a pebbly strand and a little bay, with an abundance of water flowing down from the hills. Aqueducts, pools and fountains are around us. And here is an old building that has been used for a mill. Here we obtain a complete view of the lake. The eye follows the line of the shore entirely around. Here we sit down in admiration of the beautiful view, and absorbed with the sacred and thrilling associations that throng upon the mind. Tabiga is the modern name of this spot, and some regard it as the site of Bethsaida—" House of Fisheries"—the home of several of our Lord's disciples. But if there was a Bethsaida here, there was certainly another at the head of the Lake, just over the Jordan; and it is not likely there would be two towns of the same name so near together. There are some passages of Scripture, however, that indicate a Bethsaida of Galilee and another on the eastern side, near the place of feeding the five thousand. But instead of a necessity for two, as some have supposed, the existence of one, occupying both sides of the Jordan, meets all that the Gospel narratives demand.

This spot—Tabiga—was perhaps a suburb of Capernaum, the site of which is probably marked by a few old ruins, to be found a little further along the shore, and called Tell Hûm. Dr. Thomson thinks this great fountain was the fountain of Capernaum. Here we were, as I believe, just in the border of one of the most interesting places on earth—the home of our blessed Saviour—and, as may well be supposed, I was exceedingly anxious to go on to Tell Hûm. But some of our party, being very weary and much oppressed by the heat, would consent to go no further, and desired to return at once to our tents at Tiberias. In another hour we might have reached the head of the lake; but it would hardly have been safe for one or two to venture without other protection; so with great reluctance I was obliged to stop at the border of Capernaum. But it was interesting to come even to the suburbs of such a place—to touch as it were the hem of the robe that enclosed the earthly home of Jesus— a home from which He often went out on His mission of love, mercy and salvation; going over the region of Galilee, into its cities and villages, teaching and healing, and unfolding the kingdom of God; extending His journeys down to Judea and the Jordan valley, and once at least over to the sea-coast of Tyre and Sidon. How often He came back here, worn and weary, to rest. How often He walked along this shore, where He called His disciples to be "fishers of men," where so many of His gracious words were spoken, and where such mighty works were made manifest. Across this sea He often sailed, and every wave on its surface, and every pebble and rock by its shore, seems a precious memento of Him. And how many of His marvelous works were wrought here at Capernaum, which was thus "exalted to heaven," but for the guilt of its amazing unbelief was "brought down to hell."

This home of our Lord, at the Sea of Galilee, was fitly chosen for the great and blessed work of His ministry. He came to preach the Gospel to the poor, to call the heavy laden, and to seek and save the lost. And no spot furnished better facilities than the populous cities and villages and thronged shores of this beautiful lake. Situated in the midst of the Jordan valley, on the great thoroughfare from Babylon and Damascus into Palestine, its waters were a central point of passing and gathering, by "the way of the sea," "beyond Jordan," of "Zebulon and Naphtali."

Depressed to such a depth—six hundred feet below the Mediterranean Sea—its shores have almost a tropical fertility, denied to the bordering uplands, and increased by the beautiful and abundant springs along the western coast. In this respect there is a marked contrast between the Sea of Galilee and that dismal lake into which the Jordan flows and is absorbed. If, as Mr. Stanley well observes, the southern lake is the Sea of Death, the northern is emphatically the Sea of Life—life in its waters and on its banks, and in the time of our Lord a center of population and traffic. The villages "sent forth their fishermen by hundreds over the lake; and when we add the crowd of ship-builders, the many boats of traffic, pleasure and passage, we see that the whole basin must have been a focus of life and energy, the surface of the lake constantly dotted with the white sails of vessels flying before the mountain gusts, as the beach sparkled with the houses and palaces, the synagogues and the temples of the Jewish or Roman inhabitants." It was no secluded spot that our Saviour sought for His home—no hermit-life that He lived. Nowhere except in Jerusalem could He have found such a sphere for His labors. Readily from this center "His fame went throughout all Syria;" vast multitudes were attracted by his teaching and miracles, "from Galilee, and from Decapolis, and from Judea, and from beyond Jordan," and "ran through the whole region round about," bringing the diseased in beds, "where they heard He was; and whithersoever He entered into villages, or cities, or country, they laid the sick in streets, and besought Him that they might touch if it were but the border of His garment." Such was the home of Christ with its surroundings, its scenes and "images which could occur nowhere else in Palestine but on this one spot, and which from that one spot have now passed into the religious language of the civilized world." O what an undying interest clusters around the Sea of Galilee! As we retraced our steps, I paused at Magdala for a refreshing bath in the clear waters of the lake.

It was now Saturday evening. The last two Sundays we had been in Jerusalem, so intimately associated with our Lord's sufferings, death, and resurrection; and it was peculiarly pleasant to think of passing the next here, by this beautiful lake, the scene of so much of our Saviour's life, teaching, and miracles. After the fatigue and heat of the day it was exceedingly grateful to sit down by our tents, or walk by the pebbly margin of the sea. The shadows of the high bank were thrown over us; the golden sunlight was fading from the eastern hills; and trees and rocks along the shore were mirrored in the calm, crystal waters. The crescent moon was hid behind the western bank, but might have been seen from its top, lingering over Mount Tabor. Soon the stars came out and flashed over the sea, the same as when the Holy Redeemer wandered by this shore, or sailed over the surface of the deep. It was by this lake that He said to the weary, "Come unto Me, and I will give you rest." In our tents we come to Him, commit ourselves to His loving protection, and sleep by the Sea of Galilee where He so often slept.

The first sound in the morning was the loud roaring

of the billows and breakers on the shore. A sudden change had come over the lake. So tranquil and serene at evening, now its whole surface was broken up into foam-crested waves. How vividly did this remind me of a thrilling scene in our Lord's experience when, as He was passing over in a boat with his disciples, a sudden tempest came down upon the sea—the wind rushing through some of the ravines—and tossed it into boisterous billows, which He when awaked, calmed by the word of His power.

A Sabbath by the Sea of Galilee! What a blessed privilege! It was the first day of April, and the morning was bright and warm. After breakfast our party gathered for a religious service under the shadow of an old high wall, with the green grass and sweet flowers beneath our feet, and the open heavens above our heads. We thought of home, and of the sanctuaries where we were wont to worship. We thought also of the crowds that once gathered around the Great Teacher at the shore of this sea, and we could only echo His instructions. We sang that dear hymn commencing, "How sweetly flowed the gospel sound." Several passages from the New Testament were read, all relating to incidents in the life of Jesus by or on this lake. After prayer, another hymn was sung, in which were the lines—

> "The voice that stilled the stormy waves
> On distant Galilee."

Rev. Mr. Jenkins spoke from the words of Jesus, first uttered here in calling His disciples: "Follow me." Another minister alluded to the associations of the place, pointing to the localities in view where this and that event in the life of our Saviour transpired, and where this parable was uttered and that miracle was wrought. So we could bring the scenes before us, and almost seem to be in the literal presence of Jesus. Appropriate remarks were also made by the three other ministers of our party, and we sang again—

> "Jesus, I my cross have taken,
> All to leave and follow Thee."

It was a most hallowed, precious season, and like those we enjoyed in Jerusalem and the Garden of Gethsemane, deeply impressive, spiritually profitable, and long to be remembered. For dinner we had broiled fish from the lake, reminding us of our Saviour's "showing Himself to the disciples at the Sea of Tiberias," after His resurrection, when He called to them from the shore: "Children, have ye any meat?" And "as they were come to land, they saw a fire of coals there, and fish laid thereon, and bread." Then, after "they had dined," Jesus thrice put the question to Simon Peter, "Lovest thou me?" In the cool of the evening we sat down in front of our tents and talked and sang hymns till a late hour.

The next morning, about seven o'clock, we left Tiberias for Nazareth. Up the long slope we filed away, and soon reached the top of the high western bank. Here we paused and turned about for a last look upon the Sea of Galilee, nearly all of which, with its shores, was visible. With my glass I surveyed each spot again with the deepest interest. Delightful view! Farewell, lovely Lake of Gennesareth! Thy picture, with its wonderful associations, remains in its perfection, and can never fade! No, I can never forget

THE SEA OF GALILEE.

Dear, beautiful sight! Embosomed by hills,
   How calmly reposes the Lake!
I gaze, and my soul with rapture thrills,
As the glorious scene my vision fills,
   And holiest memories wake.
     O lovely Sea
     Of Galilee,
How oft my Redeemer hath looked on thee!

All other lakes in all lands are denied
   The honors that thou dost know :
Blossoms as radiant may fringe their side,
Fountains as sparkling may swell their tide,
   But thou hast the Jordan's inflow;
     More sacred yet,
     Gennesaret,
The sandals of Christ thy waves have wet!

How oft I have come, in wondering thought,
   A pilgrim along thy shore,
Beholding the crowds that Jesus taught,
And the deeds His power and mercy wrought,
   As He walked thy margin o'er.
     O hallowed Sea
     Of Galilee,
The home of Messiah was once by thee!

And now, with thankfullest heart, I stand
   Where Jesus so often stood;
I see the same stream, and rock, and land;
The same sweet Tabor, and Hermon grand;

THE SEA OF GALILEE.

And look on the same bright flood—
    Tiberian Sea,
    So dear to me,
Because my Saviour saw these and thee!

My feet have pressed the old paths He trod,
    And crossed o'er the same clear rills;
I have sat me down on the grassy sod,
Where rested the weary Son of God,
    Who bore our sorrows and ills.
        In thee I take,
        Gennesareth Lake,
Unbounded delight for His dear sake!

Nazareth's valley and hills are fair,
    And lovely is Bethlehem;
Mount Olivet's scenes their glories share,
In the Garden shade and Bethany there,
    With precious Jerusalem:
        But, dearest Sea
        Of Galilee,
How the life of my Lord is linked with thee!

No crowds along thy thoroughfares pour;
    Silence and ruin are here to-day;
White sails on thy waves are seen no more;
The cities that flourished upon thy shore
    Have passed in their guilt away:
        But thou art yet,
        Gennesaret,
A picture unchanged in thy hill frame set!

And Christ is the same, though ascended on high,
    As when by this water He trod;
With the same tender heart, and pitying eye;

356 THE SEA OF GALILEE.

As mighty to save, as lovingly nigh—
O ever the same Lamb of God!
Adieu, sweet Sea
Of Galilee;
Thy image remains, and thy Lord, with me!

CAPERAUM AND SEA OF GALILEE.

XXXI.

Mount of Beatitudes—Cana—Nazareth.

From the Sea of Galilee our course is westward over a rich upland plain. Amidst luxuriant patches of wheat, grass, weeds, and flowers, we soon come near the southern base of a hill that rises gradually from the plain and culminates in a crest of two summits, whence its modern name, the Horns of Hattin, is derived; Hattin being the name of a village at the foot of the hill. This is the traditional Mount of Beatitudes, the supposed place where our Saviour preached the Sermon on the Mount. It is well situated for such an occasion, and there are good reasons for believing that tradition in this instance is correct. As our Lord came here, "there followed him great multitudes of people from Galilee," the surrounding region; "and from Decapolis," the ten cities near the southern extremity of the lake; "and from Jerusalem and Judea," still further south; "and from beyond Jordan," the country east of the river and lake. Here would be a natural center or converging of thoroughfares, along which to this point, the fame of Jesus would attract the thronging crowds. "And seeing the multitudes He went up into a mountain." Perhaps he ascended this southern slope upon which I look, and sat down by the level spot or hollow between the two peaks, which would be going literally "into a mountain," where the crowds might gather around and easily see and hear him. Such a Preacher, such an audience, such a Sermon!—well might the sanctuary be no temple made with hands; its floor the solid earth, its pulpit a rock, its pillars those of nature, its windows the sun-beams, its roof and dome the overarching heavens. On the east, down the vale, lay the clear waters of Gennesaret; south and southwest were Little Hermon and Tabor; west were the hills of Nazareth; and north the lower ranges of Lebanon. How sublime the scene! the Creator preaching in His own vast temple!

The Discourse itself furnishes evidences of its being spoken here. The "city set on an hill," may be Safed, in full view at the northwest on one of the highest mountains in Galilee. "The lilies of the field," common in Palestine, are very abundant here. Elsewhere I had noticed that they were always red, but here they were of various shades—red, pink, purple, and white— lovely objects to "consider." Here too are fields of "grass," which God clothes with verdure and various tints of beauty. "The fowls of the air" still fly past here from the little plain of Gennesareth near by, where are found an unusual number and variety of birds of musical notes and gay plumage. How vividly do these things remind us of the reality as well as the place of the original scene!

The bloody battle of Hattin was fought here, July 5, 1187. It decided the fate of the Crusades. The Christians, with the king of Jerusalem at their head, were overpowered by the hordes of Moslems, under Saladin; and "one more added to the long list of the battles of the plain of Esdraelon—the last struggle of the Crusaders, in which all was staked in the presence of the holiest scenes of Christianity, and all miserably lost."

We journey westward among the young wheat, which promises a fine harvest, and amid grassy uplands which afford inviting pasture-grounds to the wandering Bedawîn. Leaving the plain, we enter the outer circle of hills among which is nestled the charming village of Nazareth, now distant about six miles. A half hour's further ride amidst rocks and tangled shrubbery, and we descend into a basin among the hills, where we find the little village of Cana, which tradition makes the scene of the marriage attended by the miracle of the water changed to wine. There is another village, which I saw a little north of Nazareth, also called Cana, and which some regard as claiming the honor which the natives still say belongs to this Cana, where we have now arrived. It is a small village, and most of its houses have a neglected and half-ruined appearance. But the surrounding basin or vale is well filled with pomegranate, fig, and olive-trees—some of which are very old and venerable—a variety which gives picturesqueness if not beauty to the village. While passing through it, we were pointed to a rude, dilapidated building called a Greek church, occupying the site of the house where the marriage festival was held and the miracle wrought. As we were about leaving, a priest appeared with a bunch of keys to show us the interior, and a few remains of the identical water pots used at the wedding. But we did not think it worth while to dismount and look at the relics. We passed on a few rods and came to a fine large fountain, making quite a stream as it flowed away. Around it were gathered a considerable group of women and girls, appearing gay and cheerful, some filling their jars, and others washing and beating out clothes with clubs. Little boys gathered about us, anxious to earn a few paras by holding our horses. It was now mid-day, and we stopped for lunch under a grove of pomegranates. Our leathern bottles were filled with fresh pure water from the fountain—the same fountain if this be the true Cana—from which the water-pots were filled by the order of our blessed Lord, when He was about to work the first of those stupendous miracles that illustrated His public ministry. His mother and His disciples were here to witness this work that "manifested forth His glory," and confirmed their faith. There is no other supply of water near the village, and it was deeply interesting to see and drink of this fountain, so sacred in its associations. Nathanael, the guileless Israelite, belonged in Cana, and our Saviour was here when He healed the nobleman's son at the point of death in Capernaum.

We resumed our journey before two o'clock, and leaving the vale of Cana, we ascended a rocky slope, and going over the other side, soon reached a little village situated on the border of a fertile valley. At some distance to the right is Sefûrieh, a town prominently in view, whose old castle crowns a high eminence. Nazareth is not seen till we get close to its borders; but we are now climbing the high hill that immediately shelters it on the north-east. We reach

SKIN BOTTLES AND WATER-JARS.

its summit, and in descending its steep rocky slope, Nazareth opens upon us like a beautiful picture in its frame of hills. This moment and this vision are among those never to be forgotten. We have now seen all the Holy Places associated so intimately and wondrously with the birth, life, ministry, and death of our Divine Redeemer. Silently, joyously, and tearfully we enter the sweet and blooming vale, and come to our tents, which are pitched near a beautiful crystal fountain in the margin of the town. We wandered over this small fertile valley, shut in by green hills of wavy outline, and abounding in flowery lawns, thrifty corn-fields, and little gardens hedged around by cactus, and shaded here and there by solitary or clustering trees of olive and fig. The chief part of the village clings to the south-western side of the valley, the hill rising to the north-west of it about five hundred feet. This is "the hill on which the city is built," as stated by Luke, to the "brow" of which the angry multitude led Jesus from the Synagogue, "that they might cast him down headlong." I noticed on the steep declivity above the village, precipitous ridges of rock, down which if one were cast, it would almost inevitably produce death.

Nazareth has a population of nearly four thousand, most of whom are Greek and Latin Christians, the Franciscan Convent being the most conspicuous building in the place. There is a small Maronite church, and also a mosque with a fine white minaret. The town is one of the most thriving in all Galilee. The houses are of stone, and have a neat and substantial look. The roofs are flat as is usual. The narrow streets abound in filth, comprising dunghills, cesspools, and dead animals. The people generally have a good appearance. The men look nobler, the women are fairer, and all dress better than in any other place I remember to have seen in the land.

We visited the Latin Convent and Church of the Annunciation. They consist of a square of heavy buildings encompassed by a high wall. Some old columns of red granite lie near the large gate, admitting us to an open court around which are school-rooms, a pharmacy, and other apartments. The church is ample, and adorned with various paintings and tapestries representing Scripture scenes. The chanting of the monks and the fine organ remind us of the churches in Italy. From the audience room we go down a stairway of fifteen steps to a grotto which is the *sanctum* of the place. Here are marble walls, columns, altars, pavements, beautiful silver lamps, and a fine modern painting of the Annunciation, the gift of some European monarch. The altar and the marble slab beneath, with a cross in the center, are said to mark the spot where Mary stood when she heard the salutation of the angel Gabriel. Passing through another part of the grotto, left in its natural rocky state, we ascend a narrow staircase to a rude cave called "Mary's kitchen," where we are shown among other details the chimney and fire-place. We are next conducted across the village to the work-house of Joseph. The interior of the modern building, consecrated as a chapel, is said to contain a fragment of an old wall that belonged to the original work-shop. An indifferent painting of Joseph at work, assisted by the youthful Jesus, hangs over the altar. It was presented by a noble lady of Florence, and bears her name and coat of arms. We are then directed to another part of the town, and shown the Chapel of the *Mensa Christi*, or Table of Christ. It is a small vaulted chamber, and contains a stone slab from which, according to tradition, our Lord and His disciples often ate.

After visiting the Rev. Mr. Lundy, of Philadelphia, and his party, encamped in a grove at the south part of the town, and who were traveling under the direction of the Egyptian dragoman Achmet, who took us up the Nile, we returned to the "Fountain of the Virgin," near our tents. Here a lively scene is presented. A large number of small and full-grown girls are gathered around this crystal spring, while some are continually coming with their empty pitchers and jars, and others are going away with theirs filled. They all seem to be in a pleasant, happy mood; for their merry laugh rings out on the air. Some of them are quite beautiful. There can scarcely be a doubt that to this very fountain the Virgin Mary was accustomed to come and fill her pitcher, after the manner of her country-women, and as these Nazareth girls do now; and she might have given of the water she had drawn to the passing stranger, as they do to us. To this fountain too the youthful Jesus must often have come to drink, as others come to-day. It must be the same spring from which Nazareth was then supplied, for there is no other in the place. One of the earliest local traditions makes this fountain the scene of the angelic salutation to Mary, as she had come hither to draw water.

The sun was already behind the high hill guarding Nazareth on the west, when we gathered around the dinner-table in front of our tents. At length the vale was filled with the evening shadows, and the stars looked down upon us lovingly. The heavenly orbs, always interesting, suggestive and glorious, one surveys in a foreign land with emotions he can never feel at home. They powerfully remind him of home—of those whose eyes may now see them, of friends who once looked upon them, but have passed beyond them. When in places of historic and sacred memories, the stars bring the distant near; for you are looking upon the same serene and sublime heavens—the same constellations—the same bright gems—that those renowned and glorious men looked upon from the same locality; and the vision is the same now that it was then. You seem to be near to those heretofore so far separated in distance and time. I look from the tent-door at Nazareth around upon these encircling hills, and up from their shadowy outlines, to the beautiful skies, and I know that from this spot at the same hour of evening our blessed Saviour looked, how often! upon these clustering summits, remaining as of old, and up to these bending heavens, bright in their unchanged diadem of glory. What were His emotions when He surveyed these scenes? O thou Almighty Creator of all, and Saviour of men! here thou wast a child in one of these homes; here, in this small unhonored and almost unknown village, thou didst pass many years in a humble position—in a lowly mechanical pursuit, involving toil and weariness—that thou mightest experience all human hardships and sorrows, and that we might share in the fullness of thy human and divine sympathy! A wonderful Being is Jesus of Nazareth!

After a day of unusual weariness and a night of sweetest, profoundest repose, where the weary Jesus had so often slept, early the next morning I ascended to the top of the hill west of the town, and near the tomb or white-domed wely of Ismail, enjoyed the wide, commanding, and glorious view, one of the best in the Holy Land, even surpassing that magnificent one from the summit of Tabor. Looking to the east, the rounded height of Tabor is seen, only six miles distant. Beyond it to the left is the deep basin of the Sea of Galilee, less than twenty miles away, but the sea itself is not visible. To the right of Tabor is Jebel ed-Dûhy, or Little Hermon, with Endor and Nain dotting its slopes; and beyond them Mount Gilboa, with the site of ancient Jezreel like a speck at its base; while the broad green Plain of Esdraelon lies spread out in its beauty on the south, and comes to the very hills that encircle Nazareth. In the west, the eye rests upon Carmel, with its long, dark ridge, and on the white strand of the Mediterranean Sea beyond the plain of 'Akka, or Acre, and the town of Haifa at the best harbor on the coast. To the north are the villages of Sefûrieh, and the Cana I did not visit, and beyond are the Lebanon mountains, including the glorious, snow-crowned brow of Hermon. Grand and beautiful vision! how rich in wonderful events are the localities in view! The encircling and adjacent hills have an unusual picturesqueness and charm, in striking contrast with other hill scenery in Palestine. Except a few rocky summits around Nazareth, the hills are covered with a light growth of wood, and descend in graceful slopes to broad winding valleys of richest green. The entire landscape, in its agreeable variety, beautiful luxuriance, and soft coloring, seems almost Italian. The blessings promised to the three tribes of Zebulon, Asher and Naphtali, are inscribed here in the features of nature. Zebulon, nestling among these hills, "rejoices in his going out" to the rich plain, and from his abundant flocks in these pastures reaching to the lake, "offers the sacrifices of righteousness;" Asher, to the northwest, among the fine groves of olives, "dips his foot in oil;" and Naphtali, to the northeast, amidst the beautiful scenery and fertile soil above the Sea of Galilee, "is satisfied with favor, and full with the blessing of the Lord."

Such are the splendid views from this hill-top above Nazareth. How often must Jesus have climbed this same hill, stood on this same spot, and looked abroad over these same prospects of mountain, valley, and plain. From the hot vale below, He would come up here and behold the distant sea, and be refreshed by its cool breeze. Most of His earthly life was spent here "in the city where He had been brought up." How interesting to know more of that life, of which there is no record! Often must He have gone to that fountain with His mother—sat with His parents on the house-top at evening—traveled those streets over and over, going to His toil—and wandered along these rocky heights in meditation upon His wonderful

VALE OF NAZARETH.

mission in our world! Every spot here is hallowed by the foot-prints of the blessed Nazarene.

There had been a slight rain in the night; and now, after a succession of bright and lovely spring days, the morning sky was overcast, and the faint roll of distant thunder indicated the approach of showers. About seven o'clock we left our camping-ground, and began to wind our way up the hills that enclose Nazareth on the north. But I am looking back upon this lovely vale and picturesque village, and pause on the summit to take a last view of this fascinating spot so full of Divine images. Passing over the hill, the early home of Jesus faded from sight. Our general course is northwest among the hills of Galilee. In an hour we reach Sefûrieh, the Dio-cæsarea of the Romans, and the ancient Sephoris. Old columns, hewn stones, and other sculptured fragments lie scattered about or built into modern walls. The ruins of a Gothic church remain, according to tradition, on the site of the house occupied by Joachim and Anna, the parents of the Virgin Mary. But the most interesting relic is the immense old square tower crowning the hill. It is built of great beveled stones, indicating a Jewish origin and high antiquity.

We passed through an oak-glade into a country growing rich and fertile as we descended to the plain of Acre. Amidst hills and valleys, and groves of olive, lemon, apricot, and pomegranate, we made our way, with nothing of special or sacred interest immediately about us. Mount Carmel, crowned with a conspicuous monastery, was only a short distance from us. Indeed, we expected to ascend the mountain, but the owners of our horses refused to let them go up. Before noon it began to rain, and for two or three hours the clouds emptied their treasures upon us. Lightnings flashed down the dark canopy, and thunders rolled their heavy chariot wheels along the cloudy pavements of heaven. As they seemed to sweep over the long, bold ridge of Carmel and plunge down into the sea, their reverberations were solemnly grand. As a shower passed over us, I never was so consciously near a flash or bolt. Some of those sublime descriptions in the Psalms and elsewhere of storms, of lightnings and thunders, had their reality along these mountains and shores.

We pitched our tents by a clear, running brook on the plain of Acre, and on the borders of ancient Phœnicia. The Mediterranean Sea was before us, and the white buildings of Haifa and Acre were conspicuous. This semicircular plain, about eight miles in diameter, is one of the richest in Palestine, abounding in luxuriant crops and rank weeds, and in historical associations of great interest.

XXXII.

Phœnicia—Coast of Tyre and Sidon.

We left our camping-ground between six and seven the next morning, April fourth. We soon came into full view of the town and fortress of St. Jean d'Acre, resting on our left at the edge of the sea, with the bold promontory of Mount Carmel at the south. Acre has had a long, strange and chequered history. It is mentioned but once in the Old Testament, where it is said in the book of Judges that Asher, the tribe to whom this part of the country was given, "did not drive out the inhabitants of Accho." It was a stronghold of the Phœnicians who flourished here from time immemorial. It fell into the hands of the first Ptolemy of Egypt, who changed its name to Ptolemais. By this name it is spoken of in the account, in the Acts of the Apostles, of Paul's journey to Jerusalem: "And when we had finished our course from Tyre, we came to Ptolemais, and saluted the brethren, and abode with them one day." In the time of the Crusades, and of Napoleon I., it was an important military point, and the scene of terrible and bloody conflicts.

Continuing our course across the fertile plain, luxuriant with cornfields and wild vegetation, we soon reach the shore of the Mediterranean. Our path lay along the sandy beach for a little time, when the plain terminates on the north in the Lebanon mountains which come down boldly to the sea. We are now on the "coast of Tyre and Sidon." Here our blessed Lord once came, and perhaps our route is nearly the same as His. He looked upon this sea and these mountains, crossed this rich plain, and ascended that long flight of stone steps now before us. Here Palestine blends with Phœnicia or Syria. The little hamlet of Es-Zib, which we pass, is no doubt the representative of Achzib, mentioned in the book of Joshua. The olive groves at the base of the mountains remind us of the promise to Asher: "Let him dip his foot in oil." Right before us is a high, bold, rocky promontory, breaking down abruptly into the sea. We climb it by a long zig-zag path cut in the rocks like a staircase. The name of this height with the fountains at its base, is Ras el-Musheirifeh, and it is probably the ancient Misrephoth-maim, to which Joshua drove a part of Jabin's host from the battle at the waters of Merom. The view from the summit is extensive—Carmel and the plain of Acre being behind us, the wide and restless sea on our left, the Lebanon mountains on our right, and a long strip of the old Phœnician sea-coast before us. Over this pass our course was often on the verge of a fearful precipice, down the perpendicular side of which we could look hundreds of feet to the foaming breakers.

Descending to the narrow plain, we pass a Roman bridge, and observe the little village of Nakûrah on our right. On the same side, at the end of another hour, we find a nameless spot marked by an old building and stone foundations, with many Ionic columns scattered here and there. But a little further along on the left is a much larger mass of ruins, called Iskanderieh, the ancient Alexandroschene. Huge old walls near the edge of the sea seem like the remains of a fortification. A copious fountain flows amid the ruins, suggesting a suitable place for our noon-day lunch. This spot is named "Alexander's Tent," probably from some tradition that here the great warrior once encamped. Stretching out to the north there is a fine beach of pebbles, of various sizes and colors, intermingled with specimens of shell and sponge.

We soon reach a lofty cape, called *Promontorium Album*, from its white or chalky appearance, and more generally known as the "Ladder of Tyre," or *Scala Tyriorum*. We pass over it by a winding path cut in the rocks. This stone stairway, a mile in length, is sometimes on the very edge of the cliff, overhanging the sea, which roars and foams two hundred feet below. Some say Alexander made this path for the passage of horses and camels.

Our course is along the shore of the far-sounding sea, whose foam-crested surfs come rolling in grandly at our feet. We look on these waves, these mountain-sides, this narrow plain, and think of the riches and splendors of that ancient period when Tyre was in her glory. A mighty power were those old Phœnicians who had their home here. What teeming populations moved over this fertile soil! What magnificent cities, with their gorgeous temples and palaces, glittered along this coast! What a multitude of sails enlivened this sea! What rows of graceful palms shaded the paths, and what beautiful gardens and luxuriant fruits adorned the slopes! Against all this display of wealth and splendor the sacred prophets denounced the judgments of God, because of the idolatry and wickedness of the people; and to this day the evidences of the wonderful fulfillment of those predictions are most marked and convincing. "A mournful and solitary silence now prevails along the shore which once resounded with the world's debate."

Now along the pebbly or rocky beach, and then over the fragments of an old paved Roman road, observing perhaps a ruined tower or fallen columns, we arrived about the middle of the afternoon at Ras el-'Ain, the "Fountain Head," a group of old and remarkable fountains and reservoirs. The masonry enclosing these reservoirs is very massive. The largest, octagonal in form, is sixty-six feet in diameter and twenty-five feet high, with a slope so gradual that I could ride to the top. The stream from this fountain still carries a mill, and the remains of aqueducts show that it was carried to other mills. Running northward into a field for two miles is a Roman aqueduct supported on arches. It is said that the water supplying these fountains is brought by an under-ground canal from a distance; and there is an old tradition that these massive reservoirs were built by Solomon, and answer to the passage in Canticles: "A fountain of gardens, a well of living waters, and streams of Lebanon." They are certainly very ancient, and probably supplied the city of Tyre with water, conveyed by aqueducts nearly three miles. Near by I observed a modern silk establishment

TYRE—ITS PRESENT ASPECT. 373

which appeared well, back of a thrifty grove of mulberry-trees.

In less than an hour from the fountains, we reached our tents pitched near the solitary gate of Tyre—Tyre, so often mentioned in the Bible, so ancient and splendid, but now a desolation. In coming to it we pased over a sandy isthmus—the remains of Alexander's causeway—making a peninsula of what was formerly an island. The city is spoken of as being "in the midst of the sea." The low rocky island on which it stood is less than a mile in diameter, and was about a half a mile from the main-land. The isthmus has been widened by accumulations of sand, washing up on the north or harbor side in a fine beach. Here, near an old wreck, we found an excellent bathing-place. The present town contains about three thousand inhabitants, a part of them nominally Christians. As we wandered through the place we found most of the houses wretchedly poor, and the streets narrow, crooked, and filthy. The general aspect of desolation is partially relieved by a few green trees, mostly palm and pride of India, interspersed among the dwellings and gardens. A few rickety fishing-boats in the harbor, with a small export of cotton, tobacco and millstones, are the sole representatives of the once imperial commerce of Tyre. The old wall is broken down or has breaches here and there, and the whole appearance of the place constantly reminds one of the prophecies uttered and fulfilled against this city; "And they shall make a spoil of thy riches, and make prey of thy merchandize; and they shall break down thy walls, and destroy thy pleasant houses." "They shall lament over thee, saying, What city is like Tyrus, like the destroyed in the midst of the sea?" It is scarcely possible to describe the immense amount and confused mass of ruins lying in and around this ancient city. There are "heaps upon heaps" of them, accumulating and mingling in the repeated desolations to which it has been subjected. Every wave breaks over them, for they lie thick in the water as upon the land. Within the town there are some splendid relics, including three beautiful columns of red granite, of an ancient church, in which reposes the dust of Origen and of the Emperor Frederic Barbarossa. As I was coming out of the town I noticed some fisherman's nets stretched on the old walls, and was reminded of the striking fulfillment of the prophecy: "I will make thee like the top of a rock: thou shalt be a place to spread nets upon." Such is Tyre, the "daughter of Sidon," but outgrowing her mother; "a strong city," in the time of Joshua, and then mistress of the seas and parent of colonies in Europe and Africa. Her varied fortunes in successive ages and under different dominations, would make a long chapter. The prophet Ezekiel gives a most vivid and poetical description of her grandeur and power, her luxury and pride, and with equal vividness predicts her fall and desolation. The massive Tomb of Hiram, king of Tyre, is on a hillside a few miles east of the city.

One of Paul's voyages, as he sailed by the islands of Rhodes and Cyprus, brought him to a landing at Tyre, where the ship was to unlade her burden. Here he found congenial disciples of Christ, with whom he spent seven days of precious interest, fellowship, prayer and labor. When he and his associates departed, the loving brethren of Tyre accompanied them out of the city, so interested that they took their wives and children along to a place on that sandy beach, and there before parting they kneeled down on the shore and prayed. What a beautiful scene! How sweetly it speaks of Christian fellowship, friendship and love! How strangely in contrast with many other scenes that have transpired at this ancient city!

The next day we journeyed to Sidon, along the narrow plain, under the shadow of the Lebanon mountains and greeted by the ceaseless music of sea-billows breaking at our feet. These remain as of old, while the successive splendors and dominations of Phœnicians, Greeks, Romans and Crusaders, have passed away, leaving their intermingled ruins behind, over which the wretched Moslem rules, the very impersonation of decay. Among the streams we pass, the Leontes is the most considerable. Larger than any river we have seen in the land, except the Jordan, it rises near Baalbek, and flows down through the mountains in many a wild gorge and picturesque glen, and takes the name of Litany before it enters the sea. A few miles further on, a group of upright stones, called a sort of Syrian Stonehenge, attracts attention. A curious story is associated with it. A little hamlet is near by containing a white-domed wely in honor of some great prophet in the olden past. The prophet was once mocked by a number of men passing by, and as he cursed them in revenge, they were at once changed into stones where they still stand. The soil of the plain is dark and rich, but it is nearly deserted; the inhabitants finding it safer to live in their villages nestled on the mountain-sides which they terrace and cultivate. Old ruins, indicating the sites of former cities, lie along our path, in which are fragments of tessellated pavements, and huge columnar mile-stones, bearing various inscriptions, including the name of the Roman Emperor Septimius Severus. The neighboring cliffs are niched with numerous tombs. We crossed many little streams watering the plain from the hills, and observed graceful gazelles skipping away from their margins. These beautiful and sprightly little animals are seen in different parts of the Holy Land, and are several times alluded to in the Bible under the names of harts, hinds, and roes.

At length we come to a memorable and very interesting spot. It is the ancient Sarepta, forever identified with the poor widow and the miracles of Elijah, and it was probably the point to which our Divine Lord came when he visited the coast of Tyre and Sidon, and wrought a gracious miracle in answer to the pleadings and faith of the Syro-Phœnician woman. Thus in the Old and New Testaments Sarepta is honored and embalmed. As the prophet came hither from the brook Cherith in time of famine, he met the widow out gathering sticks to cook her last meal. I have often seen the poor women of Palestine collecting fuel on the hills and bearing home the bundles of sticks on their heads. The ancient town probably stood near the shore, where now there is nothing but scattered ruins, a wely, and an old khan. A half a mile distant, high up on a hill, is the large village of Sarafend, the modern representative of Sarepta. But here, where we are now passing, lived the widow whose story has become immortal. Her unfailing barrel of meal and cruse of oil teach lessons of confidence and trust in God. Her dead son was restored to life as a reward of her benevolence and faith, as she sustained the weary prophet, the type of the forerunner of Christ who, nearly a thousand years afterwards, in His many journeyings came once to this coast, and probably at this spot healed the daughter of the Canaanite woman, an imperishable record of simple and mighty faith and divine relief, that has inspired hope and joy in many a burdened heart. Adieu, Sarepta! Thou hast taught sweet lessons while I have lingered a little on thy ancient site, at the noontide of a lovely spring day. I shall remember thee forever. Let me pick a few leaves from this fine fig-tree to bear away as memorials of thee.

In leaving Sarepta we pass beyond where the sacred feet of our blessed Saviour pressed the soil of this Holy Land, and beyond the objects that lay beneath His holy human eye. Every day since that in which we entered Palestine, we have been treading in the footsteps of Jesus, and wandering amidst scenes, over hills, through valleys, and across streams, that were familiar to Him. And around many of those places what sacred, precious, and tender memories cling! How eloquently they repeat the wonderful incidents in the life of Jesus! How thrillingly they remind us of His gracious words and glorious works, His prayers, sufferings and tears! Every stone has a voice—every rustling leaf speaks of Jesus—every fountain murmurs His name—every flower reflects His love—every hill seems another Calvary and Olivet. O, there is something inexpressible in the associations of these Holy Places—to read the life of the Divine Redeemer in the very localities where the astonishing events transpired, and to see before you the existing and unmistakable evidences of their truth! Here are the mute but convincing witnesses of the Sacred History, and the Gospel comes home to the heart with a double power as the testimony of sight is added to your faith.

Beyond a desolate waste just north of Sarepta, we enter a shady grove and sit down to our noon repast near a sparkling fountain. Magnificent Lebanon rises above us, and the rolling sea-surf breaks at our feet. On a little promontory in the distance before us we distinctly see the city of Sidon, encircled by luxuriant gardens and blooming orchards. On that spot stood the "great Zidon" of which Joshua speaks, one of the very oldest cities of the world. To look upon such a place continuously inhabited through such a long succession of generations—through nearly all the ages of the world's history—what a train of thoughts are awakened! How the gates of history open, and you look back upon the wondrous scenes that throng the far and mighty field of vision!

In three hours more, crossing the "Flowery Stream" and the dry beds of one or two wintery torrents, whose banks are brilliant with gay and beautiful oleanders, we come to Sidon. As we enter its borders the air is laden with perfumes, and especially with odors from the numerous orange-groves, where the golden fruit looks so charming. The Sidon oranges are renowned for their excellence. In these adjacent orchards, stretching away to the roots of the mountains and abundantly watered by their streams, there is a luxuriant profusion of fruits and flowers. Nearly all varieties in the land are here—oranges, lemons, citrons, pears, pomegranates, figs, grapes, olives, dates, apples, bananas, almonds, peaches, apricots, plums, and other varieties—making a splendid forest of gardens.

We enter and pass through the town. Its population, embracing Moslems, Greeks, and Jews, is upwards of five thousand. The streets are narrow and dirty, as is usual in the East. Some of the dwellings are quite spacious and comparatively elegant, especially those on the eastern wall. There is a sort of citadel on the south and an old castle on the north, the latter connected with the city by a bridge with stone arches. Our tents are pitched just north of the town on the sandy beach. Presently a Christian family of native Syrians, connected with the American mission here, come from their house near by to welcome us. Father, mother, and three or four grown up daughters, an interesting group, in complexion, manners and dress more like Europeans than Orientals, and some of them able to speak a little English; we were very happy to see them, and to converse of precious interests and hopes that make all believing hearts one in sympathy and joy throughout the world.

Phœnicia is the oldest of civilized nations, and Sidon is "the mother of all the Phœnicians." It is supposed to have been founded by Sidon, a son of Canaan, and great-grandson of Noah. It is mentioned in the tenth chapter of Genesis, in connexion with Sodom and Gomorrah. Joshua speaks of it as a great city. Homer sang of its arts and arms. Its history is like that of many others, a story of prosperity, grandeur, and decline. Its idolatrous and wicked inhabitants, of whom Jezebel was a specimen, incurred the judgments of God, whose threatenings against it by His prophets were fulfilled. Among the ancient relics still found here, perhaps the most remarkable are the elaborate tombs and sarcophagi with which the adjacent hillsides abound, and where the early kings of Sidon were buried in rocky sepulchres and coffins of hewn stone.

The next morning, a little after six o'clock, we left Sidon for Beirût, distant about twenty miles north. The glorious heights of Lebanon were on our right, many of them crowned with snow. A few clusters of magnificent cedars are left, the lonely representatives of the great and splendid forests on the mountain slopes in the days of Solomon and Hiram. We thought of that singular woman, Lady Hester Stanhope, as we passed opposite to the place where she lived and died. Near the shore we observed a khan and a white wely. They both bear the name of Jonah. And this is the spot where tradition says the great fish "vomited out" the prophet "upon the dry land." It is at least a quiet and suitable place for such an event, and on the route from Joppa to Tarshish. Somewhere on this coast the event transpired, and it might have been here.

XXXIII.

Beirut—Smyrna—Constantinople—Athens—Home.

BEIRUT is beautifully situated on a gentle eminence or cape, and is the most flourishing city on the coast. It has so outgrown its walls that there seems to be as many buildings outside of them as within. Its commerce must be large. Our entrance to it was through fine groves of mulberry, pine and other trees. Here we spent two or three days, including a Sabbath. Here the Rev. Dr. Thomson resides, who has been a missionary of the American Board over thirty years in this country. Presenting my letter of introduction to him, he received us very cordially, invited us to spend an evening at his house, and insisted that I should preach once for him on the Lord's day. Assembled with his agreeable family, we found several other missionaries and their families, making the occasion very pleasant. The missionaries had just been holding their annual meeting, after a year of unusual prosperity. There is a good chapel in Beirût, and divine service, with preaching both in English and Arabic, is held in it every Sabbath. We found at our hotel here the Booths, whom we had met in Jerusalem, and good fortune made them our fellow-passengers to Constantinople. Before leaving Beirût, William A. Booth, Esq., of New York, with characteristic benevolence, left a very substantial token of his interest in the mission schools.

At length our arrangements are made for leaving the land of sacred memories. A journey through Palestine and Syria—how many glorious associations are connected with it! Its precious reminiscences and sweet pictures will forever remain in the mind, a constantly increasing delight. Farewell, O thou most wonderful of lands! in thy paths and palm-shades, among thy mountains and vales, by thy cities and shores, my heart is still with thee!

> O glorious Land! of all earth-realms preferred
> By Jehovah, whose voice thou so often hast heard,
> As thy valleys and hills re-echoed His word.
>
> I tread in the paths where the patriarchs trod;
> I visit the haunts of the prophets of God—
> Where the feet of bright angels have hallowed the sod.
>
> I enter thy portals, O Salem renowned!
> I walk about Zion, with towers once crowned;
> Look down on Moriah, the Temple's fair ground.
>
> I go where the Saviour, by mountain and shore,
> With the twelve He had chosen, oft journeyed before,
> Relieved the sad-hearted and preached to the poor.
>
> I gaze on the objects that He had surveyed:
> I trace His dear steps to Gethsemane's shade;
> I weep where He wept, and pray where He prayed.
>
> I stand by the Hall where false judgment was given;
> I go to the Hill where the Cross-nails were driven;
> I enter the Tomb of the loved One of Heaven.

I pass o'er the Kedron to Olivet nigh,
Where Bethany nestles so sweet 'neath the eye,
Where the Glorious Redeemer ascended on high.

O Land of the holiest memories, adieu!
My wanderings in thee I shall often renew;
Thy beautiful landscapes are ever in view.

O desolate Land! 'neath a blight to remain,
Till thy children, long scattered, are gathered again,
And thy King, once rejected, shall over thee reign

Just before sunset on Monday evening, April ninth, we sailed from the harbor of Beirût, in a fine Austrian steamer bound for Constantinople. Before going aboard, the custom-house officers subjected us to a most tedious delay and vexatious examination of our luggage. They wanted more bucksheesh than we were disposed to give, or more likely they were encouraged to trouble us by a fiery scamp named Halcel, an assistant of our dragoman, who had become offended with one or two of our party, and thus sought revenge. We had twenty-two Americans on board, making a majority of the passengers, not including a number of pilgrims, mostly Greeks, returning from Palestine, and occupying a portion of the deck with their tents. The night was clear and calm, as was the next morning, when we anchored near Cyprus, and visited the island in small boats. We called on the American Consul, a son of Dr. Barclay, missionary at Jerusalem, and were pleasantly entertained at his ample rooms. We wandered through the bazaars of the town of Larnica, visited a Greek church, and a cemetery where Mr. Pease, first missionary of the American Board to Cyprus, was buried. This island was anciently celebrated for its temples and worship of Venus by the voluptuous inhabitants; it has always been noted for its fine vineyards and wines; and it is frequently mentioned in the Acts of the Apostles, as the home of Barnabas, and Mnason, the "old disciple," and as the scene of some of Paul's labors, where he preached the gospel to Serjius Paulus, and encountered the sorcerer Elymas.

In a few hours we resumed our voyage over a fine sea. The next morning we were passing along the mountainous coast of Asia Minor. Some of the loftiest slopes and peaks were covered with snow. Here the wind rose, and the sea began to swell. A singular phenomenon occurred in the afternoon. The sky was filled with clouds of a reddish-yellow hue, and the falling rain was mixed with sand, covering our hats and coats with dust-drops. It was said the sand was blown from Cyprus, a long distance. At night the sea was very rough, and many were sick.

Early the next morning we entered the harbor of Rhodes, one of the islands mentioned in the account of Paul's voyage on his way to Jerusalem. We went ashore near the place where stood the huge Colossus, one of the seven wonders of the world. It was a statue of brass, one hundred and fifty feet high, each of its fingers being larger than a man; but it was thrown down by an earthquake after it had stood a little more than half a century. We entered the gate of a dilapidated town, amidst old fortifications, castles, and cannons, passing from the ruins of an ancient church, along the street of the Knights of St. John, the deserted stone houses being embellished with columns and slabs of marble, on which were engraved various escutcheons and crests.

Resuming our voyage, we were now in the Ægean Sea, the coast of Asia Minor and many islands in view. We passed Coos, and a little before sunset "the isle that is called Patmos," to which John, the beloved disciple, was banished, where he had glorious interviews with Christ, and caught and recorded the last accents of Inspiration. I was greatly interested in this little rocky spot, and was fortunate in obtaining a good view of it. The highest point of the island is crowned with a large monastery. The night was fearfully temptuous, and the steamer creaked and pitched prodigiously in the rough sea, environed with rain, hail, and thunder and lightning.

The next morning was clear, and we entered the harbor of Smyrna, the city and shore having a beautiful appearance as we approached them. It soon began to rain, but we went ashore, wandered through the bazaars, and entered a Greek church, which was thronged by an apparently happy multitude, kissing as fast as possible a picture of the crucifixion. It was Good Friday, and I noticed many men in the streets, carrying slaughtered lambs on their shoulders, a circumstance which the religious festival may explain. It was pleasant to see a majority of the people in European costume, and many of the ladies were quite pretty. The following day we visited the cypress-shaded cemeteries back of the town, and lingered at the remains of the ancient amphitheater pointed out as the scene of Polycarp's martyrdom. The place of his burial, and the site of "the church in Smyrna" are near by. The high eminence above, crowned with an old castle, affords a fine view of the city and surrounding country. We returned by the Caravan Bridge—whence loaded camels depart into the interior—a locality that, among several others, claims to be the birthplace of Homer.

We sailed in the afternoon and stopped a short time in the evening at Mitylene, where Paul touched on his way from Greece to Jerusalem. We had a good view of the site of ancient Ilium or Troy before we entered the Dardanelles, the narrow straits separating Europe and Asia, and then passing the Hellespont we were on the Sea of Marmora.

On the morning of April sixteenth, I was watching from the deck in the rain for a first glimpse of Constantinople, whose situation is fine, beautiful, magnificent, perhaps unsurpassed by that of any city in the world. The Golden Horn, the Bosphorus, the slopes on each side covered with buildings massed together, splendid palaces, mosques with their grand domes and graceful minarets, with gardens and cypress groves above, formed a picture not soon to be forgotten. Scutari, Pera, and Stamboul, the site of old Byzantium, combine to make a city whose position for commerce and influence as well as beauty of situation may well be coveted by the Czar. We found excellent accommodations at the Hotel de l'Europe, kept by an Englishwoman, in Pera. The bazaars of Stamboul are wonderful for the profuse variety and tempting richness and beauty of the fabrics offered for sale. Notwithstanding the rain and the wind, I enjoyed the long tramp for the attractive and curious sights and scenes it furnished. The next day we visited many places and objects of interest. It cost our large party three dollars each to enter the Mosque of St. Sophia. It is a magnificent edifice, originally built as a Christian church. You must take off your boots and enter it in slippers. You look with wonder from the vast area up to the grand domes and around on the numerous and splendid columns of porphyry and green marble or granite brought from Baalbek or from the temple of Diana at Ephesus. The Mosque of Sultan Achmet is surmounted by an immense dome supported by marble columns thirty-three feet in diameter. I noticed many boxes of baggage in the galleries said to belong to persons on the pilgrimage to Mecca. The Tombs of Sultan Mahmoud and family are very costly. In the temple or mausoleum were a number of large sarcophagi, covered with rich shawls and velvets. Copies of the Koran, elegantly printed and embellished, and wrapped in splendidly embroidered cloth, were laid in chairs around the tombs. We were next taken to a large building containing specimens of old armor, and especially curious for its multitude of life-like representations of the janizaries of the Sultan, resembling wax-fixures, in all sorts of costumes and attitudes. Our firman for the Mosque of St. Sophia and other places also included admission to the Seraglio Palace. The gardens and grounds about it are spacious and shaded by cypress-trees. It occupies a point on the edge of the Golden Horn, a beautiful situation. Time would fail to describe the various apartments we entered, their attractions, their splendors, arrangement and furniture, from the throne-room to the bath, *not* including the harem.

We were anxious for a sail up the Bosphorus to the Black Sea, and finding that no steamer was going in the afternoon, we chartered one on its arriving from some point below, and had a fine trip which we greatly enjoyed amidst beautiful scenery on both the European and Asiatic sides, as castles, palaces and mosques, fine dwellings and country seats, with gardens and groves, continually greeted us, till we got a good view of the Black Sea, when we returned. The next morning, clear and beautiful, three of us took a caique and were rowed up the Golden Horn to its extremity, and were delighted with the excursion and the scenery. The caique is a light, elegant, canoe-like boat, embellished with delicate carving inside, drawing but little water and gliding like a fish. Cushions are furnished and we sit in the bottom *a la Turk*.

We had engaged passage for Marseilles on a fine French steamer, and left Constantinople about five o'clock in the afternoon, obtaining a beautiful view of the city in our departure. The next morning we passed again by the plains of Troy and near the tomb of Achilles, a mound of earth. Mount Ida, crowned with snow, loomed up in the rear. On our right was Samothrace where Neptune surveyed the fleet, and we passed close to Tenedos, behind which the fleet lay anchored. On our left was Chios, or Scio, that rocky isle that claims to be the birthplace of "the blind old bard." We passed in view of several other islands of classic or historical interest.

By daylight the next morning, April twentieth, we

arrive at the Piræus, the port of Athens, and are soon looking out upon the soil of Greece. Our steamer remains here till afternoon; so we get a cup of coffee and hasten on shore, and take carriages for the renowned city of Minerva, distant 5 miles. It is a good road through fields of wheat and barley, and groves of olive, vine and fig. Soon the Acropolis and the ruins of ancient Athens are in view. Who can describe the associations they awaken of mighty men and great events in the olden past? We alighted near the Temple of Theseus, in and around which are numerous marble statues much broken and defaced; but the building itself is tolerably well preserved. We then made our way to the Acropolis, and ascending the marble steps through the columns of the Propylon, or grand gateway, we entered the Parthenon, the beauty and glory of all Grecian temples in its architecture and situation, and still in its shattered and ruined state exciting our unbounded admiration. The Erechtheum and the Temple of Victory, built after the battles of Marathon and Salamis, are fine structures near. The view from the lofty and commanding site of the Parthenon is enchantingly beautiful. The exquisite outline of the hills and the graceful sweep of the valleys and shores are indescribable. There are the mountains Pentelicus and Hymettus, the streams Ilissus and Cephissus, the grove of Academus, and farther off, in full sight, the Bay of Salamis. Among the interesting localities near by are the rocky prison in the side of a hill where Socrates came to his death, and the Pnyx, or stone steps, where Demosthenes and other Grecian orators were accustomed to address the people. We visited also the ruins of the magnificent Temple of Jupiter Olympus, many of whose lofty Corinthian columns still stand in their beauty and grandeur. But I was specially interested in Mars' Hill, only a short distance northwest of the Acropolis. We ascended the sixteen steps cut in the solid rock to the hewn platform where the court of Areopagus was held. Up these steps and to this spot the Apostle Paul was conducted, and addressed the philosophic Athenians in a sublime discourse of the true God and of spiritual worship. Here I read to our party the sketch of that discourse in the Acts, and looked upon some of the same temples that he saw as he declared, the "Lord of heaven and earth dwelleth not in temples made with hands." Passing through the compact modern city, we returned to the Piræus, accompanied by the Rev. Dr. King, the veteran missionary, whom it was a pleasure to meet on the field of his labors.

In the afternoon we resumed our voyage, and in two days the coasts of Italy and Sicily were in sight. We had a fine view of Mount Ætna, looming up in lofty grandeur, wearing a crown of snow plumed with a column of smoke. We stopped a few hours at Messina, the place appearing much better than it did in the rain at a previous visit. But the city was full of soldiers, and the people were greatly excited, a number of them having recently been shot down in the streets. The Italian revolution was breaking out. Here we reluctantly parted with our valued friends, Child and Howe, who took another steamer for Naples and Rome to meet their wives whom they had left on going to the East. In the evening as we were passing near Stromboli, a tall conical mountain, rising out of the sea, I walked the deck till a late hour, watching the occasional brilliant eruptions of the volcano. Our course was between the islands of Sardinia and Corsica, both in view, and we reached Marseilles early on the morning of the twenty-fifth, having had a fine voyage.

After a pleasant walk over the town, finding many of its streets beautiful and its buildings elegant, we took the railway for Paris. It was an agreeable change, and the country looked attractive in its vernal attire. We passed many fine towns, and some old Roman ruins. We reached Lyons, a large and flourishing city, about sunset, and Paris the next morning at half-past six o'clock, passing Fountainbleau a little after daylight. The gay capital of France seemed more beautiful than ever, and a week's tarry now only added to its fascinations. A visit of dear friends from Montargis, Mr. and Mrs. George M. Howell, was as delightful as it was unexpected, and their kindness is gratefully remembered.

A trip to Havre and London, with some rural excursions was greatly enjoyed, though the passage across the channel was terribly rough. On the ninth of May, after a visit to the Great Eastern, I embarked from Southampton on the splendid American steamer *Adriatic*, Captain Comstock. Of our party in the East only Messrs. Welch and Snyder were fellow-passengers. I was pleased to find Henry Trowbridge, Esq., of New Haven, and Rev. Dr. Sawtelle, of Havre, on board; and a gentleman remarked that we had also on the steamer three American noblemen, each a prince in his sphere—Mr. Hoe, of the printing-press, Mr. F. Harper, the publisher, and Mr. Webb, the ship-builder. We had a quick and agreeable voyage over a somewhat rough sea, including one Sabbath with a pleasant religious service. It was not quite ten days when we came up the bay of New York, and the beautiful verdure of Jersey shore and Staten Island greeted our joyous vision. Reaching the wharf at noon, on the nineteenth, familiar faces were a grateful sight, and soon it was a blessed realization to be with loved ones at HOME !

Appendix.

VISIT OF THE PRINCE OF WALES TO THE CAVE OF MACHPELAH.

An event which I intimated on page 236 as likely ere long to occur has already transpired. The Mosque built over the Cave of Machpelah has been opened to others besides Moslems. All Christians have been excluded from it for the last six hundred years. The following account from the London *Times* of the recent visit of the Prince of Wales and his party to that sacred locality, is of such importance and interest to Biblical scholars and others, that I insert it here:

"Jerusalem, April 9, 1862.

"You, and many others, will doubtless take a deep interest in hearing that the entrance of the Prince into the Mosque of Hebron has been effected. I will not trouble you with the long negotiations which preceded the event. Mr. Finn, the English Consul at Jerusalem, had prepared the way by requesting an order from the Porte for this purpose. The Vizierial letter, which was sent instead of a Firman, left the matter to the discretion of the Governor of Jerusalem. The Governor, as long as he could, refused to take upon himself the responsibility of a step which had hitherto no precedent, even in the visits of royal personages. By the mingled firmness and moderation of General Bruce in representing the Prince's wishes, and, I must add, through the adroitness of our interpreter, Mr. Noel Moore, the Governor's reluctance was at last overcome; and, on condition that the Prince should be accompanied only by a very small number, he consented to guarantee the safe inspection of all that was accessible to Mussulmans themselves. On this understanding the Prince and his suite proceeded to Hebron. We were joined by Dr. Rosen, well known to travelers in Palestine from his profound knowledge of sacred geography, and, in this instance, doubly valuable as a companion from the special attention which he has paid to the topography of Hebron and its neighborhood. On our arrival we found that the Governor had made every preparation for the safety of the experiment. The approach to the town was lined with troops; guards were stationed on the housetops. The royal party, which, by the final arrangement of the Governor, comprised the members of the Prince's immediate suite, was conducted by a body of soldiers up to the entrance of the sacred enclosure. It is possible that these preparations were caused by excess of caution. In point of fact, there was no appearance of disaffection on the part of the population, beyond their absence from the streets as we passed; nor was there the slightest overt act of hostility or insult.

"You, who know the spot so well, will have followed us to the point where inquiring travelers have, from generation to generation, been checked in their approach to this, the most ancient and the most authentic of all the Holy Places of the Holy Land. Let me for a moment recapitulate its history. On the slope of that hill was, beyond all question, situated the rock with its double cave which Abraham bought from Ephron the Hittite, as his earliest possession in Palestine. 'There they buried Abraham and Sarah his wife; there they buried Isaac and Rebekah his wife; and there I buried Leah' (Gen. xlix. 31); and thither, when he himself died on the banks of the Nile, his body, embalmed with all the art of Egypt, was conveyed, with a vast Egyptian escort, to the frontiers of the Holy Land, and deposited, according to his dying wish, 'with his fathers in the cave that is in the field of Ephron the Hittite, in the cave that is in the field of Machpelah, which is before Mamre, in the land of Canaan.' (Gen. xlix. 29, 30.) Of all the great patriarchal family Rachel alone is absent, in the tomb selected for her by Jacob on the spot where she died on the way to Bethlehem. We are not left to conjecture the reverence that was paid to this spot when the descendants of Abraham dwelt in that country and occupied it as their own. Josephus expressly informs us that it was surrounded by them by vast walls, existing even to this day. That these walls are the massive enclosures on the exterior of which so many eager eyes have been fixed in our own times can hardly be doubted. Their size, their beveled frames, their agreement with the description of Josephus, which became still more conspicuous as we approached them close at hand, and saw, more distinctly than could have been otherwise possible, their polished, well-wrought surface, accords with an early Jewish origin, and with no other. But beyond this has hitherto been a matter, if not indeed of total ignorance, yet of uncertainty even more provoking than ignorance in itself. From the accounts of the pilgrims of the seventh and eighth centuries we learn that already by that time a Christian church had been erected within the Jewish enclosure. This church, after the expulsion of the Christians by the Mussulmans, was known to have been converted into a mosque. Whether the cave was visible within the building is a matter on which the mediæval visitants to the spot vary so widely as to leave us in complete doubt. But that it lay within was never questioned by any, whether Jew or Mussulman ; and the tremendous sanctity with which these last occupants have invested the spot is, in fact, a living witness of the unbroken local veneration with which all three religions have honored the great Patriarch, whose title has, in the mouths of the native population, long superseded the ancient appellation of 'Hebron,' now called by no other name than 'El-Khalil'—'The Friend of God.' Within this sacred precinct, accordingly, for 600 years, no European, except by stealth, has ever set his foot. Three accounts alone in modern times have given anything like a description of the interior—one, extremely brief and confused, by an Italian servant of Mr. Bankes, who entered in disguise; another by an English clergyman (the Rev. Vere Monro), who does not, however, appear to speak from his own testimony; and a third, more distinct, by Ali Bey, a Spanish renegade. While the other sacred places in Palestine, the mosque at Jerusalem and the mosque at Damascus, have been thrown open at least to distinguished travelers, this still remains, even to royal personages, hermetically sealed. To break through this mystery, to clear up this uncertainty, even irrespectively of the extraordinary interest attaching to the spot, will, I have no doubt, appear to many an object not unworthy of the first visit of a Prince of Wales to the Holy Land, and as such it has been felt by his Royal Highness and by those who have accompanied him on the present occasion.

"To resume my narrative, which I will confine as much as possible to such points as need not involve a discussion of mere antiquarian details. At the head of the staircase, which by its long ascent showed that the platform of the mosque was on the uppermost slope of the hill, and, therefore, above the level where, if anywhere, the sacred cave would be found, we entered the precincts of the mosque itself, and were received by one of its guardians, a descendant of one of the companions of Mohammed, with the utmost courtesy on his part, though not without deep groans from some of his attendants, redoubled as we moved from one sacred spot to another. We passed (without our shoes) through an open court into the mosque.—

With regard to the building itself, two points at once became apparent: first, that it had been originally a Byzantine church. To any one acquainted with the Cathedral of St. Sophia at Constantinople, and with the monastic churches of Mount Athos, this is evident from the double narthex or portico, and from the four pillars of the nave. Secondly, that it had been converted at a much later period into a mosque. This is indicated by the pointed arches, and by the truncation of the apse. This building occupies (to speak roughly) about one third of the platform. I proceed to describe its relation to the sepulchres of the Patriarchs. It is the innermost of the outer porticos which contains the two first. In the recess on the right is the alleged tomb of Abraham, on the left that of Sarah, each guarded by silver gates. The shrine containing the tomb of Sarah we were requested not to enter, as being that of a woman. The shrine of Abraham, after a momentary hesitation, and with a prayer offered to the Patriarch for permission to enter, was thrown open. The chamber is cased in marble. The tomb consists of a coffin-like structure, like most Moslem tombs, built up of plastered stone or marble, and hung with carpets—green, embroidered with gold. The three which cover this tomb are said to have been presented by Mohammed II., Selim I., and the late Sultan Abdul Medjid. I need hardly say that this tomb (and the same remark applies to all the others) does not profess to be more than a cenotaph, raised above the actual grave, which lies beneath. But it was impossible not to feel a thrill of unusual emotion at standing in a relation so near to such a spot—an emotion, I may add, enhanced by the rare occasion which had opened the gates of that consecrated place (as the guardian of the mosque expressed it) 'to no one less than the eldest son of the Queen of England.' Within the area of the church or mosque were shown, in like manner, the tombs of Isaac and Rebekah. They differed from the two others in being placed under separate chapels, and closed not with silver, but iron gates. To Rebekah's tomb the same decorous rule of the exclusion of male visitors naturally applied as in the case of Sarah's. But on requesting to see the tomb of Isaac, we were entreated not to enter, and on asking, with some surprise, why an objection which had been conceded for Abraham should be raised in the case of his far less eminent son, were answered that the difference lay in the character of the two Patriarchs:—

"'Abraham was full of loving kindness; he had withstood even the resolution of God against Sodom and Gomorrah; he was goodness itself, and would overlook any affront. But Isaac was proverbially jealous, and it was exceedingly dangerous to exasperate him. When Ibrahim Pasha (as conqueror of Palestine) had endeavored to enter, he had been driven out by Isaac, and fell back as if thunderstruck.'

"The chapel, in fact, contains nothing of interest; but I mention this story both for the sake of the singular sentiment which it expresses, and also because it well illustrates the peculiar feeling which (as we are told) had tended to preserve the sanctity of the place—an awe amounting to terror of the great personages who lay beneath, and who would, it was supposed, be sensitive to any disrespect shown to their graves, and revenge it accordingly.

"The tombs of Jacob and Leah were shown in recesses corresponding to those of Abraham and Sarah, but in a separate cloister, opposite the entrance of the mosque. Against Leah's tomb, as seen through the grate, two green banners reclined, the origin and meaning of which were unknown. The gates of Jacob's shrine were opened without difficulty, but it calls for no special remark.

Thus far the monuments of the mosque adhere strictly to the biblical account, as given above. The variation which follows rests, as I am informed by Dr. Rosen, on the general tradition of the country (justified perhaps, by an ambiguous expression in Josephus), that the body of Joseph, after having been deposited first at Shechem (Joshua xxiv. 32), was subsequently transported to Hebron. But the peculiar situation of this alleged tomb agrees with the exceptional character of the tradition. It is in a domed chamber attached to the enclosure from the outside, and reached, therefore, by an aperture broken through the massive wall itself, and thus visible on the exterior of the southern side of the wall. It is less costly than the others, and it is remarkable that, although the name of his wife, (according to the Mussulman version, Zuleika) is inserted in the certificates given to pilgrims who have visited the mosque, no grave having that appellation is shown. No other tombs were exhibited in the mosque. Two, resembling those of Isaac and Rebekah, which were seen (by one of our party only) within an adjacent smaller mosque, were afterwards explained to us as merely ornamental.

"It will be seen that up to this point no mention has been made of the subject of the greatest interest to all of us—namely, the sacred cave itself in which one at least of the patriarchal family may still be believed to repose intact—the embalmed body of Jacob. It may be well supposed that to this object our inquiries were throughout directed. One indication alone of the cavern beneath was visible. In the interior of the mosque, at the corner of the shrine of Abraham, was a small circular hole, about eight inches across, of which one foot above the pavement was built of strong masonry, but of which the lower part, as far as we could see and feel, was of the living rock. This cavity appeared to open into a dark space beneath, and that space (which the guardians of the mosque believed to extend under the whole platform), can hardly be anything else than the ancient cavern of Machpelah. This was the only aperture which the guardians recognized. Once, they said, twenty-five hundred years ago, a servant of a great king had penetrated through some other entrance. He descended in full possession of his faculties, and of remarkable corpulence; he returned blind, deaf, withered, and crippled. Since then the entrance was closed, and this aperture alone was left, partly for the sake of allowing a lamp to be let down, by a chain which we saw suspended at the mouth, to burn upon the sacred grave. We asked whether it could not be lighted now. 'No,' they said; 'the saint likes to have a lamp at night, but not in the full daylight. With that glimpse into the dark void we and the world without must be content to be satisfied. Other entrances may exist, or have existed, and the knowledge we have acquired of the different parts of the platform would enable us to indicate the points where such apertures might be expected. But for the present it was the full conviction of those of the party best qualified to judge that no other entrance is known to the Mussulmans themselves. The unmistakable terror to which I have before alluded is of itself a guarantee that they would not enter into the cave if they could, and the general language of the Arabic histories of the mosque is in the same direction.

"The results of the Prince's visit may, perhaps, be disappointing to you and to those who hoped for a more direct solution of the mysteries of Hebron. But they are, I am convinced, all that can at present be obtained, and I will, in conclusion, draw attention to two or three indirect benefits which may be derived from the use which has been made of this great opportunity. In the first place, by our entrace, the first step has been taken for the removal of this bar of exclusion from this most sacred and interesting spot. Had the Prince and his advisers shrunk from pressing the claim which the Turkish Government had conceded, or had the Pacha of Jerusalem persisted in repudiating the responsibility which his Government threw upon him, the doors of the mosque would have been closed with a still firmer hold than before. As it is, although the relaxation may be slight and gradual, and although the advantage gained must be used with the utmost caution and forbearance, yet it is impossible not to feel that some effect will be produced even on the devotees of Hebron when they feel that the Patriarchs have not suffered any injury or affront, and that even Isaac rests tranquilly in his grave. And Englishmen may fairly rejoice that this advance in the cause of religious tolerance and of Biblical knowledge has been attained in the person of the heir to the English throne, out of regard to the position which he and his country hold in the Eastern world.

"In the second place, it will be a considerable gain to future inquirers that a survey of the mosque has been taken (however imperfectly) by persons who saw it not in disguise, or by stealth, but at leisure, and with their attention fixed on the objects most to be sought for. Perhaps the above account contains little more than might be gleaned from those of the early pilgrims, or of Ali Bey. (The latter narrative in particular is, as you will see, substantially corroborated.) But it enables us to understand them better, to correct their deficiencies, and to rectify their confusion. To do this in the present letter would require more time and space than I can command; but I am surprised to find how much light this short inspection has thrown on passages which before seemed to me irrecoverably dark. Dr. Rosen, you will also be glad to hear, has, with the help of one of our party, constructed a ground plan of the whole platform, and I trust that these results, in his hands, and in the hands of other Biblical students, will serve to render the Prince's visit not merely an occasion to be long remembered with gratitude by those whose entrance was thus facilitated, but a real advance in the knowledge of this world-renowned spot. The existence and exact situation of the cave, the closer view of the ancient enclosure within and without, the origin and arrangements of the mosque, the precise relation of the different tombs to each other, and the general conformity of the traditions of the mosque to the accounts of the Bible and of the early travelers, are now for the first time clearly ascertained. To explore the recesses of the cave and to discover within them (if so be) the embalmed remains of Jacob, must be reserved for another generation, for which this visit will have been the preparation.

"P. S. It may be observed that the shrines of Isaac and Rebekah, standing as they do in the center of the mosque, occupy a position altogether unusual in Mussulman buildings, where the corners are the places of honorable burial. This and their peculiar structure would lead us to suppose that they stand on the exact sites described by the early Christian pilgrims. The belief of the guardians of the mosque is that the massive enclosure was built by genii under the direction of Solomon. The mosque they ascribe to the Egyptian Sultan Kalarun. They account for the tomb of Joseph by saying that his body was buried in the Nile for 1,005 years, after which the secret was revealed to Moses by an Egyptian on condition that Moses should marry his daughter. Moses did so, and carried off the body to Hebron. It would seem from the account of Arculf that there were seven tombs there in his day, but that the seventh was that of Adam. The tradition of Adam's burial in Hebron, however, appears to be a Christian (not a Mussulman) tradition, founded only on the Vulgate. It occurred both to Dr. Rosen and myself that Arculf's expression about the low wall (*humili muro*) might be explained by his having seen it only from the inside of the platform, whereas modern travelers have seen it only from the outside, where its height is much more striking.

INDEX OF BIBLE PLACES.

This Index embraces every Scripture Place mentioned in this work, generally with a definition (in parenthesis), and the present Arabic name in *italics*, and with topics and Bible references of the place or of passages quoted in connexion with it. Terms explained: '*Ain*, *En*, fountain; *Beit*, *Beth*, house; *Jebel*, mountain; *Khan*, caravansary; *Neby*, prophet; *Tell*, hill; *Wady*, valley; *Wely*, saint's tomb.

Abarim (regions beyond), mountains of, 253, Num. xxxiii. 48.
Absalom's Pillar, 220, 2 Sam. xviii. 18.
Accho (heated sand), Acre, *'Akka*, plain of, 368; town and fortress of, 369; Jud. i. 31.
Aceldama (field of blood), 217, Mat. xxvii. 8; Acts i. 19.
Achor (trouble), *Wady el-Kelt*, valley of, 261, 266; Josh. vii. 24-26.
Achzib (deceitful), *es-Zib*, 370, Josh. xix. 29.
Adullam (for concealment), cave of, 232, 1 Sam. xxii. 1.
Adummim (red or bloody), pass of, 266; road from Jerusalem to Jericho, 267; Josh. xv. 7, xviii. 17; Luke x. 30-37.
Ai, Hai, Aiath (ruins), *Tel-el-Hajar?* battle of, 291, Josh. viii. 1-29.
Ajalon (field of deer), *Yalo*, valley of, 199, Josh. x. 12.
Alexandria, *Iskanderieh*, 144-150; women grinding at a mill, 148; Acts xxvii. 6; Mat. xxiv. 41.
Allon-bachuth (oak of weeping), 290, Gen. xxxv. 8.
Ammon (son of my people), mountains of, 253, Num. xxi. 24.
Anathoth (answers), *Anata*, birthplace of Jeremiah, 284, Jer. xxix. 27.
Arimathea, *Ramleh?* home of Joseph, 198; women weeping at a grave in, 199; Mat. xxvii. 57; John xi. 31.
Armageddon (mountain of Megiddo), 339, Rev. xvi. 16.
Ascalon (migration), *Askulan*, 197, Jud. xiv. 19.
Ashdod, Azotus (stronghold), *Usdud*, 197, 1 Sam. v. 1.
Asher (happiness), position and richness of, 366, 370, Deut. xxxiii. 24.
Athens, temples, beautiful site of, 389; Paul's discourse at Mars' Hill, 390, Acts xvii. 15-34.
Baal-zephon (place of Typhon), *Suez?* 188, Ex. xiv. 2.

Bashan (fruitful), *Bottein*, mountains of, 328, Ps. lxviii. 15.
Beeroth (wells), *Bireh*, village and tradition of, 287, Josh. ix. 17; Luke ii. 44, 45.
Benjamin (son of my right hand), heights and passes of, 283; aspect of, 284, Josh. xviii. 11-13.
Berachah (blessing), *Berikut*, valley of, battle at, 233, 2 Chron. xx. 26.
Bethany (house of dates), *Lazarieh*, walk to, house of Martha and Mary and of Simon, 222; tomb of Lazarus, 223; Jesus at, 268; His ascension, 269; John xi. 1-38; Luke xxiv. 50.
Bethaven (house of iniquity), changed from Bethel, 291, Hos. x. 5.
Bethel (house of God), *Beitin*, site and associations of, 288; reservoir, Abraham and Lot at, 289; Jacob's vision, death of Deborah at, 290; sanctuary and temple of, 291; Gen. xii. 8; xiii. 10-12; xxviii. 11-19; xxxv. 6, 7; 1 Kings xii. 28-32; Amos v. 5.
Bethesda (house of mercy), pool of, 279, John v. 2.
Bethlehem (house of bread), *Beit Lahm*, situation of, 227, 242; tomb of Rachel, 228; fields of Boaz and the shepherds, 242; Church of the Nativity, tombs of Paula and Jerome, 243; the stable and manger, birth of Christ, 244; city of David, 245; Gen. xxxv. 19; Ruth ii. 4; 1 Sam. xvi. 11; Mat. ii. 2, 16; Luke ii. 8, 11; 1 Chron. xi. 17; Mic. v. 2.
Beth-horon (house of caves), *Beit 'Ur*, 199, 285; Josh. x. 11.
Beth-peor (house of opening), tomb of Moses, 248; Deut. xxxiv. 6.
Bethsaida (house of fisheries), *Beit Saida*, site of, not two Bethsaidas, 348; John i. 44; Luke ix. 10.
Bethshean, Bethshan (house of rest), *Beisan*, bodies of Saul and his sons fastened to walls of, 323; 1 Sam. xxxi. 12.

INDEX OF BIBLE PLACES.

Beth-shemesh (house of the sun), *'Ain esh-Shems*, 200, 1 Sam. vi. 20, 21.
Bethzur (house of the rock), *Beit Sur*, 233; Josh. xv. 58.
Calvary (a skull), position of, 203; Via Dolorosa, 208; a new discovery confirming traditional site of, 209; covered by Church of the Holy Sepulchre, 210; scene of the crucifixion, 211; John xix. 4, 5; Luke xxiii. 33, 28, 35; Mat. xxvii. 54.
Cana (zeal), *Kefr Kenna*, appearance of, the marriage and miracle, 359; fountain at, 360; John ii. 1–11, iv. 46, xxi. 2.
Canaan (lowland), Israelites' entrance to land of, 255; Abraham's first tent in, 301; Joseph's rich possession in the heart of, 311; Gen. xii. 6, xlix. 22.
Capernaum (village of Nahum), *Tell Hum*, suburbs of, Tabiga, 348, home of Jesus, and scenes in His ministry, 349; situation of favorable for His labors, 349–351; Mat. iv. 13, 19, 25, xi. 23.
Carmel (a park), Mount, *Jebel Mar Elias*, seen from Tabor, 337; trial of Baal at, 339; view of Convent on, 367; thunder-storm upon, 368; Jer. xlvi. 18; 1 Kings xviii. 19–45.
Cherith (cutting), *Kelt*, brook, Elijah at, 260; 1 Kings, xvii. 3.
Chinnereth, Chinneroth, Cinneroth, see Gennesaret, 347. Num. xxxiv. 11.
Cyprus, landing at island of, 383; Paul's labors at, 384; Acts iv. 36, xiii. 7, 8, xxi. 16.
Daberath (a word), *Deburieh*, exploits of Deborah, 333; Josh. xix. 12; Jud. iv. 15.
Dan (a judge), Joppa a city of, 194; Josh. xix. 46.
Dead Sea, see Salt Sea, 248.
Decapolis (ten cities), situation of, 357; Mat. iv. 25.
Dothan (two cisterns), *Tell Dothain*, fine pasture-grounds, conspiracy against Joseph, pits or dry cisterns, 320; Ishmaelite caravans, Elisha and the celestial army, 321; Gen. xxxvii. 20; Jer. xli. 8; 2 Kings vi. 14–17.
Ebal (stony), Mount, *Imad el-Deen* (pillar of religion), 299; cursings pronounced on, 306; Josh. viii. 33; Deut. xi. 29, xxvii. 13.
Ebenezer (stone of help), 200, 1 Sam. vii. 12.
Egypt (limit), land of, 144: brick-making in, 158; watering with the foot, 164; "the river of Egypt," 162, 178; Gen. xli. 41, xv. 18; Deut. xi. 10.
Ekron (eradication), *'Akir*, 197, Josh. xiii. 3.
Emmaus (hot-baths), *Amwas*, 199; probable site of, 200, Luke xxiv. 13.
Endor (fount of dwelling), *Endur*, situation of, Saul and the witch, 332; Josh. xvii. 11; 1 Sam. xxviii. 7–25.

En-gannim (fountain of gardens), *Jenin*, gardens, cactus-hedges and fountain of, 323; a wounded king fled toward, 327; Josh. xxi. 28, 29; 2 Kings ix. 27.
En-gedi (fountain of the kid), *'Ain Jidy*, hills of, 238; "wilderness of," 248; 1 Sam. xxiv. 1.
En-Rogel (fuller's fountain), *Beer Eyub*, well of, 218; Josh. xv. 7, 8; 2 Sam. xvii. 17; 1 Kings, i. 9.
En-shemesh (fountain of the sun), *'Ain el-Haud*, waters of, 268; Josh. xv. 7.
Ephraim (double land), territory and fertility of, 293, 299; village of Yebrud, 293; Fountain of Robbers, 294; mountains and fruitfulness of, 299, 311; Deut. xxxiii. 14, 15; Gen. xlix. 22, 26.
Ephrath (land), tomb of Rachel, 228; Gen. xlviii. 7.
Eschol (cluster), valley, brook and fine vineyards of, 234; grape slips from, 241; Num. xiii. 23, 24; Mat. xxi. 33.
Etam (place of wild beasts), *Urtas*, vale of, 242; 2 Chron. xi. 6.
Fountain of Elisha, *'Ain es-Sultan*, 264, 2 Kings ii. 19–22.
"Fountain sealed," 229, Cant. iv. 12.
Galilee (circle), *Jeliel*, province of, 323, 324; Mat. iv. 15.
Galilee, Sea of, *Tubariyeh*, first view of, from Tabor, 335; banks of, 342; beach and fish of, 345; complete view of, 348; tempests on, 351; Sabbath services at, 352; last view of, 353; Mat. viii. 32, iv. 18, 19; John vi. 17–20, xxi. 1, 5–13.
Gath (a press), *Beit Jibrin*, 197, 2 Sam. i. 20; Amos vi. 2.
Gaza (strength), *Guzzeh*, 197, Jud. xvi. 1.
Geba (a hill), *Jeba*, 287, Isa. x. 29.
Gerizim (separated), Mount, *Jebel et-Tur*, 299, 300; blessings pronounced on, 300; ascent of, 308; Samaritan temple and shrines on, 309; fine view from top of, 300; Deut. xi. 29, xxvii. 15; Josh. viii. 33; John iv. 20.
Gennesaret, Lake of, see Galilee, Sea of, Luke v. 1.
Gennesaret (garden for the prince), *el-Ghuweir*, land or plain of, 345; fertility, trees, birds of, 346; streams of, scenes of Christ's teaching, 347; Mat. xiv. 34, iv. 21, xiii.
Gethsemane (oil-press), *Dschesmaniye*, garden of, 274, aged olive trees in, 275; services and emotions in, 277; lessons of, 278; Mat. xxvi. 36–46; John xviii. 1.
Gibeah (a hill), *Tel-el-Fulil*, birthplace of Saul, Rizpah's grief, 286; 1 Sam. xv. 34; Jud. xix, 2 Sam. xxi. 9, 10.
Gibeon (a hill), *el-Jib*, site of, 284; history of, 285; Josh. x. 12; 2 Sam. ii. 13–16, xx. 8, 9.
Gihon (a stream), Lower Pool of, *Bir-*

INDEX OF BIBLE PLACES. 405

ket es-Sultan, 217; Upper Pool of, *Birket el-Mamilla*, 272; Isa. xxii. 9, vii. 3; 2 Chron. xxxii. 30.

Gilboa (welling up), Mount, *Jebel Jilbon*, appearance of, 326; fountain at, victory of Gideon, defeat of Saul at, 328; 2 Sam. i. 21; Jud. vii. 5-20.

Gilead, Mount (heap of witness), *Jebel Jil'ad*, 311, 328, Gen. xxxi. 21,

Gilgal (rolling), camp and tabernacle at, 261; history of, 262; Josh. iv. 19; 1 Sam. xv. 33.

Golgotha (place of a skull), 210; see Calvary.

Gomorrah (submersion), 250, 251; Gen. xiii. 10, xix. 28.

Goshen, land of, given to Jacob and his family, 156, 158; Gen. xlvii. 6.

Halhul (praise), *Hulhul*, 233, Josh. xv. 58.

Hammath (warm springs), a hot bath, 344; Josh. xix. 35.

Hebron (society), *Hebrun* or *el-Khulil*, 234; Pool of David, Cave of Machpelah, 235, 393-402; tent-life at, 237; history of, 239; Gen. xxiii. 19, xiii. 18.

Hermon (summit), Mount, *Jebel esh-Sheikh*, view of from Tabor, 337; from Sea of Galilee, 343; from hill of Nazareth, 365; Ps. lxxxix. 12.

Hezekiah (strength of the Lord), Pool of, *Birket el-Hummam*, 203; 2 Kings xx. 20.

Hinnom (gratuitous), Valley of, 217; rites of Moloch in, 218; Josh. xv. 8; Jer. xxxii. 35.

Issacher (there is reward), aspect of, 324; character of, 326; Jud. v. 15; Gen. xlix. 14.

Jabbok (outpouring), *Zerka*, river, 311, Gen. xxx. 22; Deut. ii. 37.

Jacob's Well, *Bir es-Samaria*, 300; history of, 301, 302; Jesus at, 303; Gen. xxxiii. 19, xxxvii. 15; John iv. 3-43.

Jehoshaphat (God-judged), Valley of, 204, 219; tombs in, 220; Joel iii. 2, 12.

Jericho (fragrant land), *Riha*, site of, house of Zaccheus, 260; visits of Christ to, Quarantania, 262; "City of Palm Trees," 265; road to, "good Samaritan," 267; Josh. ii. 1, 22; Mark x. 46; Deut. xxxiv. 3; Luke x. 30, xix. 1.

Jerusalem (habitation of peace), *el-Khuds* (the Holy), first view of, 200; entering gates of, 201; Tower of David, 202, 280; city and walls, 203, 282; seen from Olivet, 205; House of Pilate, 207, 280; Temple area, 208; Holy Sepulchre, 211, 212; visit to a Synagogue, 213; Jews' Wailing Place, 214; remains of a great arch, 215; Jews' quarter, lepers, Palace of Caiaphas, tomb of David, Cœnaculum, 216; American Cemetery, 217; Golden Gate, 221; Hill of Evil Council, 225; Holy City past and present, 270;

tombs of the kings, 272; old quarry under the hill Bezetha, 273; stones of the temple walls, tomb of the Virgin, 274; St. Stephen's gate, 278; last view from Scopus, 281; Ps. cxxii. 2, 3; Isa. lxiv. 10; 1 Kings x. 5; Ps. lxxxvii. 1-3; xlviii. 12, 13; Lam. i. 1; 1 Kings vi. 7; Ps. xlviii. 2, cxxxvii. 5, cii. 14.

Jezreel (God will sow), Esdraelon, *Merj Ibin 'Amir*, plain of, 324; boundaries of, 325; scenes of battles, 326; view of from Tabor, 336; Jud. iv. 15, vii. 20; 2 Chron. xxxv. 22-25.

Jezreel, *Zerin*, site of the city, palace of Ahab, Naboth's vineyard, 327; death of Jezebel, 328; Bedawin camp, 329; 1 Kings xxi.; 2 Kings ix. 20-27, x. 7; Cant. i. 5.

Joppa, Japho (beauty), *Yafa*, 191, situation, houses, streets of, 192; housetop, house of Simon the tanner, oranges, 193; gate, history of, 194; Peter's vision, Dorcas, 195; 2 Chron. ii. 16; Acts x. 6-17, ix. 36-39.

Jordan (descender), *Sheriat el-Kebir*, river, 252; passage of the Israelites, 255; prophets of, 256; baptism of Christ, 257; bathing of pilgrims, 258; Josh. iii. 16; 2 Kings ii. 1-14; Mat. iii. 4-17.

Joseph's Tomb, 301, 305, Gen. l. 25; Josh. xxiv. 32.

Judah, Judea (celebrated), "wilderness of," 206, 268; "hill country" of, 232; Mat. iii. 1; Luke i. 39, 65.

Kidron, Cedron (turbid), brook, bed of, 204, 219; David passing over, 222; gorge of at Mar Saba, 246, valley of, 281; 2 Sam. xv. 23; John xviii. 1. "King's Garden," 2 9, Neh. iii. 15.

Kirjath-Arba (city of Arba), see Hebron, 239.

Kirjath-jearim (city of forests), *Kuryet el-'Enab*, Ark at house of Abinadab, 200, 1 Sam. vii. 1.

Kishon (winding), *Mukutta*, river, a source of, 323, 324; course of, 325; fatal to Sisera's army, 333; Jud. v. 21.

Lebanon (whiteness), *Libnan*, mountains of, 324, 370, 380; Hos. xiv. 5; Jer. xviii. 14.

Lebonah (frankincense), *Lubban*, 295, 297; Jud. xxi. 19.

Lod, Lydda (strife), *Ludd*, Peter healing Eneas, 197; 1 Chron. viii. 12; Acts ix. 32-35.

Luz (almond), 290, changed to Bethel, Gen. xxviii. 19.

Machpelah (portion), *el-Haram*, Cave of, 235, 236; Jews at, 240; Prince of Wales' visit to, 393-402; Gen. xxiii. 17; xlix. 29-31.

Magdala (tower), *Mejdel*, home of Mary Magdalene, 346; Mat. xv. 39, xxvii. 56.

Mamre (fertile), plain of, 237, 289, Abraham's oak, 240; Gen. xiii. 18, xviii. 1-8.

INDEX OF BIBLE PLACES.

Manasseh (a forgetter), territory of, 318, 323, hills and passes of, 23; Deut. xxxiii. 17.

Megiddo (a place of troops), *Lejjun*, site and battles of, 326; death of Ahasiah at, 328; Jud. v, 19; 2 Kings xxiii. 29, 30.

Megiddo, Valley of, see Jezreel, 325.

Memphis (grave of the good), Noph, ruined images of, 182, Hos. ix. 6; Ezek. xxx. 13.

Merom (elevation), *Huleh*, waters of, 370, Josh. xi. 7.

Michmash (hiding-place), *Mukmas*, 287, Isa. x 28.

Migdol (tower), site of, 188, Ex. xiv. 2.

Misrephoth-maim (glowings by the waters), *Ras el-Musheirifeh*, view from, 370, Josh. xi. 8.

Mitylene, 386, Acts xx. 14.

Mizpeh (watchtower), *Neby Samwil*, 200, 206, scenes of, 284; Jud. xx. 1–3; I Sam. x. 17-24.

Moab (of his father), mountains of, 206, 253; Num. xxii. 41.

Moreh (teacher), *Mukhna*, beautiful rich plain of, 299, 310; armed natives of, 300; Gen. xii. 6, 7.

Moriah (chosen of Jehovah), Mount, appearance of Temple area, 208; events of, 280; Gen. xxii. 2; 2 Chron. iii. 1.

Mount of Beatitudes, *Kurun Hattin*, sermon on the mount, 357; Safed seen from, Battle of Hattin, 358; Mat. iv. 25, v. 1, 14, vi. 26-30.

Mount of Olives, *Jebel et-Tur*, first view of, 200; position of, 203; described, 205; view from summit of, 206; resort of Jesus, 207; David fleeing over, 222; place of ascension, 222, 269; Jesus riding over, 203; Luke xxi. 37; 2 Sam. xv. 30; Luke xxiv. 50, xix. 37, 38, 41; Mat. xxi. 9.

Nain (pleasantness), *Nein*, visit to, old cemetery of, 334, Luke vii. 11-17.

Naphtali (my wrestling), 366, Deut. xxxiii. 23.

Nazareth (the branch), *Nasirah*, fertile vale of, 366; Church of the Annunciation, etc., 362; girls at fountain of the Virgin, 363; splendid view from the hill, 365; foot-prints of Jesus, 366; Luke i 26, iv. 16, 29.

Nebo (height), Mount, death of Moses, 254, Deut. xxxiv. 1.

No, No-Amon, Thebes, grandeur of, 171; Karnak, 174; Nah. iii. 8; Jer. xlvi. 25; 1 Kings xiv. 25.

Nob (hill), site of, 284; 1 Sam xxii. 9-23, xx. 24.

Noph, see Memphis, 182.

Olivet, see Mount of Olives.

On (ability), Heliopolis, obelisk of, 157, 158, Gen. xli. 45.

Ophrah (fawn), *Tuyibeh*, "city called Ephraim," 292, 1 Sam. xiii. 17; John xi. 54.

Padan-aram (plain of Syria), 310, Gen. xxxiii. 18.

Patmos, island of, seen, 385, Rev. i. 9.

Palestine (land of strangers), coast of, 191; central hills of, 322; blending with Syria, 370; Joel iii. 4.

Peor (opening), heights of, 253, Num. xxiii. 28.

Philistia, same as Palestine, 197, Ps. lx. 8.

Phœnicia (land of palms), 370, 371, 379; Acts xxi. 2, xi. 19.

Pisgah (the height), Mount, *Attarus*, 253, 254; Num. xxiii. 14; Deut. xxxiv. 1.

Ptolemais, Acre, *'Akka*, see Accho, 369, Acts xxi. 7.

Puteoli, *Pozzuoli*, Paul's visit to, 141, Acts xxviii. 13.

Ramah (elevation), *er-Ram*, of Benjamin, 287, Josh. xviii. 25.

Red Sea, first sight of, 188; passage of the Israelites, 189; Wells of Moses, *Ayun Musa*, on the Arabian side, song of Moses, 190; Ex. xiv. 15, xv. 1-21.

Rephaim (giants), plain of, or "Valley of the Giants," 227; Well of the Wise Men, 226; Convent of Elijah, 227; Josh. xv. 8; 2 Sam. v. 18-24.

Rhegium, *Reggio*, Paul detained at, 142, Acts xxviii. 13.

Rhodes, island of, site of the Colossus, houses and ruins, 384, Acts xxi. 1.

Rimmon (pomegranate), *Rummon*, retreat of 600 Benjamites, 292, Jud. xx. 45; xxi. 6, 13.

Rome, Paul's hired house, Mamertine prison, 114; Acts xxviii. 30; 2 Tim. iv. 7.

Salt Sea, Dead Sea, first view of from Olivet, 206; visit to, 248; dreary aspect of, 249; bitter waters of, great depression of, 250; Cities of the Plain, bath in the sea, 251; Gen. xiv. 3.

Samaria (watch-post), Sebaste, *Sebustieh*, fine situation of, 315; Church of St. John, old columns and ruins, 316; history of, 317, 318; 1 Kings, xvi. 24; xxii. 38; 2 Kings vi. 12-33; Acts viii. 5-24.

Sarepta, Zarephath (goldsmith's shop), *Sarafend*, Elijah and the widow, Christ and the Syrophenician woman, 376, 377; 1 Kings xvii. 9; Mark xvii. 26.

Sea of Galilee, Sea of Tiberias, see Galilee, Sea of.

Shalem (peace), *Salim*, "a city of Shechem," 310, Gen. xxxiii. 18.

Sharon (level ground), plain of, flowers and fields of, 196; yoke and plow, 197; Cant. ii. 1; Acts ix. 35.

Shechem (shoulder), Sichem, Sychar, *Nablus*, 306; valley of, 305; reading the Law by Joshua, 303; present city,

INDEX OF BIBLE PLACES. 407

307; olive groves, oil, 308; Samaritans, 312; lepers, road to Samaria, fields, shepherds, 313, 314; Josh. viii. 33; Jud. ix. 6; Isa. xvii. 6, xl. 11.

Shiloh (peace), *Seilun*, identity of site of, history of, 295, 296; Jud. xxi. 19-24; Josh. xviii. 1; 1 Sam. i, iv. 17, 18; 1 Kings xiv. 1-17; Jer. vii. 12.

Shunen (resting-place), *Sulem*, Philistines' camp at, Shumanite woman, Elisha's chamber, 329; field of the reapers, way to Carmel, 330; 2 Kings iv. 8-37.

Sidon (fishers), *Saida*, situation of, 378; fine gardens of, a Christian family, 379; history of, 380; Josh. xi. 8.

Siloam (sent), Siloah, *'Ain Silwan*, Pool of, and Fountain of the Virgin, Neh. iii. 15, Isa. viii. 6; John ix. 7.

Siloam, *Silwan*, village of, 220, Luke xiii. 4.

Smyrna, appearance of, Polycarp's martyrdom, 385; "Church in," 386, Rev. i. 11.

Sodom (burning), 250, 251; apples of, 263; Gen. xiii. 10, 12, xix. 28.

Solomon (pacific), Pools of, *el-Burak*, 228-231; Eccl. ii. 6.

Syria (upland), 350, 370; Mat. iv. 24.

Taanach (sandy soil), *Ta'annuk*, site of, defeat of Jabin and Sisera at, 326; Jud. v. 19.

Tabor (quarry), Mount, *Jebel et-Tur*, first sight of, 330; beauty of, 331; ascent of, 334; summit of, grand views from, 335, 337, 339; scene of the Transfiguration, 338; Ps. lxxxix. 12; Mat. xvii. 1-9.

Tekoa (tent-pitching), *Tekua*, 232; 2 Sam. xiv. 2; Amos i. 1.

Tiberias, *Tubariyeh*, appearance, tombs, baths of, 344, John vi. 23.

Tophet (timbrel), 218; Isa. xxx. 33; Jer. xxxii. 35

Tyre (rock) *Sur*, situation of, 373; prophecies of fulfilled, ruins of, 374; Paul at, 375; Ezek. xxvi. 12, 14, xxvii. 32; Isa. xxiii. 12; Josh. xix. 29; Acts xxi. 3.

Tyre and Sidon, coast of, power of the old Phœnicians, "Ladder of Tyre," 371; gazelles, 376, Jonah and the great fish, 370; Beirut, 381; Mat. xv. 21; Jonah i. 10.

Zebulon (habitation), position and richness of, 366, Deut. xxxiii. 18, 19.

Zion (sunny place), Mount, standing on, 202; situation of, 203: "plowed as a field," 218; English Church on, 221; preaching on, 224, :81; Ps. xlviii. 2; Jer. xxvi. 18; Mic. iii. 12.

Zoan (low region), "in Egypt," 235, Num. xiii. 22.

www.ingramcontent.com/pod-product-compliance
Lightning Source LLC
Chambersburg PA
CBHW022143300426
44115CB00006B/326